Manny Shwab
and the George
Dickel Company

Manny Shwab and the George Dickel Company

Whisky, Power and Politics During Nashville's Gilded Age

CLAY SHWAB

Forewords by Ridley Wills II
and Kay Baker Gaston

McFarland & Company, Inc., Publishers
Jefferson, North Carolina

Frontispiece: Victor Emmanuel Shwab, circa 1915
(courtesy of George Shwab IV);
an ad for "the famous Cascade whisky," circa 1915
(courtesy of Kay Baker Gaston).

Library of Congress Cataloguing-in-Publication Data

Names: Shwab, Clay, 1949– author.
Title: Manny Shwab and the George Dickel company : whisky, power and politics during Nashville's gilded age / Clay Shwab ; forewords by Ridley Wills II and Kay Baker Gaston.
Description: Jefferson, North Carolina : McFarland & Company, Inc., Publishers, 2024 | Includes bibliographical references and index.
Identifiers: LCCN 2024007870 | ISBN 9781476692777 (paperback : acid free paper) ∞
ISBN 9781476651088 (ebook)
Subjects: LCSH: Whiskey industry. | Distillers—Biography. | Whiskey—Tennessee.
Classification: LCC HD9395.A2 S48 2024 | DDC 338.4/766352—dc23/eng/20240327
LC record available at https://lccn.loc.gov/2024007870

British Library cataloguing data are available
ISBN (print) 978-1-4766-9277-7
ISBN (ebook) 978-1-4766-5108-8

© 2024 Clay Shwab. All rights reserved

No part of this book may be reproduced or transmitted in any form or by any means, electronic or mechanical, including photocopying or recording, or by any information storage and retrieval system, without permission in writing from the publisher.

Front cover: (top) V. E. "Manny" Shwab, circa 1915 (courtesy George Shwab IV); background photograph © 2024 Joe Prachatree

Printed in the United States of America

McFarland & Company, Inc., Publishers
 Box 611, Jefferson, North Carolina 28640
 www.mcfarlandpub.com

To my sons, Keats and Reilly, for caring,
and to Abraham Shwab, for taking the chance

Table of Contents

Acknowledgments ix
Foreword by Ridley Wills II 1
Foreword by Kay Baker Gaston 3
Preface 5
Introduction 9

1. Abraham, 1841–1857   13
2. Knoxville's First Jewish Bride; Knoxville's First Jewish Divorce   21
3. Parson Brownlow versus A. Schwab & Co.   25
4. Civil War   29
5. George A. Dickel & Co.   36
6. The Growing Temperance Movement   48
7. The Saga of Bell Nance   51
8. 1881–1889   54
9. Cascade Hollow and the Silver Dollar Saloon   71
10. Diversification and Family   82
11. Temperance and Law Enforcement: Captain Clack   89
12. The Tennessee Election, 1894   102
13. George Augustus Dickel, 1818–1894   110
14. Siblings   112
15. 1897–1898   121
16. Full Ownership of the Cascade Hollow Distillery   127

Table of Contents

17. 1900–1905	135
18. The Southern Electric Company and "A Harmless Shooting Affair"	140
19. The Killing of a Senator on Union Street	147
20. 1909: The Largest Federal Seizure in History	150
21. Distilling, Prohibition, and Shifting Plans	159
22. That Reif Letter: Legislators Flee to Alabama	166
23. Manny and Boss Crump: Liquor by the Drink	173
24. Nashville's Largest Office Buildings: Dueling Newspapers	179
25. The Final Game: U.S. Supreme Court: *Shwab v. Doyle*	185
Epilogue	195
Appendix	197
Chapter Notes	215
Bibliography	225
Index	233

Acknowledgments

I suppose anyone who finds themselves on the odyssey that is writing a book must become obsessed with its subject. It has been my good fortune that many people have forgiven my obsession with Manny Shwab and the history of the George Dickel company, and many have helped channel that obsession to keep my odyssey from becoming a total shipwreck.

I have had a notion to write this story for many years. But only after spending time with authors and historians Ridley Wills II and Kay Baker Gaston did I become motivated enough, and persistent (stubborn) enough, to go from notion to sitting down at a computer. Ridley has written over thirty books about the history of Tennessee—specifically Nashville and the people and institutions that make up its skeletal frame. When I asked him why Victor E. Shwab was absent from the literature, he exclaimed, "Because you need to tell the story!" Since my introduction to Ridley in December 2017 (thank you, Mary Brockman, who has also served as an effective muse), he has given me invaluable direction, encouragement, and information.

Kay Baker Gaston knows everything that can be known about Tennessee whiskey and has written extensively on the subject. It was her 1998 *Tennessee Historical Quarterly* article on the Dickel company and her encouragement that convinced me there was a tale for me to tell; this article also provided a model (albeit an intimidating one) of thorough, exhaustive scholarship. Kay has provided inspiration and made available her arsenal of research.

My sons, Dr. Reilly Shwab and Dr. Keats Shwab, have contributed their editorial, artistic, and research acumen in addition to providing inspiration and much-needed patience with their father's obsession.

Acknowledgments

Reilly has provided many hours of research and was responsible for the chapter on Flora Shwab. Keats has labored over the many images in this book. My sister, Muff, has provided much-needed encouragement and a base from which I could research Nashville. Linda Venable has likewise been a patient source of encouragement, reality checks, and image editing.

Thanks to cousin George, who made available original photographs, documents, stories, and even whiskey that filled needed gaps.

Archivist Lindsay Hager and the staff at the Tennessee State Library and Archives have been responsive, informative, and persistent, as have the staffs of the Nashville Metro Archives, National Archives, Nashville Public Library, and Knox County Archives.

Copyeditor Nancy Harless devoted exhaustive hours and a positive attitude to making things consistent and right. And thanks to Mary Weaver, who provided invaluable reality checks, editorial support, and knowledge of how to make Microsoft Word behave. Thank you, Walter Green, for directing me to the excellent McFarland & Co. and guiding me through their processes.

I am indebted to the journalists of the mid–nineteenth to early twentieth centuries, who, unlike many of their modern counterparts, made moments come to life with descriptive accounts (even with—shudder—adjectives!) and contextual insight.

I am grateful for my Maryville College senior thesis students. Remembering their year-long perseverance and patience with my demands for scholarly research guilted me into being more diligent. And thanks to Professor Rebecca Treadway for encouraging me to embark on this odyssey.

I raise a glass of 2005 Dickel whisky to my dear friends Craig Williamson, Pat Scofield, Judge Tommy and Julia Brothers, Mikey and Jerrie Lynn Martin, Howard Siegel, Robin Dow, Mary Brockman, and David Burkhalter and to Blue, Ava, and Max Dean for putting up with my obsessing over all things Dickel.

Foreword
Ridley Wills II

In the fall of 1962, I began working as a volunteer in the 1963 United Givers Fund of Nashville. My assignment in the Small Firms Division was to walk up and down Dickerson Pike in the 100, 200 and 300 blocks, where I called on fortune tellers, used-car dealerships, small loan companies, used-tire stores and a Howard Johnson restaurant. I had no idea that the hill paralleling Dickerson Pike to the west was Bowman Hill and that the richest man in Nashville, Victor Emmanuel "Manny" Shwab, lived on top of it for thirty years, from 1870 until 1901. Shwab, whose address was 221 Dickerson Pike, had as his next-door neighbor George Dickel, who lived there until his death in 1894.

In 1888, Shwab purchased controlling interest in the Cascade Hollow Distillery and one hundred acres near Tullahoma, Tennessee. He made enough money from this acquisition that he was able to give, in 1890, ten acres on Dickerson Pike for a school named after him. Shwab, an entrepreneur, also invested heavily in Cumberland Telephone and Telegraph (where he was on the board), owned the Climax Saloon on Cherry Street in Nashville, and built the Silver Dollar Saloon on the corner of Market Street and Broadway. Later, he purchased the five-story Castner-Knott Department Store, one of the city's best.

Although vilified by Prohibitionists, Shwab remained a major figure in Nashville charitable, financial, and social circles for his entire active life, which ended on November 2, 1924, two years after he suffered a debilitating stroke. Because Manny Shwab is almost unknown today, his great-grandson, Clay Shwab, has spent years

Foreword by Ridley Wills II

researching Manny and has written his biography. It not only tells Manny's life story, including his fight with the IRS and the confiscation of his distillery, but also covers his relationships with such prominent Nashvillians as George Dickel, James E. Caldwell, Frank O. Watts, Edward Ward Carmack and others. Clay's interesting and accurate book is one any Nashvillian interested in local history should read.

Ridley Wills II is an author and historian living in Nashville. He has written over thirty historical and biographical books. He received the Tennessee History Book Award in 1991, is the past president of the Tennessee Historical Society, and was given an Honorary Doctorate of Humane Letters from the University of the South. He has been on the boards of trust for Vanderbilt University and Montgomery Bell Academy prep school.

Foreword

Kay Baker Gaston

My interest in Tennessee whiskey grew out of my family's ownership of distilleries in Robertson County, Tennessee, beginning in 1792 with the arrival of the Pitt and Woodard families from Edgecombe County, North Carolina. Thomas Woodard and his wife Elizabeth Pitt established a distillery on our farm, and Elizabeth's brother, Arthur Pitt, established one on his adjoining farm. Wiley Woodard continued the business his parents had established. His daughter, Josephine Woodard, married Jordan Stokes Brown, who established a distillery on Wartrace Creek that became known as the Wartrace Distillery. The history of these and other Robertson County distilleries is documented in my article "Robertson County Distilleries, 1796–1909" (*Tennessee Historical Quarterly*, Spring 1984).

Before moving to Woodard Hall, the homeplace farm in Robertson County, my husband Joe and I lived on Signal Mountain, Tennessee, where a good bit of informal distilling before and during Prohibition produced colorful stories. But I was more interested in legal distilleries and turned my attention to Jack Daniel's and George Dickel, the two Tennessee distilleries that were revived after Prohibition. I was particularly interested in George Dickel's distillery because of his and the Shwab family's association with Nashville, where I grew up and graduated from Harpeth Hall and Vanderbilt University. My father, Thomas B. Baker, Jr., was a Nashville native who relished stories of the goings-on during the days of Prohibition and the growth of the city, as did his friend Louie Phillips. They and William Waller, a prominent attorney and historian, helped me arrange an interview with a Shwab family member who

Foreword by Kay Baker Gaston

shared information about George Dickel and his relationship with the Shwab family. This and other research resulted in the publication of my article "George Dickel Tennessee Sour Mash Whiskey" in the Fall 1998 *Tennessee Historical Quarterly*.

Jack Daniel's and George Dickel, the major distilleries to survive Prohibition, have both had an impact on Tennessee's economy, but Victor Emmanuel Shwab and his family have also played a key role in the development of Nashville. Only a family member could have documented this process fully. Now, one with academic credentials and expertise has undertaken the task. My hat is off to Clay Shwab. I only wish my dad, Louie Phillips, and William Waller were still around to read his book!

Kay Baker Gaston is a historian and author who lives in Springfield, Tennessee. She has researched and written extensively about Tennessee whiskies and distilleries for the Tennessee Historical Quarterly, *the Tennessee Historical Society, and others. She published the biography of Appalachian naturalist, artist, and author Emma Bell Miles.*

Preface

I don't remember when I first learned that the George Dickel whisky company had anything to do with my family, and I did not learn of Cascade Whisky until I was in my forties. When six or seven, I was aware of the imposing family homes scattered around the Nashville suburb of Belle Meade, and when driving around the city, my father would make references to buildings and sites downtown that the family had once owned. He seemed most interested in three buildings: the Climax Saloon, the Silver Dollar Saloon, and the huge Castner-Knott building. His father had shown him the hidden rooms on the third floor of the Climax, where customers and prostitutes would hide during police raids.

But it was the long talks I would have with my grandmother in her grand home on Jackson Boulevard, in front of a clinking, coal-burning fireplace, that sparked my interest in the family history. I would stay with her once a week (when her paid companion was off) and for weeks at a time when my parents were traveling. We would slowly go through the many ancient scrapbooks, and she would tell me long stories about each person, and I would write the stories on the backs of the photographs. When I was around thirteen and she began sharing her sherry with me, the stories became much more interesting and even a bit bawdy: her honeymoon had been three months at the Waldorf Astoria in New York, where she loved meeting in secret behind a department store with her wealthy aunt, who, according to her, had left Nashville to "become a public prostitute."

But few (in fact, almost none) of her tales were about her father-in-law Victor Emmanuel "Manny" Shwab, who, after all, was the sole source behind her homes and lifestyle. They certainly had

Preface

not come from her husband, who "worked one day in his life" (a story for another day), or from my father. I had no idea what my father did until my time in the third grade at Parmer Elementary, when we were given the assignment of interviewing our dads (that's how long ago it was) about what they did and telling it to the class. I was told to say mine "legally retired at twenty-one"—embarrassing (but gratifyingly short). I remember only two of my grandmother's stories about Victor Emmanuel and the George Dickel company. One was that Victor's wife, Emma, would occasionally call my grandmother to ask, "Is Buist [her husband] drinking again? Manny is redoing his will." Of course, her disingenuous answer was always "Not a drop." The other was about a family meeting at her home in 1937 after the end of Prohibition to decide what to do with the Dickel company. My grandmother, who was in the meeting, said they decided a liquor company was "just not socially acceptable" and to sell it. "None of them needed the money."

So, what had this man done that could support multiple generations of Shwabs, some obviously containing representatives not inclined to add to the common good (believe me, that train is no longer running)? There was virtually nothing written about him—and very little about the Dickel company—in the histories of Nashville and Tennessee from the 1850s up to Prohibition. So, around ten years ago, I set out to find V.E. "Manny" Shwab and the George Dickel whisky company.

But as I got deeper into the research, it became impossible to detach the stories of Manny, the Dickel company, and the Cascade Hollow Distillery from the Tennessean epoch in which they struggled and thrived. Their stories are a direct reflection of the times. What started as curiosity about my great-grandfather; the man who I learned was my great-granduncle, George Dickel (they married sisters); and their company became almost an obsession with the era. I also became intrigued by a sour mash whiskey brand, Cascade, which (at the time) dwarfed Jack Daniel's and made George A. Dickel & Co. one of the most profitable firms (possibly *the* most profitable firm) of its kind for four decades.

I have spent well over four thousand hours researching in an

Preface

attempt to be as factual and thorough as possible. This research has, in part, included interviews with Tennessee historians; visits to the Tennessee State Library and Archives, the Davidson County Metro Archives, the Knoxville Historical Society, and the National Archives; dozens of newspapers and hundreds of articles from the 1850s through 1925; books concerning the Civil War and Tennessee history; discussions with the current general manager and distiller of the Cascade Hollow Distilling Company (George A. Dickel & Co.); and untold hours googling anything I could think of to google about the subject.

Much of the available information comes from newspaper articles and books, which drip with delightfully descriptive narratives of political trench warfare usually fought along Prohibitional (rather than party) lines, devastating fires, survival in occupied Nashville during the war, saloons and brothels, and social events. Directly quoting many of these articles gives insight into not only the events but also the journalistic coverage of those events, which is so much more descriptive (albeit subjective) than modern reporting. I hope that depicting the challenges facing a pre-war, Jewish immigrant family in the South and the closeness of immigrant Tennessee families provides further insight into the era.

Nicole Austin, the general manager and distiller for the George Dickel company, remarked that although much is known and written about Jack Daniel, George Dickel and Manny Shwab are "shadow figures." I hope to change that. When told of this book, Frances Turnbell, the editor of *Tennessee Historical Quarterly*, wrote, "What you've outlined here is a real gap in the literature that your book is going to fill." That is my intent.

Introduction

On a recent trip to England, when told we were from Tennessee, our Uber driver beamed and exclaimed, "Elvis and Jack Daniel's!" Worldwide, those two names are synonymous with the state. Elvis forever stands alone, but before the rise of Jack Daniel's, there was a much better-known and predominant Tennessee sour mash label, distributed by George A. Dickel & Co.: Cascade Whisky, "Mellow as Moonlight." By 1909, Victor Emmanuel "Manny" Shwab's Cascade Hollow Distillery had become so prominent that when seized by the federal government, it was the largest seizure of any kind in history. Newspapers around the country, covering the event, declared Cascade Hollow "the most valuable property of the kind in the state."[1] To demonstrate Cascade's importance to Tennessee, the April 6, 1909, edition of *Nashville American* pointed out that the distillery's four-year tax burden amounted to $1,200,000 ($34 million in today's dollars), which represented 25 percent of taxes paid by all the distilleries (including Jack Daniel's) in Middle and West Tennessee combined.

Cascade Whisky had acquired a national—and even international—reputation as the premier American whiskey. Famed distiller and whiskey aficionado Pappy Van Winkle (whose whiskey today sells in excess of $1,000 a bottle) called it "the great Cascade whiskey," stating that "its like has not been seen since Prohibition."[2] In addition to the whisky's excellence, resulting from the skills of master distiller McLin "Kie" Davis, its recognition was due to the business acumen of Victor Shwab and his subsequent use of the newly founded ad agency D'Arcy. At the time, D'Arcy's other significant endeavor was the launch of a nonalcoholic (yet quite stimulating) libation: Coca-Cola.

Introduction

George A. Dickel & Co. letterhead, circa 1910. The image of the distillery that they most likely commissioned appeared in several advertisements (author's collection).

Today, however, Jack Daniel's is a household name around the world; Shwab's George A. Dickel & Co. (GDC) and Cascade Whisky are not. The Dickel company, now owned by the British spirit behemoth Diageo, has slowly come back to a level of prominence, but Cascade Whisky and Manny Shwab have faded into obscurity. And, while much is known about Jack Daniel, the man, and other historic distillers, Shwab and George and Augusta Dickel are, as noted by GDC's general manager, "shadow figures." Reviving their story enriches the history of Tennessee, its whiskey, and the state's relationship with that whiskey. In addition, Manny's and his family's journey from the 1850s through the Civil War, World War I, and the monumentally divisive (and sometimes brutal) fight against Prohibition opens doors to fascinating, often forgotten events that shaped Tennessee and the South.

Manny Shwab had a profound impact on the politics, economics, and the modernization of Tennessee. Having learned the business of spirits from his Alsatian Jewish immigrant father, he rose from his origins as a sixteen-year-old, decidedly successful (alleged) smuggler of whiskey, weapons, medicines, and clothing through the Union lines of occupied Nashville to become a founder and eventual sole owner of GDC and Tennessee's most prosperous distillery, Cascade Hollow. As he, more than any other Tennessean, fought the relentless encroachment of Prohibition, he would repeatedly be described as "owner" of Tennessee politics for almost four decades.

Introduction

In addition to GDC, he was a developer and director of several prominent banks, the Nashville Power Company, Nashville's first telephone organization, and three railroads. Shwab was also the owner of the most successful and architecturally renowned saloons (and brothels) in Nashville as well as more than a dozen downtown Nashville properties. His obituaries declared him the wealthiest man in Nashville, if not the entire South. But, except for newspaper accounts and legal records, he is virtually absent from the histories of the region.

Drawing from delightfully embroidered, pre–Hemingway newspaper articles and police records to track events and stories associated with the Shwab family, from the immigration of Manny's father, Abraham, through Manny's death in 1924, glimpses of nineteenth- and early twentieth-century life in Knoxville, Nashville, and the South are revealed. Stories emerge of a Jewish immigrant to the prewar South with Confederate involvement and his introduction of fine wines and spirits from France to the region. The tales include smuggling, brothels, and police raids; devastating fires, a thwarted lynching, and the killing of a senator; police and political manipulations, the best whiskey in America, and the nation's obsession with alcohol (both pro and con); and the largest federal seizure in American history. At the center of it all is a man known as a "one-man Tammany Hall," who capitalized on the opportunities arising from the explosion of postwar ideas, technologies, and political divisions. While Manny Shwab was creating an individual empire, his siblings were making waves in their own, more narrowly defined arenas: theatrical entertainment, classical music, and whist.

1

Abraham, 1841–1857

On November 3, 1924, the front page of the *Nashville Tennessean* (along with other newspapers across the South and Midwest) announced the passing of Victor Emmanuel "Manny" Shwab, "generally reputed to be the city's wealthiest resident" and "one of the wealthiest men in Tennessee and the South." The articles would continue from a full column on the front page to a second page, describing Manny as a capitalist; owner of the Cascade Hollow Distillery and George A. Dickel & Co.; cofounder and director of several major banks; director of the Nashville, Chattanooga & St. Louis Railway; cofounder and director of the Nashville Railway & Light Company and the Cumberland Telephone & Telegraph Company (the future Bell South); director of the Pullman Train Co.; owner of the famous Climax Saloon and the Silver Dollar Saloon; and owner of two "V. E. Shwab" buildings, the Castner-Knott Building, and over a dozen downtown and other "less valuable" properties as well as homes in Charlevoix, Michigan.[1]

There was no mention that Manny was the son of a resourceful Alsatian Jew whose family, in reaction to the death of their Confederate son and brother (as well as for financial gain, earning the equivalent of $50,000 a week), had been at the center of the "nest of smugglers" that, according to Nashville's Union occupiers (1862–1865) proved "impossible to prevent."[2] Nor was it mentioned that, for over three decades, Manny was the driving force of Tennessee Democratic politics and decried as a "one-man Tammany Hall."

Thus, there was much more to the compelling story of Manny Shwab than could be found by reading the two columns of the *Nashville Tennessean* that day. His family's story chronicles the challenges that many nineteenth-century Jewish immigrants faced when integrating into the New World, as well as the rise of a wildly successful and influential, multifaceted capitalist. This tale also contains the true history of GDC and the whisky it distributed, Cascade, as opposed to the prevailing version being promulgated today.

VICTOR E. SHWAB, BANK AND PUBLIC SERVICE HEAD, DIES

Nashville Capitalist Had Many Eminent Friends.

AIDS WAR WORK

Pneumonia Causes His Death at Age Of 77.

Victor, E. Shwab, capitalist and senior director in several of the largest public service and banking corporations in the state died of pneumonia at his home, 3100 West End avenue, Sunday night. He was 77 years of age.

Mr. Shwab had been practically retired from business for the past two years, due to a stroke of paralysis, but had continued a general supervision over his affairs until a few days ago when pneumonia set in. Death came at 8:30 p. m., while local members of his family were gathered at his home.

During his 50 years of participation in the Southern business field, Mr. Shwab had been connected directly or indirectly with a large number of corporate enterprises, and was generally reputed to be the city's wealthiest resident.

Directed Large Banks

He was a director of the American Bank, the Nashville, Chattanooga & St. Louis Railway, the Nashville Railway and Light Company, the Cumberland Telephone & Telegraph Company, and was a former director of the First and of the Fourth and First National banks.

Born in Youngstown, Ohio, January 18, 1841, Mr. Shwab came to Tennessee in his youth to study at Crocker School, formerly located at Crocker Springs. He became so attached to Southern life that he remained after graduation and entered business here with George A. Dickel & Co., famous wholesale liquor dealers, who dealt in the Cascade brand.

He was married in July, 1871, to Miss Emma Banzer, a Davidson county woman, whose parents came to this county from Germany and advanced by rapid steps to a directorship in the firm, and continued as one of the heads of the business until the prohibition law was enacted.

In his earlier years, Mr. Shwab became closely associated with several men who have risen to eminent prominence in the local realm of finance, and continued the associations until his death.

Had Many Business Associates

Among these were James E. Caldwell of the Fourth & First National Bank, with whom he and others originated the Cumberland Telephone & Telegraph Company. Mr. Shwab was a director of the company while Mr. Caldwell was its president, and became interested with Mr. Caldwell later in the First National Bank. He withdrew from the directorship of the last corporation a few years ago.

Other friends with whom he was associated are J. H. Ambrose, Whitefoord R. Cole, Robert Orr, Walter Pulmer, Paul M Davis, local industrialists and financiers and John S. Runels, former chairman of the board of the Pullman Company.

Mr. Shwab won distinction as the kind of business associate who never forsook a fight in the face of opposing odds, and was much sought by men seeking to establish new enterprises. His sense of humor and his innate courtesy made him many friends.

Following the withdrawal of active participation in the George A. Dickel & Company, Mr. Shwab turned over the major part of his interest to his son, George Shwab, who continued to manage its affairs for many years.

Coming from a family of Alsatians, Mr. Shwab was particularly

(Continued on Page 8.)

Victor E. Shwab, Bank and Public Service Head, Dies

(Continued from First Page.)

anxious at the declaration of war in 1917 that the United States should carry the fight to a finish as rapidly as possible. To this end he bought heavily of government securities from his private fortune, and through the local banks financed a large part of the bond distributions in Middle Tennessee. This interest was not abated by the fact of his wife's German descent, but after the war much assistance was rendered to relatives of her family still remaining in Germany.

Until the first years after 1900, Mr. Shwab's home was located on the Dickerson pike. He removed then to Broad street, and from there to Acklen park where he died. He also owned a summer home in Charlevoix, Mich.

His real estate holdings included the Castner-Knott building, the southeast corner of Church street and Eighth avenue, and valuable business property in Fourth, Fifth and Sixth avenues, in addition to numerous less valuable pieces of property.

Mr. Shwab was a Democrat in political sentiment and a communicant of the Vine Street Christian church.

He is survived by his wife, Mrs Emma B. Shwab; four sons, Felix E., George A. and J. B. Shwab of Nashville, and Hugh M. Shwab of Louisville; three daughters, Mrs Paul M. Davis of Nashville. Mrs Ben Tate of Cincinnati and Mrs. Otto H. Lindenberg of Columbus Ohio, and a sister, Miss Flora Shwab of New York, living temporarily in Switzerland.

Funeral arrangements are awaiting the arrival Monday morning of his sons and daughters from the north.

Front-page obituary for V.E. Shwab from the *Nashville Tennessean* (November 3, 1924).

1. Abraham, 1841–1857

Manny's life and diverse spectrum of accomplishments are woven into the historic fabric of Nashville and Tennessee from before the Civil War through decades of Tennessee politics, history, and business. His and his family's story encompasses wartime smuggling; the long and sometimes deadly struggle against Prohibition; prostitution and saloons; trains and banks; the advent of telephone and power companies; the U.S. Supreme Court; and even the wildly popular card game whist, forerunner of bridge. The chronicle begins with his father's immigration from the Alsatian region of France.

* * *

Abraham Schwab, circa 1870 (courtesy of Shwab family).

In Philadelphia, on March 30, 1841, Abraham (also Abram) Schwab, an Alsatian Jew, became an American citizen. He came from an area in France where Jews had historically been barred from most cities, living instead in small villages, adhering to historic customs and Talmudic law enforced by their rabbis, most likely speaking Yiddish, French, and Judeo-Alsatian. During the French Revolution, official tolerance of Jews grew, with full emancipation coming in 1791. But mainstream anti–Semitism was on the rise, to the point that, in 1806, Napoleon imposed a one-year moratorium on debts owed to Jews. Since about a third of all mortgages in Alsace were financed by Jewish lenders, this decree had a profound effect on the region.³ Given Abraham's weighty involvement with French wines and liquors, he may well have come from (or at least was associated with) the winemaking regions of Alsace. Growing up in this economic and social environment, his evident wine and liquor connections—and the promise of opportunities overseas—may have given the twenty-two-year-old Schwab the impetus to try a new life in America.

For forty-three years, like many Jewish immigrants, Abraham's family was consistently on the move, establishing successful wine and liquor stores in Youngstown, Ohio; Louisville, Kentucky; and Knoxville and Nashville, Tennessee, as A. Schwab & Co. Abraham was in Youngstown in 1842, the year his first child, Cecelia, was born. She was followed by Joseph in 1844 and Emmanuel (Manny) in 1846. According to the *Early History of Temple Beth El, Knoxville, Tennessee*, Abraham Schwab was a devout Jew. In 1848,

Abraham Schwab's 1841 citizenship declaration. Schwab identified as a citizen of France or Alsace, although this declaration lists him as a citizen of Germany. The Alsace region was for centuries politically and culturally contested between France and Germany, with French culture dominating during Schwab's lifetime (courtesy of Kay Baker Gaston).

1. Abraham, 1841–1857

he established minyans at the home of Isaac Garritson in Nashville (a minyan, which consisted of ten male adults, was the quorum required for Jewish communal worship). This group was to develop into Nashville's first Jewish congregation.[4]

The 1850 census shows Abraham Schwab living in Louisville with Cecelia, eight; Joseph, six; Emmanuel, four; and Henry Dryfous, his brother-in-law from New York, twenty-one. The census lists Abraham as a merchant from France.[5] He was involved with the city's new Jewish congregation and was elected as its president. He then moved back to Nashville and was elected to serve as the third president of the Shield of David congregation and the president of the Magen David Society.[6] In addition to providing a means to practice his religion, these faith-based associations undoubtedly gave a young man in a foreign (and sometimes unwelcoming) land a sense of community and belonging.

In the 1853–1854 Nashville city directory (Nashville's first), Abraham appears as "A Shwab, 100 Cherry Street: merchant."[7] By 1857, he had moved his family to Knoxville and established Schwab & Co., wholesalers of brandies, whiskies, and wines. His daughter became the city's first (and second) Jewish bride, and his oldest son, a future Confederate soldier, would eventually be the first Jew buried in Knoxville. The year 1857, however, would prove to be a formidable one for Abraham Schwab: fifteen-year-old Cecelia would marry his thirty-four-year-old business partner, Meier Salzkotter, and the state would sue him for selling liquor to a slave.[8] The court records and testimonies provide insight into prewar life in the South and, specifically, life in Tennessee for an immigrant Jew.

A law was passed in 1813 by the Tennessee legislature assessing a fine of $5–$10 for each offense of selling liquor to slaves without a permit from their master. Failure to pay would result in jail confinement. A slave who sold liquor to another slave was to receive five to ten lashes (plus another three for being found in possession of liquor). By an act of 1832, a dealer receiving a license to traffic in alcoholic liquors was required to take an oath that he would not sell to a slave without a written permit from the slave's master.[9] One can assume that Abraham was well aware of these restrictions when he opened his Knoxville and Nashville stores. And although anti-slavery sentiment was much more prevalent in East Tennessee than in the rest of the state, the institution was far from absent in Knoxville in the years leading up to the Civil War. Weekly ads were run in the local newspapers for slave sales just steps away from Schwab & Co.'s store on Gay Street.

At 7:00 in the evening on February 3, 1857, the moonlight reflected on the courthouse and storefronts along the city's main thoroughfare, Gay Street. Officer H.B. Smith later testified that he watched from the shadows as Lisbon, an enslaved man, furtively made his way toward the door of A. Schwab & Co. The policeman had suspected Schwab of selling liquor to slaves. Lisbon abruptly turned back as two white men stepped up and entered the store; he then made his way to the courthouse, ascended the steps, and stood some

VALUABLE NEGROES
For Sale.

I HAVE IN KNOXVILLE, Tennessee, next door to the

REGISTER OFFICE,

for sale:

FIFTY VALUABLE NEGROES,

just received from Virginia and North Carolina.

They are of various ages, and are very valuable. They consist of

HOUSE SERVANTS, FIELD HANDS AND MECHANICS,

and will be sold low for cash.

dec13&tf
W. S. ROGERS.

A slave sale ad from the *Knoxville Register* (December 14, 1862). Notices about slave sales on downtown Knoxville's main street were frequently run in the local papers in the 1850s up until the Civil War.

1. Abraham, 1841–1857

ten minutes concealed in the shadows of the courthouse vestibule. The white men left the store, at which time Lisbon approached and entered. The policeman moved to the window and saw that Schwab and Lisbon were alone. Schwab handed Lisbon two bottles in return for something that Smith described as sounding like "a piece of silver dropped into a drawer."[10]

As Lisbon left the store, Smith confronted him and confiscated two pint bottles of whiskey. Lisbon explained that he had been sent from the Mansion House Hotel by a man named Erni with a note to Schwab requesting whiskey for a hotel guest named Solomon. A second officer, Carloss, arrived at the scene. They sent Lisbon on his way, and he, according to Smith, "disappeared" as he trotted toward the hotel stables where he served as a hostler (someone looking after the hotel guests' horses). Carloss left to talk to Erni, and Smith entered the store. Schwab produced the note, which read, "Please deliver to bearer, bottle of whisky for Mansion House. Knoxville, 3d Febry 57."[11]

Despite this, Schwab was arrested for illegally selling whiskey to a slave. He was convicted, after which he appealed the verdict; on being convicted again, he appealed to the Tennessee Supreme Court. Court records of the August appeal show a witness for the state, R.D. Turolman, who said that he was Lisbon's owner's "agent," who "controls the negro, hires him out and, at the time this occurred, the negro was hired to Mr. Smith, the proprietor of the Mansion House." According to Turolman, he gave no permit to anyone to sell liquor to Lisbon. The policeman, Carloss, stated that he saw Lisbon shortly before the confrontation coming from the direction of the stable and not the hotel. He assisted H.B. Smith in the arrest and attested that he could see by the moonlight that Lisbon walked past the Mansion after being released.[12]

One witness for Schwab, Erni, was a clerk at the hotel. Smith, the hotel's owner, was away and Erni was in charge of the servants, "the negro Lisbon included." A man named Solomon, assumed to be staying at the hotel, asked Erni to send Lisbon to get the whiskey from Schwab's store. The witness wrote the note to that effect, which was submitted as Exhibit B. Erni took the note to Lisbon, who had gone to bed complaining of a headache, and "dispatched the boy with the order across the street a short distance to the grocery of Schwab." He stated that Lisbon returned in five or six minutes without the whiskey. Another witness, Crawford, corroborated Erni's testimony. However, in what most probably was the result of anti–Semitic and racist sentiment, three twelve-man juries in three court cases found Abraham guilty, fining him $10, $5 and a week in jail, and $32.55, respectively. Fines had been assessed and justice served because, it would be said, "to the annoyance of the citizens of Knoxville ... spiritous liquor" had been given to a slave, even though merely for delivery.[13] The evidence and testimony, however, clearly supported the contention that Schwab was selling whiskey to the hotel at their request and with permission from the person in charge of Lisbon.

2

Knoxville's First Jewish Bride; Knoxville's First Jewish Divorce

Knoxville, Tennessee, was morphing into a booming "modern" city in 1857. The population in the 1850 census was 2,076; it more than doubled during the following decade and would more than quadruple to 8,682 by 1870.[1] This growth spurt was the result of the city finally getting railroad service—via the East Tennessee and Georgia Railroad—in 1855.[2] A hint of the flavor of the city leading up to this boom can be found in a letter written in 1794 by Abishai Thomas, who was impressed by the city's "modern frame buildings," though, sadly, "the town had seven taverns and no church."[3] As advertised almost daily in the *Knoxville Register* from 1859 through 1861, A. Schwab & Co., "wholesale dealers in pure brandies, whiskeys, wines and other liquor," would be the highly visible supplier of alcohol to taverns and the public from its prominent location on Gay Street.

The 1860 census shows that forty-two-year-old Abraham's Knoxville household consisted of A. (Annie, his wife), fifty-eight; Cecelia, eighteen; Joseph, sixteen; Emmanuel, thirteen; Harry, six; Emily, six; and M. Salzkotter, thirty-one. It is interesting to note the mistakes in the census: in 1860, Annie was 38, Harry was 8, and Meier Salzkotter was 34. Also, "Emily, f" (female) was in fact Abraham's six-year-old son, Emile (misunderstood Emile would be listed as Amelie [sixteen, female] in the Louisville, Kentucky, 1870 census).[4] The name Emile seems to have been problematic for the census takers, as was spelling in general (Salzkotter also had an age discrepancy, but his may well have not been the fault of a census taker).

In a little more than a decade, members of this household would become the inspiration, foundation, and core of George A. Dickel

Manny Shwab and the George Dickel Company

& Co. Emmanuel, Salzkotter, and Emile would work there along with George Dickel (who was listed as a shoemaker in the 1855 and 1860/1861 Nashville directories). By 1867, Meier (as cofounder of the company), Manny, and, logically, Abraham provided the necessary experience, international contacts, and capital for supply, marketing, travel, and management. The initial funding would come from Civil War smuggling.

As Knoxville's population approached 3,000, only seven Jewish families counted the city as home.[5] At the beginning of 1857, Cecelia Schwab was fourteen years old. She would not have known that before the year was over she would become Knox County's first Jewish bride or that within two years she would become its second, as well as its first Jewish divorcee.

On August 5, 1857, Cecelia and Meier Salzkotter were married. At this time, there were no temples, synagogues, or even rabbis in Knoxville, so the ceremony was conducted by a justice of the peace, William P. Seay. Meier sued for divorce in October of the following year. According to testimony, Meier and Cecelia "lived together in peace and harmony until September last [1858]." Meier had promised Cecelia she could travel with him as he "started to the eastern cities" to buy goods for the company, to which she "cheerfully agreed." According to him, he felt it would be an interesting and pleasant trip for his wife. It was certainly to be interesting. Their first stop was in Philadelphia for "a time" at the plush, five-story American Hotel, across from Independence Hall. They then went on to New York City for a few days before returning to the American Hotel for a week. On a Friday morning, Cecelia left the hotel, not to return. Meier was left in "great suspense."[6]

According to the July 20, 1859, testimonies of detectives Charles W. Wood and Edward Schlemin, Meier reported Cecelia missing on Friday. Hearing that the wife of the hotel's owner had identified her in the company of James Bilger, "a boarder at the American Hotel," Wood stated that he followed Bilger to the 1514 Chancellor Street home "kept by a woman known as Ida Penrose ... that had the reputation of being a house of prostitution." The detectives entered the home and pushed into a bedroom to find Cecelia and Bilger in bed

2. Knoxville's First Jewish Bride and First Jewish Divorce

together. An apparently defiant Cecelia told Wood "that she had slept with Bilger and had sexual intercourse with him." Detective Schlemin was descriptive with his testimony, stating that "they were undressed in a bedroom together and I saw one of them getting out of bed." After finding her in a "house of ill fame," the detectives took Cecelia to her husband at the hotel. Meier Salzkotter's petition stated

1859 testimony of Philadelphia detective Charles Wood for the Salzkotter divorce hearing in Knoxville, Tennessee. He and another officer confronted Cecelia Schwab Salzkotter in Ida Penrose's "house of prostitution" in Philadelphia, Pennsylvania (courtesy of Knox County Archives).

that he felt it was his duty to her parents, who lived in Knoxville, "to return her to them," as he "always had great respect for her parents."[7] He petitioned for divorce on October 14, 1858. The case was not heard until early April 1859, and the marriage was dissolved on October 15, 1859—almost exactly one year from filing. The wheels of mid-nineteenth-century justice turned slowly, as they were dependent on the judges' circuit.

Six months later, in April 1860, Cecelia Schwab became the second Jewish bride in Knox County when justice of the peace R.D. Jourlman performed the ceremony for her and Meier Salzkotter once again, with Abraham's brother-in-law, Henry "Dreyfoos," "posting bond"[8] ("Dreyfoos," like many of the family's names, would have multiple spellings in various documents over the decades). It can only be speculated, but Meier may truly have been in love and eighteen-year-old Cecelia obedient to her traditionalist father.

3

Parson Brownlow versus A. Schwab & Co.

While there was familial drama at home, Abraham's business was apparently thriving and the company's reputation growing. He had attracted the attention of the famous hellfire-and-brimstone preacher, newspaper editor, anti-secessionist, pro-slavery, pro-temperance future governor of Tennessee, W.G. "Parson" Brownlow. Brownlow had moved his newspaper, the *Tri-Weekly Whig*, to Knoxville's Gay Street in May 1849, from which he raged and waged his battles against Baptists, Democrat secessionists, immigrants, and alcohol. At one point, Brownlow famously predicted that drinking would "bring down upon us, as a State, Sodom's guilt and Sodom's doom."[1] Since Schwab, a few doors down Gay Street, represented at least 50 percent of Brownlow's four societal evils, he rose quickly on his neighbor's radar.

Typical of newspapers at the time, Brownlow opened the August 9, 1859, edition of the *Whig* with two fabricated letters to the editor from politicos bemoaning the loss of the election for Congress to Horace Maynard. Brownlow supported the anti-secessionist Maynard, who would go on to represent Tennessee in Congress after secession in 1861 and eventually become U.S. postmaster general. In one of the letters, with "communications strictly confidential" under the heading, the losing candidate bemoans:

> Dear Shin! With the help of a soaped pig, I have pulled up among these d---d foreigners. Received a dispatch from Father dated yesterday—substance "I have lost all faith in the perpetuity of the union.... Managed bad in Knox—ought to have promised every voter in the county to make him a Juror! ... Taylor's liquor give out, he got drunk on day of election, and went to sleep in a pile of rags in the store! ... This g-------d wooden nutmeg Yankee, Maynard, has pulled the wool over the eyes of the Democrats.... Tell

Manny Shwab and the George Dickel Company

Schwab & Co, that if I am not elected, they must fall a snake or so in their liquor bill."[2]

One can only surmise how a soaped pig helped the author slide in among "these d----d foreigners," but it was a direct reference to Schwab and his logical support for a "liquor bill." Both letters give poignant examples of the dangers of alcohol.

Ramsey Drawn out of Overton by a Soaped Pig.
Sends a Dispatch by Jarnagin's Line—Maynard Elected by 2000 Votes!

Clinton and Wortsburg Telegraph Line!
Communications strictly confidential.
WORTSBURG, Aug 6—9 P. M,

Dear Shin!—With the help of a soaped pig, I have pulled up among these d—d foreigners. Received a dispatch from Father dated yesterday—substance, "I have lost all faith in the perpetuity of the Union." What the Devil does this mean? If things went wrong in Knox, it is on account of my refusing to resign my office to Elliott and Jo Lewis! Shin, your d——d fool remark that you wanted me beat, to get me out of the way, has met me every where! Managed bad in Knox—ought to have promised every voter in the county to make him a Juror! Played the Devil in Clinton—Jarnagin bragged too loud! Taylor's liquor give out, he got drunk on day of election, and went to sleep in a pile of rags in the store! Morrow and Bolling did not reach Jacksboro', or I would have gained in Campbell! The Cullom's and McHenry's played hell with me in Overton and Fentress! This d——d wooden nutmeg Yankee, Maynard, has pulled wool over the eyes of the Democrats—he is stronger than ever he was! They ought to have sent more funds from Washington. Tell Schwab &

Co., that if I am not elected, they must fall a snake or so in their liquor bill.
J. CROZIER RAMSEY.

Old Bullen Leaving Cocke and Sevier—Defeated by 1000 Votes—Saves One Barrel of Liquor in the Scramble!

A fictional, "strictly confidential" letter run by Parson Brownlow in his Knoxville, Tennessee, *Tri-Weekly Whig* on August 9, 1859. It refers to Schwab & Co.'s "liquor bill."

3. Parson Brownlow versus A. Schwab & Co.

From 1859 through the first year of the Civil War (1861), A. Schwab & Co. ran large weekly ads in the *Knoxville Register*, East Tennessee's dominant newspaper from 1816 to 1863. The ads promoted the company as wholesale dealers in "pure brandies, whiskey, wines and other liquor," stating that their product was inspected daily, which "will save the trouble and expens [sic] of having them re-inspected." Drinkers needed to be judicious with their consumption choices in those times. Abraham's contacts for "imported wines and liquors" (many from his native France) would prove invaluable in the years ahead as A. Schwab & Co. morphed into underground activity and then into George A. Dickel & Co. In one ad, Schwab sought the "finest hops" in the region (it would seem he had an interest in production as well as distribution). Business was so good that during this time, Schwab opened another store in Nashville, with Salzkotter becoming a partner. Abraham traveled frequently between the two cities.³

Disaster was avoided on April 7, 1860. According to the *Nashville Republican Banner*, the grocery of Fitzgerald & Co. in Knoxville was "occupied by three drunken Irishmen," and a fire broke out, consuming and destroying the grocery and two other buildings. The fire most threatened the livery stable of William Lackey, which contained thirty horses, as well as Schwab & Co. As the flames spread, "the windows of heaven opened, the rain

A. SCHWAB & CO.
Wholesale Dealers
IN PURE
BRANDIES,
WHISKEYS,
WINES,
AND OTHER LIQUOR.

PERSONS WANTING

PURE LIQUORS

Should patronize this house. Their Liquors have been duly

INSPECTED,

AND WILL SAVE THE TROUBLE AND EXPENS of having them re-inspected.
April 25 '61

An A. Schwab & Co. ad in the *Knoxville Register* (June 11, 1861) for "pure" and inspected brandies, whiskies, and wines. Liquor consumers needed to be careful, as unregulated alcoholic beverages were often poisonous.

descended in torrents and checking its ravages" (it would be seventy years before journalism benefited from Hemingwayian minimalism). Mr. Lackey "had a valuable watch and $20 in money taken from his vest pocket," but all the horses were saved.[4]

In that same year, W.G. Brownlow appealed to his *Whig* audience to "pray against the wicked leaders of Abolitionism and the equally ungodly advocates of Secessionism."[5] His stance on these issues seemingly embraced both sides of Civil War positions. But his statement reflects the conflicting attitudes permeating East Tennessee leading up to, during, and after the war. In 1860, the heavy storm clouds of war affected every American, immigrant or not. Abraham's citizenship papers declared his obligation to uphold the Constitution and to "denounce forever, all allegiance and fidelity to any foreign Prince, Potentate, State, or Sovereignty whatever, and particularly to the King of Bavaria." It's impossible to know Abraham's political allegiances as of 1860 and his position relative to the North and South, having moved from Youngstown, Ohio, to Tennessee, but it would soon become concretized and clear as Meier and Cecelia Salzkotter and Cecelia's sixteen-year-old brother, Joseph Schwab, moved to Nashville to manage Schwab & Co.'s second store.

4

Civil War

After much contentious debate, with East Tennessee voting two to one against seceding, Tennessee seceded from the Union on June 8, 1861, becoming the last of the eleven states to do so. On August 15, Joseph Schwab, just seventeen years old, joined Nashville's C Company (the Rock City Guards) of the 1st Tennessee Infantry Regiment under George E. Maney. This unit fought in the earliest battles with Thomas "Stonewall" Jackson and Robert E. Lee and took a leading role in forcing Union troops from their positions at Bath, Virginia. In September 1861, they participated in Lee's first campaign of the war (the Cheat Mountain Campaign march to the Potomac) and then returned to Winchester, Virginia. On January 1, 1862, Jackson took command of the Army of the Northwest, which included the 1st Tennessee. The regiment had been decimated by disease from its inception. From April until June 1861, during training exercises, the regiment went from 1,250 men to 944.[1]

While in Winchester, Joseph Schwab contracted typhoid. He died on March 5, 1862, ten days after his eighteenth birthday, attended by a Confederate physician from Nashville: Dr. John Buist. A bereft Abraham Schwab took the train to Lynchburg, Virginia, and on to Front Royal, before boarding a carriage to Winchester to retrieve the body of his son. Dr. Buist must have made a deep impression on the Schwabs, as evidenced by the fact that Joseph's younger brother, Manny, named his third son—this writer's grandfather—John Buist Shwab (he was subsequently known as "Buist").

On March 11, Joseph was buried with full "military honors by Company C, Col. Maney's 1st Tennessee Regiment."[2] He was the first to be buried in Knoxville's tiny new Jewish cemetery, which had been donated in anticipation of war casualties by Solomon Levy. Joseph's gravestone was made of brilliant white sandstone engraved with a Jewish prayer and the words "In memory of Joseph M., son of Abraham Schwab member of the Rock City Guards 1st Tenn Regiment born Feb'ry 1844 died March 5, 1862 in Winchester." Like Joseph, many other young Tennessee Jews volunteered to defend their native or adopted state.[3]

* * *

On February 25, 1862, General Don Carlos Buell's Union army marched into Nashville after the rebel army retreated to Murfreesboro (accompanied by, according to the *Chicago Post* and *New York Times*, the exodus of about half of the city's population). Those whose businesses remained open were required to take an oath of allegiance to be restored to the status of

The Knoxville, Tennessee, gravestone of Confederate soldier Joseph Schwab. A cemetery plot had to be procured for him, as, at the time, there was no Jewish cemetery in the area. He was buried on March 11, 1862, with full Confederate military honors.

4. Civil War

loyal citizens of the republic, swearing that they had not furnished material to aid the rebellion.[4] Few could honestly take the oath; Salzkotter and the Schwabs certainly could not.

Nashville's provost judge during the occupation, John Fitch, devoted an entire chapter of his *Annals of the Army of the Cumberland* to "A Nest of Nashville Smugglers." He documented the success of the smugglers, especially Abraham Schwab and Meier Salzkotter, and the extreme difficulty involved in capturing them:

> For many weary months after its occupation by the Federal army, Nashville was the great center to which thronged all the hordes of smugglers, spies, and secret plotters of treason, whom a love of treachery or of gain had drawn to the rebel cause.... Their shrewdness and secrecy seemed to defy every attempt at detection. The regular pickets, do what they would, found it impossible to prevent the transportation of contraband goods beyond the line ... mounted policemen were stationed on every road leading from the city.[5]

They finally did apprehend a boy, a "German Jew, not yet sixteen years old." He was riding on one of the incoming wagons when he was spotted by two pickets on a Nashville pike. He jumped off and escaped into the woods. Several days later, they caught him. The boy, who falsely gave his name as James Wilson, had $600 on him (over $15,000 today). His testimony led to the apprehension and testimony of several groups of smugglers, and the authorities slowly closed in on "Schwab & Co, a heavy firm in Nashville [that] had been engaged in smuggling." One smuggler named Keller had been making runs for two Jews named Friedenberg and Besthoff. He stated that each load would net $15,000 ($412,000 in today's money).[6] It has been speculated that the boy might have been Manny, as he fit the description, but it seems unlikely that he would have given testimony that would have implicated his family.

It was determined that Keller had not engaged in smuggling "for the purpose of aiding the rebellion but rather through actual fear of coming to want" and that he might be made of some service to the government by helping to capture the Friedenbergs and Bestoffs. The noose was beginning to tighten on Salzkotter and Schwab. Isaac and Mike Friedenberg were arrested and their goods confiscated.

Manny Shwab and the George Dickel Company

Mike's testimony led to the arrest of a carpenter named John L. Smith. Smith testified that in early March 1862, "a Mr. Salzkotter, of the firm of Schwab & Co. ... called at the shop and requested him to make a false bottom in a light spring-wagon" for $5. He made several of the wagons at Salzkotter's request. Each had a gap of three inches to accommodate product beneath the floorboards. Smith stated that after finishing one of the wagons, Salzkotter sent to his shop a "dray loaded with boxes, the contents of which he said he wished to pack into his wagon," which they did overnight. One of Smith's workmen, Mahlon Jones, testified that while he was helping remove the boxes from the dray, one box fell and broke open, exposing quinine and other medicines. Judge Fitch wrote:

> It was now Salzkotter's turn to receive the attention of the police, as a smuggler and dealer in false-bottomed wagon-beds; and some three or four thousand dollars [$105,000 today] worth of liquors and domestics were seized as belonging to him. He was immensely indignant, of course, and unblushingly endeavored to lie out of the scrape in which he found himself.[7]

Salzkotter testified that Abraham and Henry Dryfous had returned to the Knoxville branch of the business, and he denied that either he or Schwab had ever had such wagons constructed or had connections with anyone running goods through the lines. When he was about to swear to this statement, a Colonel Treusdail intervened to stop Salzkotter from perjuring himself and called several witnesses against him. One stated that Salzkotter had claimed he was making $1,800 ($52,000 today) per trip to Louisville and that Schwab and he were moving goods between Nashville, Atlanta, and Louisville, trading both ways. One witness against Salzkotter was William Muller, a former clerk with Schwab & Co., who stated that Meier and Abraham were running knives, pistols, and medicines through the federal lines. Salzkotter attempted to cross-examine the witnesses,

Opposite: **Alton Union Prison roll from 1863. Meier Salzkotter was sentenced "indefinitely" but was released after only eight weeks on "oath and bond." There was a serious smallpox outbreak at the prison, but the significant bond available from Salzkotter's smuggling successes may have been the prison's primary incentive for early release (National Archives).**

4. Civil War

but his "case was now hopeless.... His liquors were turned over to the United States Marshal for libel and confiscation, his domestic goods were put to immediate use in the hospitals."[8]

In January 1863, Meier Salzkotter was sent to Alton Prison in Illinois "indefinitely," but, in a testament to his resourcefulness, he returned to Nashville eight weeks later, released due to good conduct and, most likely, well-placed lucre ("oath and bond"). In addition, a severe smallpox outbreak occurred there that year, which may have induced his captors to minimize the prison population.[9] Isaac Friedenberg, however, was imprisoned in irons. He and his brother, Mike, were paroled and sent north "not to come south of" the Ohio River. Their goods and belongings were confiscated. The false-bottom carpenter, Smith, was released. The police carried out several "long and thorough searches" but never found the sly Salzkotter's substantial holdings; Meier later said they came "within an inch or two" of discovering it. According to Fitch, the hidden stash was at least $23,000 ($356,000 today);[10] however, considering the many successful smuggling runs over a long period of time, as well as the immediate

THEN AND NOW.—1862 AND 1882.

"OH, NOW YOU WEEP, AND I PERCEIVE YOU FEEL THE DINT OF PITY. THESE ARE GRACIOUS DROPS."

1882 political cartoon reminding voters of Grant's 1862 General Order No. 11, banishing Jews from the occupied South and prohibiting them from joining the army (Library of Congress).

4. Civil War

ascent of the soon-to-be George A. Dickel & Co. from startup to leading Nashville enterprise, it can be assumed the Schwab & Co. partners stashed away much more than that.

General Ulysses S. Grant was in charge of the Union-occupied territories. Smuggling, conducted in many cases by Southern Jews, became such a problem that in December 1862 he issued Order No. 11, declaring that all Jews were to abandon their property and leave the "western" front—Mississippi, Tennessee, and Kentucky. A couple of weeks later, Lincoln heard of the order; incensed, he revoked it. Order No. 11 would come back to haunt Grant and the Republicans as they attempted to woo the Jewish vote in the coming years.[11]

5

George A. Dickel & Co.

George Dickel was born in 1818 in Grunberg, Germany. In a 1983 interview conducted on behalf of historian Kay Baker Gaston, Parson Bremer of Grunberg's Lutheran church provided the following translation from the church's 1818 church register:

> Grunberg page 506   Year: 1818
> In the year of our Christ, 1818 February 2nd, in the night at one o'clock gave birth, according to authentic announcement, Elisabeth, unmarried daughter of Ernst Dickel to an illegitimate son, who has been baptized on

Opposite: Map of downtown Nashville, circa 1897. Map Legend: 1. *12 S Market.* Original addresses (1865–1867) for "George Dickel, liquor" were on Market and College streets. 2. *2 & 4 N Market St. at the corner of Church.* George A. Dickel & Co. was located here from 1868 to 1917. The company did relocate for one year (1881–1882), as the headquarters building was destroyed by fire in 1881 and rebuilt the following year. Shwab sold the building (which still stands) in 1917 due to Prohibition. 3. *2nd and Broad.* The Silver Dollar Saloon/V.E. Shwab building. Two giant silver dollars in round windows greeted customers; hundreds of silver dollars were embedded in the bar and floor. 4. *210 N Cherry.* The Climax Saloon— Shwab's elaborate, four-story "sporting house" in the heart of the Men's Quarter (which included today's Printer's Alley) complete with small, hidden rooms on the fourth floor, available during police raids. Shwab was credited with the building's design. 5. *Union and 7th.* Senator Edward W. Carmack was shot and killed on the street at this location due to animosity surrounding Prohibition. 6. *Dickerson Pike.* For thirty years, the Dickels and Shwabs lived on the pike two miles from downtown. Shwab donated two acres of the property for a school that bears his name to this day. 7. *215 Church St.* The Southern Electric Company, purchased from Cumberland Telephone by Manny for his son, Felix. 8. *Broad Street becomes West End Ave.* The Tennessee Centennial Exposition of 1897 and, for twenty years, Shwab's grand Victorian home were just two miles from the Dickel headquarters. (Tennessee State Library and Archives).

5. George A. Dickel & Co.

the 21st of the same month. He was given the name Georg Adam. Alleged father is Anton Fischer, legitimate son of Adam Fischer, cooper (master) in Marktheidenfeld in the area of Wurzburg.

Godfather was: Georg Adam, son of Adam Fischer. He was represented by Philipp Wolf, citizen and baker of this place.

Signed: Philipp Wolf   Signed: H. Georgi[1]

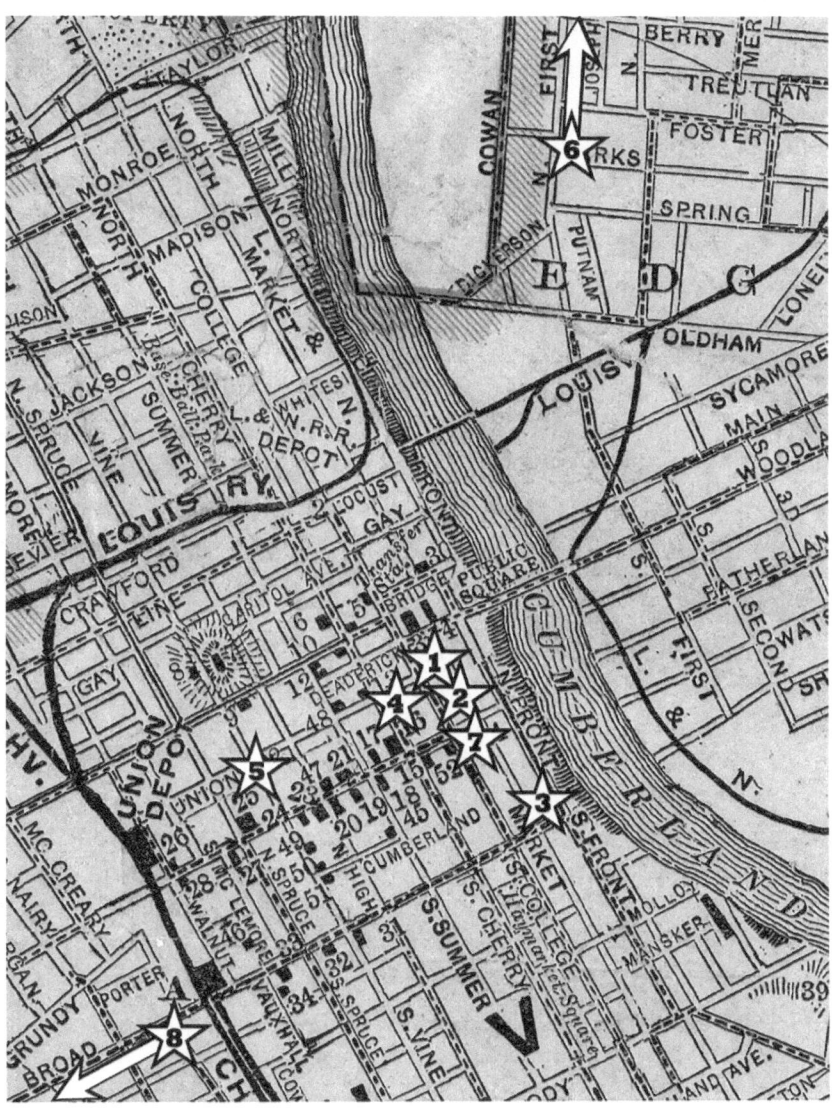

Manny Shwab and the George Dickel Company

The interviewer engaged by Gaston went on to write, "As I know that many people, coming from Germany to the USA, change their family names somewhat slightly, but keep their initials always, I am perfectly sure that this child is the Mr. Dickel (George August Dickel) you asked for." As seen above, his father's brother, Georg Adam, assumed the very significant role of godfather for young George, acknowledging responsibility for the boy. Being the son of Adam Fischer, it can be assumed Georg Adam was himself illegitimate.[2]

Dickel's obituary states that he immigrated to the United States in 1844, when he would have been twenty-six. It goes on to state that he was active in the Masons beginning in the 1850s (becoming a master Mason in 1852). He was also a member of the "famed Deluge Company No 3," a volunteer fire department. In those days, firemen had significant status in the community, influencing elections, holding entertainments, and using the fire halls as clubhouses while wearing their distinctive uniforms.[3]

On June 30, 1860, at forty-two years old, Dickel married Augusta Banzer, age twenty-two. She was the daughter of a confectioner from Hanover, Germany, and sister of Emma (future bride of Manny Shwab).

George Dickel was listed as a shoe- and bootmaker in the 1855–1856 Nashville city directory and again in the last directory before the war, 1860. In 1865, at forty-seven, he began his new career as a liquor wholesaler. In 1867, Dickel's residence was in Edgefield, a more rural suburb east of Nashville, two miles from downtown and, coincidentally, a mile from the home of George Maney, the leader of the Rock City Guard, Joseph Schwab's regiment.

Dickel apparently had a green thumb and soon developed a knack for growing high-quality produce. Living on his small farm two or three miles from Nashville, he began producing small, prize-winning crops of barley and pears. He won awards for "best barley" and "best wine vinegar" in 1868, and an 1871 article declared that Dickel's "Mammoth Pears" were "some of the largest we've seen."[4] The barley award came from the largest brewery in Nashville, Stifel and Pfeiffer, which became a major supplier for the Dickel company in subsequent years. The brewery was founded and operated

5. George A. Dickel & Co.

by two German immigrants and eventually became the Gerst Brewing Company, which operated until 1954 as one of the most popular breweries in the country. They had closed operations during the Civil War.[5]

Apparently, during the war years, Nashville's German population grew close. An example of this closeness and George Dickel's generosity (as well as an apparent fondness for gold-headed canes) was his presentation of a cane to a fellow German immigrant prior to the friend's return to the fatherland.[6] In May 1885, he would run a notice in the *Daily American* offering a liberal reward for his own gold-headed cane lost "between Dickel's residence and the bridge."[7]

> **Off for Europe.**
>
> H. Metz, the clothing merchant on South Market street, departs for the Fatherland to-morrow morning to be absent for several months. He was yesterday the recipient of a magnificent gold-headed cane, presented to him by George A. Dickel in the presence of a select party of friends, when the best of wishes was extended to him, and hopes expressed that his trip would be pleasant.

George Dickel presents a traveling friend with a gold-headed cane (*Nashville Union and American*, May 22, 1870).

* * *

The 1859 Nashville city directory stated that out of eighty economic categories, wine and liquor sales were the third highest (behind dry goods and groceries) at $1,442,200. The 1859 and 1860 Nashville city directories, the last produced before the war, included "Dickel, Geo A shoemaker" on Union Street. The next city directory, printed in 1865, the first after the tumultuous war and occupation

39

Manny Shwab and the George Dickel Company

years, had "Dickel, G.A. liquor store" on College Street and "Schwab & Company clothing," also on College Street. That would be the last time a Nashville city directory included a Schwab & Co. and the only time since Abraham's landing on American shores that Schwab & Co. was listed as a clothing company. Appearing in the next year's directory (1866) was "Salzkotter, M superintendent" at 12 S. Market Street, the same address as the George A. Dickel liquor store. The morphing of George Dickel, shoemaker, into "George Dickel Company, liquors," as well as the transition of Schwab & Co., fine wines and liquors wholesalers, to clothing store to Dickel liquors, was complete. Officially, it had taken less than a year.[8]

Dickel's knowledge of the Schwab/Salzkotter smuggling activities is unknown, as is his reason for abandoning a two-decade-long shoemaking business to open a liquor store immediately after the war. But given the cultural and physical closeness of Nashville's German immigrant population and the imminent blending of the Schwab and Dickel families, it can be assumed that George was well aware of the smuggling as well as its financial success. Dickel had, for more than twenty years, been identified as a Nashville shoemaker. The Schwabs had, for the same period, been identified as successful wine and liquor importers and dealers, with Meier Salzkotter joining in the 1850s. Schwab & Co. emerged from the war posing (albeit for one year) as a clothing store neighboring Dickel's new liquor enterprise. Given the publicized inability to locate Salzkotter's (and, presumably, Schwab's) war gains and the almost immediate success of the Dickel company, could the families also have been starting a laundry business?

By 1867, forty-nine-year-old Dickel was apparently still not fully knowledgeable of the requirements of the liquor trade. In May, he was arrested and charged in federal court for rectifying liquor without a license and posted a $1,000 bond. Interestingly, the charge appearing in the paper immediately after his circuit court listing was "United States vs 73 barrels of whisky."[9] Let's hope the barrels prevailed.

Manny Schwab, now nineteen years old, would appear in the 1867 directory as "E. Schwab bookkeeper" and Salzkotter as "superintendent." In 1864, after attempts in the *Nashville Daily Press* to locate and serve the missing Cecelia, Salzkotter was granted another

5. George A. Dickel & Co.

United States vs. Geo. A. Dickel, conducting business of rectifying liquors without license. Bound over in the sum of $1000 for appearance at October term.

United States vs. seventy-three barrels whisky. Continued.

Circuit court notice of George Dickel's arrest for rectifying whiskey without a license (*Nashville Union and American*, May 1867).

divorce from Cecelia (again on the grounds of adultery) as well as custody of Felix, their three-year-old son. There are no known references to her after this time, but Shwab family lore held that she had, in line with family tradition, started her own business—as a "public prostitute" in Louisville. Chancery court records confirm the rumor.[10]

In April 1866, Meier Salzkotter renewed his passport and began spending several months at a time overseas. His passport description perhaps gives a little insight into Cecelia's disappearance: "five foot, three inches tall; forehead, prominent and bald; mouth, large; chin, short; eyes, black; nose, Roman; hair, black." According to advertising, he was in France procuring wines, brandies, liquors, and Champagnes for the new company, presumably from the same producers Abraham had engaged for decades to supply his three stores. Coming from the general area of Abraham's youth, these suppliers may have been family or friends. The significant resources necessary to finance expenditures for this startup business—supplies, extended international travel, salaries, and storefront—in the wake of four years of economic, human, and infrastructure devastation can be assumed. The aspirations of the diminutive Meier Salzkotter, Manny Schwab, and George Dickel were large and visionary. The "fine" wines and liquors Abraham Schwab had been hawking for almost two decades were hardly the mainstay of the weary, postwar South. But the nascent GDC brain trust focused on quality, wholesaling, and marketing as the keys to future success, as had Abraham. This focus is evident in their advertising, and it soon paid off.

Manny Shwab and the George Dickel Company

Minutes from Davidson County Chancery Court declaring Meier and Cecelia divorced due to her abandonment of the family and plying her trade as a "public prostitute" in Louisville, Kentucky (Tennessee State Library and Archives).

The 1870 census found "Abram Shwab" and his family back in Youngstown, Ohio. He is listed again as a liquor dealer, and he and Annie are shown (probably incorrectly) as both being from France. Three children are listed: Harry, eighteen, a clerk in the store; Flora, five; and misunderstood Emile, shown again as a female, age fifteen, all born in Tennessee. In the home are also listed Emanuel Guthman, "liquor dealer and [his] wife, clerk," both from Baden, and two "domestics" from Ireland. This is the second occasion of Abraham being officially listed as "Shwab," sans "c."[11]

Manny is also listed as "Shwab" in the Nashville census of 1870. He was apparently coming into his own at this time, experimenting

5. George A. Dickel & Co.

with his given name as well as with his surname, as indicated in the city directories, in which he went from Emmanuel to Vesuvius E. and finally to Victor E. It has been surmised that he was trying to distance himself from his Jewish heritage by dropping the "c" from his last name, but that does not explain his father's choice to

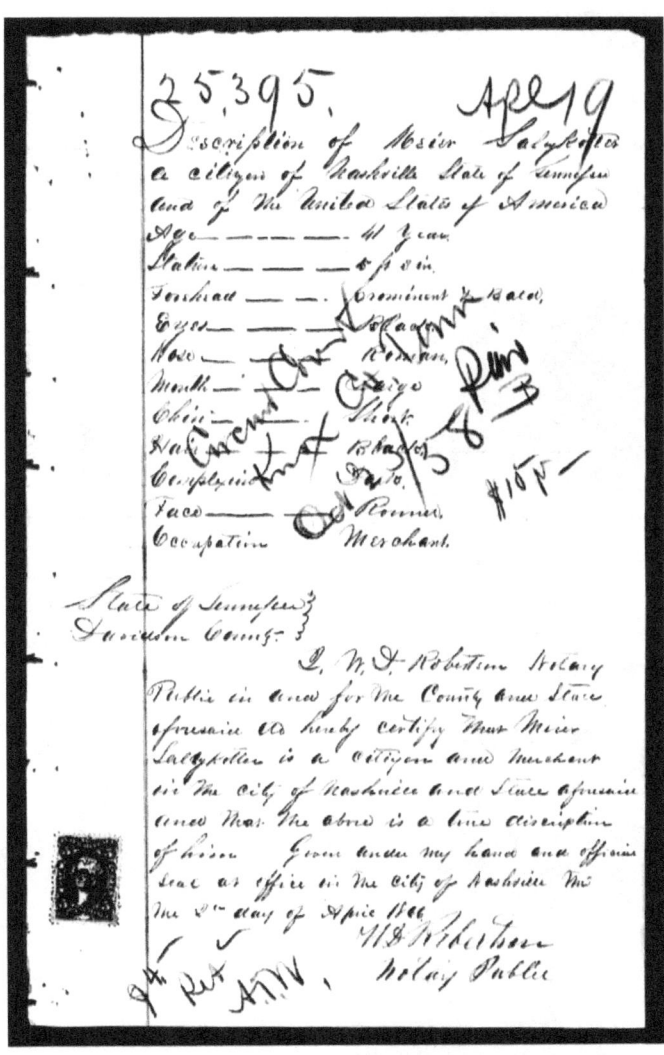

Meier Salzkotter passport (1866).

DIED

SALZKOTTER—Died, yesterday morning, at ten minutes past twelve o'clock, after a painfull illness, Felix H., son of Maier Salzkotter, in the eleventh year of his age.

The friends and acquaintances of the family are invited to attend the funeral from the residence, No. 359 North Vine Street, at 9 o'clock Sunday morning.

Top: Eleven-year-old Felix Salzkotter's obituary (*Nashville Tennessean*, October 5, 1872). Manny named his first son after his nephew. *Bottom:* Salzkotter memorial in Nashville's historic Jewish Temple cemetery. Meier commissioned a famous Louisville sculptor to create the white marble depiction of Felix, a rarity for a Jewish cemetery.

5. George A. Dickel & Co.

do the same while serving as president of a Jewish congregation in Youngstown. On July 25, 1871, Manny married Emma Banzer, the twenty-two-year-old sister of Augusta Banzer Dickel, and they moved into the Dickel home on Dickerson Pike. Meier Salzkotter had married Rachel Essenger, the daughter of a prominent German rabbi. With nepotism being their customary practice, the Shwab family drew indistinct lines between family and business: Abraham,

Statue of Felix Salzkotter.

Manny Shwab and the George Dickel Company

Manny, George Dickel, Salzkotter, Henry Dreyfous, and later McLin Davis as well as Emile, George, Felix, and Buist Shwab all worked for the family companies. Trust was a concept that nineteenth-century Jewish immigrants may have found hard to embrace.

* * *

On October 3, 1872, the deepest of all tragedies struck Meier Salzkotter, the Dickels, and the Shwabs with the death of eleven-year-old Felix Salzkotter, after "a painfull [sic] illness."[12] Indicative of the deep love and devotion he had for the child, Meier commissioned Flavius Cardoni, a well-known Italian sculptor living in Louisville, to create a white-marble statuary likeness to mark Felix's grave in Nashville's historic Temple Cemetery. The statue still exists and is the only one of its kind in the vast cemetery, as it is very rare for a likeness of any sort to be erected in a Jewish cemetery. (Jewish tradition does not favor displays of opulence.) A 2004 *Tennessean* article describes the statue: "The boy may have been a handful poised as he is with one leg cockily bent and an elbow leaning on a marble

Fine Wines.

Geo. A. Dickel & Co. have received a large shipment of superior Champagne wines and other imported liquors, and will be receiving others every few days, including fine brandies and other French wines. These goods were purchased for the house by M. Salzkotter in person, in France the past summer and fall, and every article is not only pure but is fine as represented.

Announcement of a large shipment of Champagne, fine brandies, and other French wines bought by Meier Salzkotter while traveling in France (*Nashville Union and American*, December 18, 1873).

tree. His face is sweet, with just a dash of the devil in it." In describing Meier, the article erroneously states that he served in the Confederate Army (unless his smuggling activities could be deemed "serving") but accurately refers to Cecelia's infidelity and their divorce.[13] Meier Salzkotter is buried next to his only child. Evidence of little Felix's significance to the Shwab family is exemplified by Manny's name for his first child: Felix Emile Shwab ("Emile" for his brother).

Meier's role at GDC may have served to ameliorate his grief somewhat, as, according to frequent newspaper advertisements, he spent many months at a time in Europe, primarily France, acquiring "choice" Champagnes, liquors, wines, cordials, and absinthe. The company was still concentrating on the Schwab & Co. products and relationships; focus on Tennessee sour mash was yet to come.

George A. Dickel & Co. ad for high-end Champagne and French liquors (*Nashville Union and American*, December 18, 1873).

6

The Growing Temperance Movement

The fight against the anti-liquor advocates would be a long and arduous one for the Shwabs, extending from the late 1850s until the start of Prohibition in 1920. The "Dry" newspaper press in Tennessee had begun long before Abraham's first Tennessee store and his conflicts with Parson Brownlow. For decades, the conflicting sides were designated "Wets" and "Drys." In 1824, the state had restricted liquor sales near churches; five years later, in 1829, the first Tennessee temperance societies met in Kingsport and Nashville. The 1831 Tennessee General Assembly began to regulate the liquor trade by authorizing licenses for operating saloons (the number of saloons increased 500 percent under this law). In 1838, the assembly repealed the 1831 law and passed a "Quart Law," which restricted the sale of alcohol to containers of one quart or more. However, this law applied only to liquor; as had been the case previously, wine, beer, and cider could be sold without restriction. In 1846, the 1838 law was replaced by legislation that again licensed saloons to sell liquor by the drink. Saloonkeepers could not sell to minors if parents forbade it in writing or to slaves without permission from their owners (hence Abraham's troubles in 1857). In 1877, the legislature enacted a law forbidding the sale of alcohol within four miles of chartered rural schools—the "four mile law."[1] This was the environment in which George A. Dickel & Co. was developing.

By 1874, the company had a multi-state reputation and had rapidly expanded its physical presence. A March 1875 *Nashville Union and American* (*U&A*) article stated that the company was "pleasantly located at Nos 2 and 4 South Market Street," occupying the entire

6. The Growing Temperance Movement

premises, and that the "trade of the house extends to every section of the country [and] no house of any character in the city is more wide-reaching in its extent." So, according to the paper, after only nine years, GDC's national scale exceeded that of any other Nashville company. Its "stock" of old whiskies and other choice liquors and imported wines, the article maintained, was "enough to make one bibulously inclined, no matter what his prejudices."[2] Interestingly, the article's author said the Salzkotter/Dickel business relationship began in 1859—while George was making a living cobbling and selling boots. The nature of Dickel's early relationship with Salzkotter and the Schwabs is vague but obviously close. And the families' ties were to get even closer.

Reflective of things to come, the article explains that "the great specialties of Dickel & Co. are copper distilled, sour mash whiskies and [C]hampagnes and other choice wines [and that] they virtually control the product of different distilleries."[3] Indeed, the company's importing impact was such that authorities in Nashville were urged to develop their own customhouse and not rely on the houses of New York and other established customhouses. A *U&A* article on November 8, 1872, stated explicitly that the city's surveyor of customs was being stressed by Dickel's importation of bonded Holland gin and Irish and Scotch whiskies.[4]

The company had moved in 1871 to secure the wholesale distributorship for the highest-quality beer and ale available. Stifel and Pfeiffer brewed "bottled ale and lager beer ... a pure and healthy beverage [for] general and family use ... acknowledged to be the best in the South." It was brewed in the massive South Nashville Brewery (later the Nashville Brewery) in voluminous underground caves. An 1871 ad in the *Nashville Tennessean* stated, "For full particulars, please call on or address Geo. Dickel & Co."[5] Their beer—later known as "Gerst," after future master brewer and owner William Gerst—would be a national staple for decades.

A hint at the scale of the business by this time is reflected in an 1874 *Tennessean* article covering a 2:00 a.m. fire, witnessed by Meier Salzkotter, at the Dickel warehouse on the corner of Church and Market streets. The article described the appearance of "disheveled heads, and forms clad in thin drapery" who threw open their windows, as well as "nervous women shouting in terror, wringing their hands and crying frantically for help.... The animals at Tealey's livery stable being released with horses running up and down the street neighing and snorting with affright." Fortunately, within an hour the fires had been extinguished. The rescued warehouse contained 900 barrels of whiskey, 150 of which had just been received from Lincoln County, valued at $100,000 (over $2 million in 2021 dollars).[6] Of note is that Lincoln County is only a few miles from Tullahoma and Lynchburg, future homes for Cascade Whisky (today's George Dickel/Cascade Hollow) and Jack Daniel's. Someone in the area was producing a lucrative product.

* * *

Manny and Emma wasted no time starting their family while living with Emma's sister, Augusta, and George Dickel on Dickerson Pike. Felix Emile was born in 1873, when Emma was twenty-three and Manny twenty-six, followed by George Augustus in 1874, John Buist in 1876, and Louis Banzer in 1878. Insight into Manny Shwab's character and familial devotion is shown by his naming his first child after his deceased nephew, Felix, and his brother, Emile; his second after his brother-in-law, George; and his third, John Buist, after the doctor who had cared for his dying brother, Joseph.

The 1873 city directory lists "Shwab VES salesman GAD and Co[.], residence country," and the 1877 directory lists Meier Salzkotter and George Dickel as owners of George A. Dickel & Co. The 1879 city directory shows "Shwab V Emmanuel, salesman 2 [N.] [M]arket St, living on Dickerson Pike."[7]

7

The Saga of Bell Nance

As stated previously, George Dickel was active in community affairs such as the volunteer fire department, produce competitions, and local issues in his rural community of Edgefield, two miles from GDC headquarters. He played a small role in one such issue—an interesting but explosive affair in the summer of 1877 that involved murder, mob violence, and a potential lynching a mile or so from the Dickel/Shwab household. This story gives insight into the times and the social environment of Shwab, Dickel, and their company.

According to *Nashville Union and American* (*U&A*) newspaper accounts and later court testimony, on the night of June 1, 1877, about fifty men met in Edgefield, "at the hall of Cherokee Tribe No. 21, Improved Order of Red Men, North Edgefield, in regard to the death of Capt. Leonard K. Hooper." (Despite the name, this fraternal organization was open only to white men, and it appropriated stereotyped ideas about native cultures.) The local mayor, A.S. Hill (later to serve as the mayor of Nashville in 1904–1906), was "called to the chair" of the meeting and the *U&A* reporter called as secretary (a reporter being part of the story was apparently not as surprising then as it would be today). The mayor stated to the assemblage that their task was "to take action, not to say whether the killing was or was not justifiable." The police had been warned that a mob was planning to descend on the jail to lynch twenty-two-year-old Bell Nance, who had been arrested for the murder of Leonard Hooper. The mayor appointed George Dickel to "draft a suitable resolution[,]" which he did. He later read it to the gathering.[1]

Seven years prior, A.C. Nance, Bell's father, had leased property for a scheme to erect a toll house and gate that would block White

Manny Shwab and the George Dickel Company

Creek and Dickerson Roads (address of the Shwab/Dickel residence), which he successfully did. According to later witness testimony, the community "patiently" paid the tolls, coming and going to Nashville. A year before Hooper's death, the state legislature passed an act prohibiting Nance's blockage of the roads, but he persisted. Some community members cut a small road bypassing the toll booth and gate, but A.C. and Bell erected a fence blocking the workaround. On May 31, 1877, Captain L.K. Hooper, a decorated Confederate cavalryman and respected community member, began disassembling the fence. A.C. and his son approached Hooper and asked "by what authority" he was tearing down their fence. Hooper walked to the nearby blacksmith shop and returned with an axe. Words were exchanged. Hooper planted the axe in A.C.'s head and the latter fell to the ground. Bell then pulled out a gun and shot Hooper, who dropped dead at the scene. One witness stated about the gunshot that they heard "some sort of report, but I thought it was the sound of Mr. Nance's skull bursting." But A.C.'s skull did not burst: a doctor testified that the paper stuffing in his hat saved him from death, though he did suffer a two-inch gash in his skull.[2]

Word spread of an attempt to congregate the next evening to storm the jail and lynch Bell, who had been arrested for murder. In reaction to this rumor, the National Camp of Pale Faces, No. 106, and five other camps of this national order—another extreme white supremacist organization with which the Nances were apparently associated—met and "adopted resolutions ordering out as much strength as the Order could muster to prevent the lynching of young Nance." One hundred fifty to two hundred members were in the assembled mass of five hundred on the street, awaiting a signal should the crowd descend on the jail. But apparently the Nances were being "kept in concealment by an officer."[3]

Dickel read his resolution to those gathered on June 1, simply stating that the "community have suffered in death the loss of one of our best and enterprizing [sic] citizens" and that it was resolved that "we tender our entire and heartfelt sympathy" to his family. After reading the resolution, Dickel and others spoke regarding Hooper's character. According to the *U&A*, "In less than fifteen minutes after

7. The Saga of Bell Nance

[Dickel read his resolution,] the toll house and toll gate were discovered to be on fire." The mob watched as the structure burned. The *U&A* article continued:

> It is also stated that it was not intended to burn the house but to cut it [the gate] down. For this purpose eleven men with sharp axes ... were on the way to the house when the flames burst forth and saved them further trouble.... [T]he negroes residing on the Nance place have vacated their cabins through fear that they may be burned over their heads.[4]

Several weeks later, a hung jury resulted in the release of Bell Nance. Seven jurors voted to acquit; five voted to find Bell guilty of second-degree murder. By a plethora of eyewitness testimony and many character witnesses for Captain Hooper, Bell, and his father (the governor testified on A.C.'s behalf), Nashville was entertained for the summer.[5]

8

1881–1889

The future portfolio of Manny Shwab's ventures, investments, and many backstage endeavors illustrates his focus on—and indeed obsession with—recognizing and embracing trends and associated opportunities and controlling as much of the business landscape and points along the supply chain as possible. An example of his and the Dickel company's vision can be seen in Meier Salzkotter's overseas explorations for "the best" products. They were not solely focused on wine and spirits, also taking into consideration anything associated with their distribution and sales. An 1880 item in the *American* and a subsequent advertisement announced the company's carload shipment and availability of "the Queen of Table Waters," Apollinaris, a German sparkling-water sensation discovered twenty years before that was trending throughout Europe, where a popular drink was "whisky and a small Polly." Most likely, George A. Dickel & Co. had obtained distribution rights and would provide the product wholesale.

The Nashville Fire

In 1881, the company was again greatly impacted by fire. In May, a massive inferno gutted downtown Nashville, destroying "one of

---
ONE car-load of fresh Apollinaris Water just received by Geo. A. Dickel & Co.

Announcement of shipment of Apollinaris water (*Daily American*, March 28, 1880).

8. 1881–1889

Above: Dickel ad for Apollinaris, the "queen of table waters," with caution to buy only the authentic brand (*Daily American,* May 29, 1880). *Right:* A poster (circa 1890) by Philip May, a nineteenth-century English illustrator. "A whisky and a small Polly" was an international favorite drink at the time, consisting of Apollinaris sparkling water and whiskey.

the finest blocks in the city." The *Nashville Banner* estimated that the fire destroyed 1,350,000 square feet of the city. The conflagration started in a large paint and oil warehouse and quickly engulfed the surrounding buildings. The Maxwell House Hotel occupants "stampeded away from the hotel with their baggage." At a wholesale liquor warehouse (not Dickel's), "whisky began to explode like small artillery."[1] An article from the *Nashville Banner* read, "It seemed the whole population were out on the thoroughfares. Add to our 50,000 inhabitants the 25,000 strangers in the city and readers can have some idea of the excitement that prevailed."[2] Many of the bystanders formed "bucket and broom brigades" to assist and "threw bricks through the windows to admit the stream" of water from firehoses. The building of one of the city's largest newspapers, the *Union and*

American, was threatened by the flames. One bystander, waxing eloquent, stated, "I have always been opposed to the *American*, but look at her, she stands like a rock and it seems God is with her, and, by the Eternal, so am I."[3]

The George A. Dickel & Co. building at the corner of Market and Church streets was entirely destroyed, and the company's loss was the greatest of the thirty-four buildings affected: $2 million in today's dollars.[4] As early as 1869, the company's address had been 2 North Market, later changed to 2nd and "Mkt" (which is today's 2nd Avenue and Church Street), but they did not originally own the building.

The company purchased the property in 1881 and began construction on a new building. The period of 1881–1882 would be the only time the company was not listed at that address, moving down the street to 36 South Market while the new headquarters was built. Geo. A Dickel & Co. remained at that location until Manny sold the property in 1917. The building stands today with a marker under the gable reading "1882."

The Citizens' Reform Ticket

The city election of October 1883 served as the first public indication that GDC was actively involved in local politics. Nashville Democrat merchants developed a "radical reform" ticket (the Citizens' Reform ticket) and a new system of government in response to the perceived incompetence of Nashville's electors, who were accused of grossly mismanaging public works and city operations (as well as associated high taxation). An October 6 *Nashville Banner* article titled "Reform: A Strong Pull and a Long Pull All Along the Line" described the merchants' ticket. GDC was one of the companies closing down on the day of the election to encourage employees across the city to get out and vote.[5] The front page of the October 12 *New York Times* highlighted the importance of the election to the city:

> NASHVILLE, Tenn., Oct. 11.—The election for Mayor and 10 Councilmen, under the new system of government, resulted in favor of the Citizens' Reform ticket, which has a majority of probably 1,500. The contest

8. 1881–1889

The headquarters (still standing) for George A. Dickel & Co. from 1882 until 1917. The company had been at the same address since 1869, but the original building was completely destroyed in the "great Nashville fire of 1881."

was the most exciting in the history of the city, and to-night bonfires are blazing and the streets are filled with thousands of enthusiastic citizens.[6]

Abraham

On March 24, 1884, Abraham Schwab died at the Tod House Hotel in Youngstown, Ohio, with his daughter, Flora, by his side. Immigrating from Alsace at twenty-two to a country unknown to him, most likely unable to speak the language and not knowing what reception he would receive as a Jew (a religion especially strange to the mid-nineteenth-century South), Abraham became a force in fledgling Jewish communities in Youngstown; Louisville, Kentucky; and Knoxville and Nashville, Tennessee. He was part of the first Nashville minyans and president of its Magen David Society, president of Youngstown and Louisville congregations, and part of the first minyans in Knoxville as well as the father of the city's first Jewish bride and of the first Jew buried in the county. He also established successful imported liquor businesses in four cities, in addition to fathering and mentoring several influential children and associates.

Abraham's passing was noted in the *Pittsburgh Post-Gazette* as that of a "most esteemed Hebrew citizen."[7] An announcement to Manny's "many friends" in the *American* of his father's death was an indication of Manny's growing reputation in the city.[8]

However, an editorial tongue-in-cheek aside in the February 20, 1885, *Nashville Banner* showed Manny was also gaining notoriety:

> We observe with pain that the old form of putting the name of a hotel first is going out of style, and that they now put it "Hotel English," "Hotel Anderson," etc. Soon we shall see such signs as "Butcher Shop Jones," "Gin Mill Schwab" and the like. What is the country coming to?[9]

* * *

In August 1885, another indication of Shwab's rising prominence in the city was the newspaper coverage of his wife Emma's "Distressing Accident" and its aftermath for days in detail. The coverage of this incident, like so many newspaper stories at the time, detailed everyday life in Nashville in the late 1800s in a style that

The many friends of Mr. V. E. Shwab, will regret to learn of the death of his father, Mr. A. Shwab, at Youngstown, Ohio.

Abraham Schwab death announcement (*Daily American*, March 26, 1884).

8. 1881–1889

> Abraham Shwab, for many years engaged in business at Youngstown, O., and a most esteemed Hebrew citizen, died suddenly of heart disease at his room in the Tod House yesterday afternoon. Deceased leaves three sons, Emanuel Shwab, Nashville, Tenn.; Emil Shwab, Louisville, Ky.; Harry Shwab, formerly of Pittsburgh, now in Cincinnati. His only daughter, Miss Flora, was with him when he died.

Abraham Schwab obituary (*Pittsburgh Post-Gazette*, March 25, 1884).

would be lacking in today's dry journalism. In describing the August 28 accident, the *American* reported that Emma would often bring Manny the two and a half miles along Dickerson turnpike in a buggy early in the morning, letting him off at "the eastern approach, on First Street, to the pontoon bridge"; he would proceed on foot to GDC at the corner of Market and Church streets and then be picked up by Emma after work.

> Mrs. Shwab had turned her horse in the direction of home and, with her little son [ten-year-old George] started back, when she heard a streetcar coming up behind her, and attempted to drive to the edge of the street in order to allow the car room to pass. Driving too near the embankment, the vehicle struck a deep gully running along the side of the street and the buggy was overturned throwing the lady with great force against the embankment. The little boy escaped unhurt, but when his mother was picked up it was found that the bones of her left leg above the ankle were both terribly crushed.

Emma was taken, in "excruciating pain" and greatly depressed, to a neighboring home, where she was surgically attended by a Dr. Menees. According to the paper, the next day Emma was home resting "as comfortably as could be expected [and] her many friends seriously fear that amputation of the limb will yet be necessary."[10] Fortunately, as it turned out, amputation was not necessary.

On October 12, 1886, "Vict E Shwab and wife" sued the mayor and city council for $40,000 ($1,125,000 today) as a result of the accident. At the time, over a dozen suits against the city were pending for accidents caused by the poor conditions of the city streets and other public works. A newspaper report describes lawsuits for various injuries sustained: people falling into an open sewer on Demonbreun Street; a cart breaking into a sewer; a fall due to changes in the road's grading; a leg broken due to falling into a "cut in the street"; a lady falling into an "open water box"; and so forth.[11] Apparently the city (especially the Board of Public Works) could indeed benefit from a "Reform Party." The Shwab case was "compromised" (settled) for an unknown amount, with court costs paid by the city.

Very interestingly, on October 12 the Circuit Court heard the Shwab suit as well as the George Dickel company's proceedings against one Jack Daniel for a $2,000 debt ($536,000 today). The details of the latter suit apparently no longer exist. It was dismissed in December.[12]

George Dickel apparently had to withdraw from an active role in the company bearing his name around 1886 due to being thrown from his horse and, according to his 1894 obituary, never fully recovering. The specifics of the accident and his injuries are unknown. In addition, while the roles of partners Meier

CIRCUIT COURT.

Proceedings on yesterday—A. R. Castleman vs. T. W. Castleman, motion to dismiss petition for certiorari and supersedeas, overruled and cause set for trial at special term; J. M. Guardian, road commissioner, vs. James Burchett, justice's judgment affirmed; Chas. H. Redmond vs. Dan Hanifin, plaintiff took non suit; Ed. Lisle, commissioner, vs. J. S. Greer et al., continued by consent; Vic E. Schwab and wife vs. the Mayor and City Council of Nashville, passed until special term; Maay Altmyer vs. same, same entry; McGuire, Scoggins & Co. vs. Louisville & Nashville Railroad Company, pending.

Call of docket to-day—B. F. Champ vs. George Beech, W. H. Lasley vs. Charles Nelson, T. H. Young vs. John Forte, Howard Bell vs. T. H. Young, Wm. Winters vs. Order of Iron Hall, S. H. Husler vs. Jacob Tugendrich, W. L. Fonville vs. G. H. Wessel, Leon Lewis vs. C. A. McLean. The call to-morrow, 66 to end of docket jury.

Geo. A. Dickel & Co. commenced suit yesterday in the Circuit Court against Jack Daniel for a debt of $2,000.

Circuit court proceedings. Manny and Emma sue the mayor and city council and the Dickel company sues Jack Daniel, the individual (*Daily American*, October 13, 1886).

8. 1881–1889

Court minutes showing Dickel/Daniel suit dismissed. The Dickel company declines to further prosecute (Minutes of the Davidson County Court, December 23, 1886).

Circuit court record of dismissal.

Salzkotter and Manny Shwab in GDC are well documented, the role of Dickel in the business, other than serving as an early rectifier and—on rare occasions—as a spokesperson to the media, has little documentation. He is quoted in an August 1889 newspaper article about the effect of a good corn crop on the business.[13] However, he was never involved in the Cascade distillery that Shwab would soon purchase or in the operations of the Climax Saloon (purchased the year after his accident) or in the other establishments purchased by Shwab. The company's role in Cascade Whisky was as exclusive distributor and eventual bottler. There is no record of Dickel having ever visited the distillery. The Shwab family has an undated photograph of him, titled "the Cascade Club," which must have been taken after Shwab's purchase of the distillery in 1888 and the active marketing of "Cascade Whisky." So, although Dickel withdrew from active participation in the company, he apparently was not fully incapacitated until two years before his death.

The Climax Saloon

Shwab seemed to have had a passion for controlling as much of the supply chain as possible. Not content with operating one of

8. 1881–1889

Previously unpublished photograph of George Dickel (front left) and Victor Shwab (front right) (assumed) at the Cascade Club, others unknown, circa 1890 (courtesy of George Shwab IV).

the most successful liquor wholesale operations in the South, his focus moved to the end user: retailing. His first effort must have been unsatisfactory. In 1886, GDC advertised for sale a "first-class saloon in a good location" about which there are no records.[14] But Manny decided to create his own outlet. On January 11, 1887, the property at 210 Cherry Street was sold by John Burkholz to Manny Shwab, George Dickel, and Meier Salzkotter, individually, for $27,000 ($585,000 today).[15] That was a lot for a nondescript building. But the Climax was to become the first, most famous, and most elaborate of the many saloons and gambling houses (also known, perhaps more suitability, as "sporting houses") that arose in the Men's Quarter, along Broadway, in Hell's Half Acre, and in Black Bottom. The Men's Quarter included what was later known as Printer's Alley. Whereas the area was well known and patronized by many of the most prominent men in Nashville, their ladies stayed away, knowing whom they would see leaving the various establishments.

Manny Shwab and the George Dickel Company

Climax Saloon street scene, circa 1895 (Tennessee State Library and Archives).

Manny would be the saloon's sole owner and promote it as the company's headquarters. Its profitability extended into the twentieth century up until Prohibition. He was to add other successful "end user" establishments to his holdings, but none as elaborate or artistically designed as the Climax. He has been described as its "builder" and "architect."[16] The establishment was to be frequented by many of Nashville's movers and shakers (including the mayor, the chief of police, and the Public Works "Big Three") and, if rumor spoke true, even entertained a president of the United States.

This area, between Church and Union, was the political, economic, and recreational center of Nashville. So, the four-story Climax's proximity to the Maxwell House Hotel and other upscale establishments was no coincidence. The Maxwell had a convenient back door opening into the area. The building was completely renovated. Four enormous angels on its exterior greeted customers as they entered. The basement floor was a saloon and theater for cancan dancers and other acts. Infamous dancers were employed, such as Gilda Gray (the "Shimmy Queen") and Eva Tanguay (the "I

8. 1881–1889

The Climax Bar interior, circa 1890 (Tennessee State Library and Archives).

Don't Care Girl"). The first floor boasted an elaborate bar with marble floors—modern and elegant for the times. The second floor was dedicated to gambling, with card, craps, and pool tables as well as boards for horse racing. A large mural of the First Street riverfront was painted behind the elegant bar. A notorious craps croupier, Spot McCarthy, ran the table and barked out his well-known announcement: "Put your money where your mouth is. If you can't get them in, you can't get them out!"[17]

The stairs up to the third floor were often adorned by ladies greeting incoming customers. The rooms' walls were covered with embossed wood or papier-mâché wallpaper, each with a cast-iron mantel. In anticipation of unwelcome visits from the police, each room featured a false wall with a hidden panel in the closet that, when pressed, opened to a small room with a bench where customers and the ladies could wait out inspections (the author's grandfather, Buist Shwab, showed the hidden rooms to the author's father). The Gay Nineties, indeed.

Manny Shwab and the George Dickel Company

Legalized Prostitution

Perhaps the casual, "look the other way" attitude of many Nashvillians concerning prostitution was influenced by the fact that, just a little over twenty years before Manny Shwab built the Climax, the profession was legal in the city. Nashville was the first city in the United States—indeed, on this continent—to experiment with legalized and regulated prostitution. And, according to the doctors tasked with managing the associated medical care, "it seems to have been a remarkable success."[18]

The Climax Bar exterior, circa 1890 (Tennessee State Library and Archives).

The marshals for the Nashville federal census of 1860 identified 207 women who listed their profession as "prostitute," though there were likely many other ladies of the night who officially identified otherwise (this in a city whose population was approximately 14,000). The Smokey Row district, positioned just below the capitol building, was an area two blocks wide and four blocks long—eight blocks of bordellos. Most houses were poorly constructed and maintained, but a few were luxurious, such as that belonging to Rebecca and Eliza Higgins at 101–103 North Front Street in the census, showing seventeen resident prostitutes. Martha Reeder listed $15,000 of personal property at 72 North Street, making her one of the city's wealthiest citizens.[19] The residents of Smokey Row may not have been too disappointed when, in February 1862, thirty thousand Union soldiers descended on the area.

Cases of venereal disease among the Union occupiers became so prevalent that Captain Ephraim Wilson wrote, "During the winter of 1862–1863, the Army had a social enemy to contend with which seriously threatened its very existence.... [T]he women of the town ... fifteen hundred of them at a single time were gathered up and placed aboard a train" and sent to Louisville. They came back. Lieutenant Colonel George Spaulding then used the police force and provost guard to round up "all known women known to be of vile character" and placed them on a steamer headed out of town.[20] Once again, they came back.

So Colonel Spaulding proposed a system of licensed prostitution. Each prostitute would be issued a recorded license and her residence documented. A surgeon was appointed as a Board of Examination; each prostitute was examined weekly and then either given a certificate of soundness or ordered into a hospital if "in the slightest degree diseased." While in the designated "Hospital Number Eleven," located on Market Street, they would do the Army's laundry until deemed disease free and "returned to duty." Those arrested without a license served no less than thirty days in the workhouse.[21] This approach worked.

By April 30, 1864, 352 women were licensed and 92 infected women had been treated. The surgeon general noted, "Under these regulations a marked improvement was speedily noticed in the manner and appearance of the women. When the inspections were first enforced, many were exceedingly filthy in their person and apparel, and obscene and coarse in their language, but this soon gave way to cleanliness and propriety." Apparently the women were treated well and attention given to their comfort and medical needs. The doctor noted that a "better class" of prostitutes had been drawn to Nashville, and there had been a notable increase in the ladies of the night.[22] One result was that the ladies no longer needed the cloak of nighttime. Soldiers, notably officers, became open in their relationships.

According to Nashville's *Daily Press*, officers were often seen with their ladies in carriages, and one was seen riding into downtown "nude from the waist heavenward," which caused quite a stir.[23]

Dr. William Chambers, the physician in charge of Hospital Number Fifteen (the Soldiers Syphilitic Hospital), noted that in early 1863 he had ten to twenty officers under treatment at all times. After the regulation of prostitution, the number dropped to one per month. As of December 31, 1864, 2,330 men had been treated in his hospital. Of the first 999 admitted, only thirty had contracted the disease in Nashville.[24] Surgeon R. Fletcher was in charge of the women's hospital. In a letter dated August 15, 1864, he concluded,

> We have here no Parisian "Bureau des Moeurs" [morals], with its vigilant police.... This much, however, is to be claimed, that after the attempt to reduce disease by the forcible expulsion of the prostitutes, had, as it always has, utterly failed, the more philosophic plan of recognizing and controlling an ineradicable evil has met with undoubted success. Among the difficulties to be overcome was the opposition of the public women. This has so effectually disappeared that I believe they are now earnest advocates of a system which protects their health and delivers them from the extortion of quacks and charlatans. They gladly exhibit to their visitors the "certificate."[25]

As the war ended, according to Dr. Chambers, many of the women rapidly left Nashville, "looking out for situations where more money can be obtained wherewith to bedeck and bedizzen themselves."[26] Certainly, many Nashvillians, along with young Manny Shwab, witnessed this successful experiment, which may have resulted in a greater tolerance for the profession's practitioners.

Tolerated or not, as this author's grandmother, Louise Shwab, explained, the wives of Nashville knew to steer clear of the Men's Quarter to avoid identifying the businesses' patrons.

Meier Moves On

Meier Salzkotter, after thirty years in the (legal and illegal) business of wholesale spirits with the Shwabs and marrying into the family twice, retired in 1888. That was the last year he was listed in the

8. 1881–1889

Female Venereal Hospital #11 in Nashville, circa 1863. During Nashville's Union occupation, venereal disease was finally brought under control after prostitution had been made legal—a first in the Americas (National Archives).

city directory as a partner in GDC. The 1889 directory listed him as "capitalist." He invested in several real estate properties and was listed in 1891 as having paid taxes on $23,500 of real estate—almost $1 million today. He also evidently became quite involved with the Masons, presumably with George Dickel's lodge. Meier died August 3, 1891, of a "heart clot," and his obituary stated that the "Masonic fraternity will conduct the service of the order at the cemetery."²⁷ He was buried in the Nashville Temple cemetery next

DIED.

SALZKOTTER.—At his home, 1503 Hays street, at 7 a. m. yesterday, M. SALZKOTTER, aged 65 years.

His funeral will take place at the Vine-street Temple, on Wednesday, Aug. 5, at 10 a. m.

Burial at the Jewish Cemetery. The Masonic fraternity will be in attendance, and will conduct the service of the order at the cemetery.

Carriages from Cornelius'.

Meier Salzkotter obituary (*Daily American*, August 4, 1891).

Manny Shwab and the George Dickel Company

to his beloved Felix. An interesting side note is that drama seemed to follow Salzkotter till the very end. On the day of his death, his "house boy," Jim Ross, was arrested for murder at Meier's home. He had apparently been in a rock fight the night before with a drunken nineteen-year-old man who ran at him with a knife. Ross confessed that he had shot and killed the man.[28]

9

Cascade Hollow and the Silver Dollar Saloon

Having secured a significant place at the end of the supply chain with the Climax Saloon (the whiskey chain extending from raw materials, distillation, aging in barrels and their storage, packaging [bottling], marketing, wholesale distribution, and ultimately retailing to the consumer), Shwab turned his focus to its beginning. According to the Nashville *Daily Union*, in 1886 the distilling industry was the largest manufacturing industry in Tennessee, having consumed 750,000 bushels of corn and 500,000 bushels of apples and peaches in that year.[1] So distilling was logically Shwab's next step.

Cascade Hollow

The company had continued to expand on the business plan developed by Abraham Schwab, specializing in imported items, including French brandies and Scotch whisky, as well as local whiskey. Since before the war and until the early 1880s, in order to maintain their image as providing a high-quality product, the family had to "rectify" the various available local whiskies to achieve acceptable and consistent quality. In the process, they could easily identify the better distillers. Manny's attention was on one in particular in Coffee County.

The future Cascade Hollow Distillery was located on property granted by the State of Tennessee. According to Jerry Cook's *Historic Normandy*, by 1810 a settler named John Gage had established water-powered grist mills and a sawmill on a branch later known as Gage Creek and eventually as Cascade Creek. Gage sold one hundred acres in 1812 to the heirs of Joseph Ake.[2] We can assume a distillery

Manny Shwab and the George Dickel Company

1890 photograph of Cascade Hollow Distillery in operation. View is looking north. The stillhouse is on the left, the aging barn and cistern room on the right (United States Department of the Interior, National Park Service).

was present by the Civil War when Confederate General Braxton Bragg's Order No. 146 was issued a few miles away in Tullahoma, outlawing consumption of grain by distillation (grain for the troops was becoming scarce), resulting in the confiscation of all grain and whiskey in the area. Matthew Sims bought part of the property (including distillery equipment) from John Brown in 1879. Sims is shown in the 1880 census as a distiller.[3]

By 1883, McLin "Kie" Davis had partnered with Sims and F.E. Cunningham to complete the three-hundred-acre parcel, purchased for $4,400, which eventually became the Cascade Hollow Distillery (IRS listed as the Cascade Distil. Co.). In addition to the distillery, the purchase included a flour grist mill, three warehouses, stables, and even a sawmill. The property was beautiful, set in deep woods full of white oak and sugar-maple trees. The oaks were harvested for the sawmill to cooper whisky barrels and the maples burned for charcoal. The Cascade name originated from the stream's eighty-foot waterfall. At its base, the water filtered through limestone, which, it was said, removed the iron, resulting in pure water perfect for whisky distillation. The stream then flowed through the distillery.[4]

9. Cascade Hollow and the Silver Dollar Saloon

Photograph of the Cascade Falls, circa 1905. This may be the distillery employees at a Fourth of July celebration. Shwab owned the property, including the falls, at this time (Tennessee State Library and Archives).

Manny Shwab and the George Dickel Company

In 1888, the Internal Revenue Service listed the distillery in the name of M.B. Sims as number 392. In 1892, it was listed as the same number but in the name of "Davis & Co., as Cascade Distil. Co." However, Kie Davis was the distiller from 1883 until his death in 1898, a master whose product, due to its exceptional quality, almost immediately became known as "the famous Cascade whisky." Davis is credited with several innovations, but the most marketed was his insistence that cooling the mash by moonlight gave the whisky its distinctive mellowness. "Mellow as Moonlight" became the catchphrase printed on every label.

It was a bustling, efficient operation. In her definitive article on GDC in the Fall 1998 *Tennessee Historical Quarterly*, Kay Baker Gaston quotes Sweetwater native David McQuiddy, assumed to have worked at the distillery: "I now see in my mind's eye the mule teams hauling the Cascade whiskey in large, square unfinished wooden boxes, with the picture of a still burned into the wood, and loading them into [boxcars] on the siding across the main track from our home."[5] In 1888, Manny purchased Sims' share of the distillery and additional adjacent property, increasing the acreage to approximately six hundred and securing two-thirds of the distillery in his own name while Davis retained a one-third share. GDC became the whisky's sole distributor.[6]

The distillery's reputation grew exponentially, a result of Kie Davis' wizardry and Manny Shwab's marketing through GDC. In December 1889, the *Nashville Banner* sent a reporter with Manny to Cascade Hollow to write about, according to the reporter, the "best" Tennessee whiskey distillery, its processes, and the difference between true Tennessee sour mash and the "lesser sweet mash" and "sweet wines" being peddled as Tennessee sour mash. (Because of his history, it may have been Manny who insisted on spelling *whisky* without an "e" in a nod to the alleged superior quality of Scottish whisky.) The *Banner*'s reporter attempted to explain why the reputation of Tennessee whiskey was not as great as that of other whiskies. The result was an in-depth, instructive, and detailed (though obviously biased) look at the making of "true" sour mash and what made Cascade whisky so distinctive. The following quotes are condensed

9. Cascade Hollow and the Silver Dollar Saloon

notations and excerpts from the very detailed article, included here (for the whiskey nerds out there) as a primer on nineteenth-century Tennessee whiskey distillation as well as examples of the era's journalistic style.

The author began by stating that much of Cascade's competition was "a flood of common, impure, and poisonous liquors" and "rectified high wines" and that it was an "incontestable fact" that many of the odors and flavors in Bourbon, Scotch, Irish, and other whiskies were due to the presence of fusel oil and amylic alcohol "poisons," which were purified out of sour mash due to true sour mash processes and percolation through fine charcoal. The writer's leanings were apparent in the argument that Tennessee sour mash was "incomparably less obnoxious in its effects than Bourbon, rye or any other known whisky" and that "more of it can be drunk than any other kind.... [T]he toper who confines himself to it will live longer than he who drinks Bourbon, as it has not an obtrusive flavor like other whiskies which cannot be disguised." Sour mash was described as a

> mixture of meal and water prepared for fermentation. It comes from natural fermentation, without the aid of chemicals or artificially destructive agents, when the action of the diastase in the malt converts the starch in the grain to sugar and then into alcohol.... [S]weet mash comes from sulphuric acid and other destructive elements being added to get the most starch into glucose then into alcohol. So, sour mash comes from the intent to create the best quality spirits whereas, sweet mash from the intent to create the greatest quantity of spirits without special regard to quality.[7]

As one explanation for the cutting of corners by competition, the reporter said that the IRS required accountability of only two and a half gallons of whiskey from a bushel of grain for sour mash but four to five gallons from a bushel for sweet mash. So there were much greater profits from sweet mash. Distillers could get twice as much sweet mash from a bushel of corn. According to this writer, the majority of whiskey sold as sour mash in bars and dispensed from drugstores was the doctored stuff, which ruined sour mash's reputation. Cheating distilleries would get certification for both varieties and then distill sweet mash but advertise with their sour mash certification.

Manny Shwab and the George Dickel Company

The article then moved to the Cascade distillery:

> This distillery is beautifully situated in a picturesque region at the foot of high reaching hills, by which it is nearly surrounded. Its machinery is run by water power supplied by an abundant flow of pure freestone water which gushes from springs above to the turbine wheel. The water is pellucid and cold and sent to the flake stand and other parts of the distillery. This distillery is under the constant personal management and supervision of Mr. [M. H.] Davis who takes a great pride in making the finest and purest whisky. He understands the minute details of the process. No trouble or expense is spared by him to maintain his whisky at the highest attainable standard. This effort is seconded by Mr. [V. E.] Shwab, the active manager of the firm of Geo. A Dickel & Co[.] who is determined to make this whisky the model brand of pure whisky.[8]

Cascade used only the cleanest white hominy, which was finely ground and weighed out by "the government storekeeper" (federal agents had someone permanently on site at every major distillery). The reporter then launched into the details of making sour mash:

> Sixty-three bushels [of grain] are weighed and delivered every day into a large hopper just over the great mash tub. They add a small portion of rye meal as determined by the distiller's long experimenting as to exactly what is necessary for the best quality whisky. Then into the mash tub is injected a certain quantity of hot potale from the still [residue left from the first distillation] and the meal is flowed into the tub while a wooden rake revolves to thoroughly mix the meal and water. This is cooked into a mush. It is then cooled via cold spring water flowing through copper pipes coiled in the tub. A certain quantity of pure corn malt and a little yeast from one of the fully fermented mashes is added and then it is all deposited in one of four large fermenting vats and kept at a certain temperature to naturally ferment.[9]

The specific process that Kie Davis developed to filter the mash was explained as follows:

> There are four large leach tubs about 10 feet high and six feet diameter. Into these tubs is packed and pounded compactly and firmly a quantity of the finest wood charcoal until the tubs are nearly full. The charcoal is maple wood and made in the open air. Even the best kiln-made charcoal contains a trace of creosote and other wood extracts used by most distillers, but not allowed by Mr. Davis. The open air charcoal is very pure but very expensive and difficult to keep the wood from going to ashes before

9. Cascade Hollow and the Silver Dollar Saloon

the fire can be extinguished. Davis will not even allow the sprinkling of water to extinguish the fire as the water's contact with the ashes gives a perceptible trace of lye to the charcoal which would be detrimental to the quality of the whisky.

Into the closely packed leach tubs the new whisky is conducted by the pipe and it percolates slowly though the charcoal. This ground charcoal is packed so closely it takes several days for the whisky to make its way to the cisterns below. When it does get through it is thoroughly purified as can be easily demonstrated by comparing some of the whisky after it comes through with the whisky before it is leached.

The liquor is a limpid, crystal fluid without any color and without any trace of verdigris or fusel oil or unpleasant odor. Because of these processes, the whisky made by this distillery is unsurpassed in quality by any made anywhere else. The cistern and leaching rooms are kept under lock and key by the government storekeeper.[10]

The author then explained the final process:

The barrels are thoroughly charred on the inside to prevent the taint of tannin from the oak. No coloring matter whatever is added, but the liquor gradually is colored by the charred barrels. The coloring corresponds with the age of the whisky, becoming richer and darker as the years go by. In the "high wine" establishments, coloring is added, but not here. The whisky remains in bond in charge of the storekeeper for three years then taken out, and stored in Nashville to get still more age and mature into the richest and finest bouquet.

Finally noted was Manny's determined goal:

Some dealers who know the quality of this whisky buy it while still in bond and leave it there to mature, but Shwab prefers to store the bulk of it himself to hold for supplying an old whisky to their rapidly extending trade in this specialty of liquors. They propose to make this the peerless whisky of Tennessee, and by the most scrupulous care and ample outlay of money in storying, maintain its reputation as a whisky to be sought after by all who want the purest article for drinking or for medical or family use.[11]

This author can attest to the whisky's exceptional flavor. In 2021, I tasted 109-year-old "Exceptionally Special" Cascade with my sister, Olivia; my son, Reilly; and my cousin, George Shwab IV. This drink was from extremely limited production reserved for the family. The whisky was best summed up by Olivia, who claims to drink only Miller Light ("anything else makes me misbehave"): "I could drink this all day." Using the "Kentucky Chew" method (according to which one swishes the liquor around in the mouth and breathes through it), distinct flavors, one by one, became discernible. There was no bite whatsoever in the Cascade whisky. It was, indeed, mellow as moonlight. George's family had set aside some whisky from 1912 that was brought out for generations on very special occasions. He described family gatherings at which his aged great-grandmother, Gene Mason "Gunga" Shwab (wife of Manny's son George), would quietly sit back in a rocking chair with the bottle in her lap as she occasionally sipped from a tiny shot glass.

The current distiller and general manager of Cascade Hollow Distilling Co. (George Dickel), Nicole Austin, kindly reviewed the above description of the Cascade process. According to her, the sour mash process is now the standard in most commercial distilleries. The use of "backset" (liquid from a previous sour mash distillation) provides an ideal environment for fermentation and has benefits for sustainability. Today, both the sour and the sweet mash processes allow one to get five gallons of product from one bushel of corn. She noted that one major difference is that today barley malt is used, not corn malt, which is "incredibly rare and difficult to find." She speculated that "corn" may have been used as a general term for grain. The final process of filtering the mash is very similar, except for Davis' insistence that the charcoal be made in the open air, the fire never extinguished by water, and then the mash cooled in the moonlight. Ms. Austin stated that she didn't "know how they did it." Today the fires are extinguished with water, but they "definitely don't notice any soapy or lye characteristics."[12]

The Silver Dollar Saloon

The Men's Quarter and the Climax Saloon catered to Nashville's more affluent patrons, but Manny was not content with capturing that limited section of the market. He knew GDC products, especially Cascade, had a much broader appeal. He had the crème de la crème saloon in the quarter. He moved on to develop the premier

9. Cascade Hollow and the Silver Dollar Saloon

saloon near the bustling waterfront to cater to the river and steamboat trade. He bought, in Emma's name, property a block from the wharf at Broad and North Market streets (today's Second Avenue) around 1892. The three-story structure became known as the V.E. Shwab Building. Manny commissioned architect Julius G. Zwicker

V.E. Shwab Building/Silver Dollar Saloon, circa 1905 (Tennessee State Library and Archives).

Manny Shwab and the George Dickel Company

Huge silver dollars in the Silver Dollar Saloon windows, circa 1900. The building and (empty) windows exist today in the heart of Nashville's honky-tonk nightlife (Tennessee State Library and Archives).

to draw up his vision for a marketing spectacle. The very distinctive, still-in-use building has terra-cotta wreaths and garlands, decorative brickwork, and an octagonal turret and lookout. In the saloon's heyday, the tile floors and bar contained hundreds of embedded silver dollars, and outside, next to the entrance, were two large round windows, each filled with a giant silver dollar. In addition to being a saloon, it served as a lodging house where one could get a bed for 25 cents and a hot lunch for 10 cents. Now affiliated with the Hard Rock Café, the building exists today alone as an island, in the midst of dozens of nightclubs and music houses—but the round windows stand empty and the embedded silver dollars have long since disappeared.

Substantial, consistent, and increasing cash flow, gained from Manny Shwab's control of the raw materials associated with whisky making through its end user, gave him the ability to venture well beyond that industry. While diversifying his holdings and spheres

9. Cascade Hollow and the Silver Dollar Saloon

Silver Dollar Saloon (the V.E Shwab building), with rooms for rent and hot lunches for 10 cents, circa 1900. The figure at the front in the center is assumed to be Manny's brother, Emile Shwab; the other men are unknown (Tennessee State Library and Archives).

of influence, for the next three decades he aggressively (both directly and indirectly) sought to thwart—or at least keep at bay—the ever-growing temperance movement. Manny astutely created leverage via influence in politics and law enforcement as well as through his association with the banking, utilities, railroad, and steel industries to keep the "Drys" at bay.

10

Diversification and Family

1890s

As the years went on, Manny began expanding his real estate portfolio. He bought two lots in 1889, one at North High and Cumberland and one on North Cherry, for a total of $2,700 ($80,000 today).¹ The property on High Street may have been purchased for his sister and brother, Flora and Emile, as they were listed as residing there. In 1890, he bought property through GDC with the United Electric Railway Company (UER) to, according to the *Banner*, "join with the railway company and erect an arcade. There will be a restaurant and general store."² UER was chartered in 1889 and consolidated the extensive Nashville streetcar system; in April of that year, it introduced Nashville's first electric streetcar. Also in 1890, for $29,500 ($885,000 today), as trustee of GDC, Manny bought two adjacent lots on the southeast corner of Broad and Walnut, one of them from James E. Caldwell, with whom he was to have a close business and personal relationship for the rest of his life. Caldwell would be one of his pallbearers.³

All This, for a Penny

If nothing else, Manny Shwab was persistent. The May 1, 1890, *Memphis Commercial Appeal* published a front-page article demonstrating this characteristic (along with his pugilistic nature) as the family's property on Dickerson Pike came to attract statewide

10. Diversification and Family

Inaugural run of Nashville's first electric streetcar on April 30, 1889 (Tennessee State Library and Archives).

interest. The article described a test case that was "the first time ever raised in Tennessee." No one had before attempted to sue an abstract company to test the liability for furnishing a defective abstract title. Shwab and Dickel had been offered an additional twenty-one acres on Dickerson Pike, but they required an abstract of the title before purchasing. The Nashville Abstract Company provided one, tracing the acres' history from 1852 until 1890. The property had been surveyed multiple times, and the abstract showed the same twenty-one acres after each sale as shown in 1852. Manny paid $200 an acre for the parcel. He had it surveyed after the sale, only to find that four and a half acres had vanished. He contracted another company to provide a title abstract, which showed the Nashville Abstract Company had failed to account for two sales that had reduced the property. Shwab and Dickel sued for $900 to recover the $200 paid for each of the missing four and a half acres.[4]

Manny Shwab and the George Dickel Company

The court battles resulted in a final appeal to the Tennessee Supreme Court by the abstract company, hoping to reverse $900 in damages found against it. The Supreme Court held that Dickel and Shwab knew well the land they were buying. "[I]n fact, one of the complainants lived on one of the small conveyances which had been made [so] they purchased exactly what they intended to purchase"; furthermore, an "abstract is not a guarantee of area." The court declared that the previous chancellor was in error to the measure of damages. However, it found that there was a technical breach, and "for this complainants are entitled to nominal damages." "The decree of the Chancellor is reversed and a decree of 1 cent and costs is given."[5] One cent. At least Shwab and Dickel were not shackled with court costs.

Chief Justice Peter Turney, future governor and Shwab ally, wrote a dissent in an article carried by the *Daily American*, expressing that buyers depend on abstract companies for the details of their purchases.[6]

Manny Shwab's Dickerson Pike property received a more positive spin when, in 1890, he donated two acres for the construction of a school bearing his name; he also served on the school's board. At the time, it was the only ten-month school in Davidson County.[7] It was in the county's seventeenth district, which the *Banner* described as one of the largest and best-equipped districts in the county. Manny must have been closely associated with the school, as evidenced by a *Nashville American* article that covered "V. E. Shwab, one of the school directors of the district," taking the pupils on an annual outing with the teachers as chaperones.[8] The Shwab School still exists on Dickerson Pike, attended by "Shwabees."

In April 1892, Manny's interest in North Cherry Street (today's 4th Avenue) expanded through his purchase of four lots at auction for $40,000 ($1,200,000 today). The *Banner* stated that the price was considered small since an offer for the property for $50,000 had been made less than a week before. The article concluded, "It is not known what Mr. Shwab's plans are."[9]

GDC newspaper ads appeared regularly in the Nashville papers

10. Diversification and Family

Shwab School, home of the "Shwabees," Dickerson Pike. Manny donated two acres for the school.

during the 1890s, highlighting Cascade Whisky, touting it as the "best and purest" sour mash in Tennessee. At the same time, the company continued to advertise European shipments of gin, port, wine, and cognac, but, interestingly, the ads now said that the spirits were "for medical purposes."[10] Under one of these Cascade ads was an ad for the First National Bank, "Capital Stock $1,000,000," showing V.E. Shwab as a director. In 1890, at the annual meeting of the Nashville Merchants Exchange, it was noted that Shwab and Charles Nelson represented the "standing committee on liquor."[11] Charles Nelson was the owner of Nelson's Green Brier Distillery.

A curious exchange between presumably fictitious personalities "Buck" and "The Situation" in the *Nashville Banner* and *Knoxville Journal* involved Cascade and Manny. In the January 16, 1892, *Banner*, "The Situation" in Knoxville asked "Buck" in Nashville to "[p]lease see Shwab and forward a gallon of 'Old Cascade.' The weather up here is hard on my by-laws."[12] The result of the request appeared in the January 18 *Journal*: "Dear Buck: Thanks to you and Shwab, The Cascade reached me safely this morning. I have surrounded

CASCADE DISTILLERY.
Best and Purest Sour Mash Whisky in Tennessee

NASHVILLE, TENN., Oct. 24, 1890.
HON. D. A. NUNN, COLLECTOR INTERNAL REVENUE, FIFTH DISTRICT, TENNESSEE:
DEAR SIR—Will you kindly state whether or not the Cascade Distillery, No. 392, is registered, operated and known as a Sour Mash Distillery.
Respectfully, GEO. A. DICKEL & CO.

UNITED STATES INTERNAL REVENUE COLLECTOR'S OFFICE, FIFTH DISTRICT, TENN., NASHVILLE, Oct. 25, 1890.
MESSRS. GEO. A. DICKEL & Co., Nashville, Tenn.:
GENTLEMEN—In reply to your inquiry of the 24th inst., I have to say that this distillery, No. 392, is now and always has been known to this office as a Sour Mash Distillery. Respectfully, D. A. NUNN, Collector.

GEO. A. DICKEL & CO.

Cascade Distillery ad declaring Cascade the best and most pure Tennessee whisky, run in the *Nashville Banner* (October through December 1890) and nationally.

one quart of it already, and the kinks have returned to my tail. You will be glad to hear of this, for it will give you a new hold. Shwab is both a patriot, scholar, and a rare judge of good liquor, as I was truly informed by Gid Baskette [editor of the *Banner*]."[13] This dialogue may have been banter between editors or even placed by Manny, but that would have been a rare display of personal propaganda for the publicity-shy Shwab.

Manny and his family were becoming known in Nashville beyond their relationship with GDC. In 1889, a blurb in the *Tennessean* stated that Manny's sister, Flora, had moved to Nashville from Boston, where she had been studying piano at the prestigious Boston Conservatory of Music.[14] She eventually matriculated at

THE SITUATION DRY.
Knoxville Journal: Dear Buck: Please see Shwab and forward a gallon of "Old Cascade." The weather up here is hard on my by-laws.   THE SITUATION.

Request from "The Situation" in Knoxville to "Buck" in Nashville for Shwab to send a gallon of Old Cascade to Knoxville (*Nashville Banner*, January 16, 1892).

10. Diversification and Family

> DEAR BUCK—Thanks to you and SHWAB. The "Cascade" reached me safely this morning. I have surrounded one quart of it already, and the kinks have returned to my tail. You will be glad to hear this, for it will give you a new hold. SHWAB is both a patriot, a scholar and a rare judge of good liquor, as I was truly informed by GID BASKETTE. THE SITUATION.

A note of appreciation in the *Knoxville Journal*. Shwab is declared a "patriot, scholar, and rare judge of good liquor" by Gid Baskette, editor of the *Nashville Banner* (*Knoxville Journal*, January 18, 1892).

Columbia University, following her major professor, Edward MacDowell, a renowned composer and pianist. She became close, lifelong friends with Professor MacDowell and his wife (as discussed later). Flora lived on High Street in Nashville, as did her brother Emile, who was listed as a salesman at GDC. In 1891, the postmaster general recommended a new post office on Dickerson Pike to be named "Shwab," as "[t]his will be satisfactory to the people of the neighborhood ... he being a leading citizen in that neighborhood and very influential."[15] Thereby, "Shwab, Tennessee" was created.

However, familial publicity was not always positive. A March 7, 1890, article stated that Shwab's sixteen-year-old son, George Augustus (named after his uncle Dickel and perhaps his aunt as well), and a friend were being sued by P.M. Carroway for $10,000 damages ($300,000 today) for "carelessly riding their bicycles."[16] Carroway claimed the boys frightened his seventeen-year-old mule, causing the animal to run away, thus injuring the mule, Carroway, his wife, and their daughter. We can only imagine the conversation poor George had with Emma and Manny when he returned home that day. The bicycle—perhaps a big-wheel, "penny-farthing," version popular in the late eighteen hundreds—was probably garaged for a spell. George was ultimately exonerated; his friend was not.

Newspapers frequently carried blurbs about the Shwab family such as George and his brother Hugh representing Montgomery Bell Academy at a speech contest and the Shwabs and Dickels "vacationing together at the Virginia shoreline."[17]

11

Temperance and Law Enforcement
Captain Clack

Radical societal divisiveness comes in many forms. At the time of such divisiveness, each side passionately clings to the righteousness of its position, but often, in retrospect, the prevailing side seems ludicrously and obviously correct: slavery, women's suffrage, segregation, even seat-belt regulation. The cavernous societal divide of late nineteenth- and early twentieth-century America—the gilded age of Nashville—was Prohibition. The divisiveness resulting from this issue dramatically impacted the city's and the state's, political, social, and economic development. According to newspaper accounts across Tennessee, Manny Shwab was the single most bothersome and effective break in the tracks. His focus was on the "tippling" (drinking of alcohol) laws and political influence.

Captain Clack: Chief of Police

The year 1893 provided a rare peek under the invisibility cloak that concealed Shwab's behind-the-scenes policy and political influence. That year (as many to follow), Manny's relationship with the chief of police, Captain J. Hadley Clack, came under heavy and very public scrutiny. Given the persistent questions concerning their relationship, it is worth taking a close look at Captain Clack.

In the latter half of the nineteenth century, the Nashville City

Council elected the powerful Board of Public Works—the "Big Three." Most of the city department heads, including the chiefs of police and fire and the street overseer, were hired and overseen by the three men chosen for the board. In 1887, they elected twenty-seven-year-old Captain J. Hadley Clack chief of police. He was the youngest chief in any American city at least the size of Nashville. Clack was from Brentwood (just outside Nashville) and a graduate of Montgomery Bell Academy and the University of Nashville. He had

J. Hadley Clack, Nashville's chief of police and first city judge (*Daily American*, May 14, 1893).

the reputation of being capable, fearless, tough, and hard nosed—"a terror of crooks and evil-doers ... an artist in his line," according to his 1904 obituary.[1] On several occasions, Clack tracked down criminals who had fled Nashville and physically brought them back for trial. One episode involved A.L. Landis (a.k.a. J.G. White), a forger who had created and sold sixteen $1,000 United Electric Railroad bonds (half a million dollars today); Clack, in disguise, tracked him down in Cincinnati and arrested him at a bank. On another occasion, Clack tracked down Pink Huckleberry, who had been accused of knifing another man, and arrested him in Louisville.[2]

In 1893, the *Banner* and other papers covered an example of Clack's toughness. The incident involved Mose C. Byrum, "a figure in the *Chicago Sunday Sun* cases."[3] The *Sun* was a notorious newspaper rag known throughout the United States for its supposed exposés of local notables for immoral and/or illegal behavior—something like the *National Enquirer* on steroids. Most cities in 1892–1894 had *Sun* "agents and correspondents" who sold copies of the paper and dug

11. Temperance and Law Enforcement

up dirt on local celebrities. The paper was sued dozens of times for obscenity and indecency; many postmasters refused to deliver the issues, and its attorneys were arrested on obscenity charges.[4] The six-foot-tall, two-hundred-pound Byrum had been convicted of murder and sent to prison but was ultimately pardoned by the governor. Since leaving prison, he had been the Nashville agent for the *Sun* and was arrested but let go several times for selling it. On September 27, 1893, Clack's wife had been "annoyed" by Byrum's persistent and "rude" stares in the Bijou Theater in Nashville. She felt he was "playing the spy" by following her as she left the theater. She called her husband, who, in full uniform, hurried to her side. When he arrived, Mrs. Clack saw Byrum "peep out from his hiding place" at a law office. The chief ran to him, seized him by the collar, and dragged him back into an office. "Someone" locked the door and closed the blinds, and then, according to the newspapers, Clack "administered a series of kicks and blows Byrum will not soon forget." Byrum made no attempt at self-defense, and Clack later said he did not want to shoot a man who did not have the courage to protect himself. The chief then dragged Byrum to the door and kicked him into the street. A large crowd had gathered, and Public Works had to investigate the incident. Clack was fully and completely exonerated, with one member stating, "I think the highest evidence a man can hear in matters such as this kind are statements of his wife, and therefore I voted to excuse the Chief." Coincidentally, surely, Clack had received an anonymous letter the week before this incident stating that the *Sun* was going to publish an exposé on him and his family.[5]

During his eleven-year tenure as chief of police, the (according to the *Banner*) "tall, handsome, well proportioned" Clack was investigated and arraigned by the Public Works Committee multiple times for objections over such issues as the disappearance of stray funds ($50) resulting from the sale of rounded-up stray cattle; "official oppression" (being too rough) on officers; public moral misconduct; failure to raid gambling houses; and frequenting houses "of ill repute" with the mayor. One investigation witness as to the last objection stated that when he saw the mayor and Clack outside Minnie Perry's well-known establishment, Clack told him to go into the house. His reply had been "I am too old for that" but that he "had gone with the two men at such houses during the day for business, but never at night." On another occasion, an officer filed a complaint that Clack had aggressively confronted him about a missing firearm that the officer had confiscated from a "Negro lady." She had complained to the officer that her husband had come home with a stolen gun and threatened to shoot her. He reassuringly replied, "[T]hat's all right, if he does, we'll get him." Clack was always exonerated, usually the result of overwhelmingly positive witness statements. For instance, one witness declared that there was "a man who looked just like Clack and was often mistaken for him," explaining why he might appear to be where he should not be.[6]

But the most frequently repeated complaint and rumor, and the one receiving the greatest public notice, was that Clack had "daily conferences with the head of the whisky front," that he "confers with Shwab with a view of favoring his interests," and that his "actions are shaped by these conferences."[7]

In June 1893, D.C. Kelley, the revered senior pastor of McKendree Methodist Church, referred in his Sunday sermon to Clack's association with the liquor industry. Kelley was well known for his relationship with General Nathan Bedford Forrest, having been a colonel as part of Forrest's escort and staff throughout the Civil War. Kelley had gone to the Big Three for information about Clack's associations and was referred to the police. On arriving at the station, he was told that Clack was not there. He speculated in his sermon that Clack had been in one of his daily conferences with "the head of the whisky front." This public accusation prompted Clack to write two open letters to Kelley appearing in the *Banner* on June 19 and 23. These letters shed direct light on the cavernous cultural schism surrounding Prohibition that was deepening both in Tennessee and nationally at this time and the position in which this rift placed the police. It was a time when disputes were often publicly and personally battled in newspapers.

In his first letter, dated June 19, Clack complained about Kelley's preaching the previous Sunday. The chief had been told that the reverend stated, on hearing of Clack's absence from the station, "I

11. Temperance and Law Enforcement

don't know where he was, but there is a rumor that at some hour of almost every day he is in conference with the head and front of the whisky element of Nashville." Clack asked, "Are you insinuating that I receive private instruction from this 'head and front' or that I am controlled in my official action by the person? I respectfully request you give to me the name of the person."[8]

Receiving no reply, Clack penned a much longer (and quite eloquent) letter on June 23 titled "An Open Letter From the Nashville Chief of Police." Clack addressed Kelley as follows: "Your protracted silence compels me, in my own defense, to address this open letter to you." He began by saying, "The Bible teaches you that the words of a tale-bearer are as wounds [and] a slanderous rumor had been repeated in the very pulpit of god." The chief then explained that "the way of a policeman is hard—damned if you do or don't. Some want you to suppress, others acclaim their right to do whatever they please." He referenced past attempts to depict him as an oppressor and the issues surrounding policing and suppressing gambling and liquor. His expressive statement was prescient of the coming shortfalls of Prohibition:

> The propensity in man to drink, to game, and to indulge his passions, has never been eradicated. Noah drank. David was not a eunuch, and soldiers gambled for the raiment of the Son of God. These propensities were strong then, and they are strong now. The theorist expects the police to suppress them. Police know all they can do is restrain. When he attempts to suppress and fails, men like you impugn. When he persists, [those affected] cry out they are oppressed.
>
> The worst of them cry out for [the officers'] heads.... [W]e deal with humanity in its shirt sleeves, and you deal with it in its Sunday clothes. I don't expect you to read this or desist from tale-bearing.... [A] dog barks.... You of course knew that a stab at my official integrity was worse than a stab at my life. If the Board of the Public Works believed you, they could not retain me. But you struck like an adder ... but blindly. You were informed by Sgt[.] Reed that I had gone home to take some medicine to my daughter.[9]

Clack then hit at the specific rumor:

> Now, as to the rumor that I had daily conferences with the head and front of the whisky interest. I am informed that you mean Mr. V.E. Shwab. He is a member of the George Dickel Company who deal in wholesale

liquors. If they have saloons, I am not aware of the fact. I do know that Mr. Shwab owns and rents out the house where the Climax Saloon is kept. I am informed he has no interest in the business. Your insinuation is that I confer with Mr. Shwab with a view of favoring his interests, or I confer with him ... to know what he desires us to do as to all the whisky men. It is absolutely false in fact. As Chief, I give orders to lieutenants who convey orders to officers. I'd have to give orders directly to officers. The officers would have to ignore gaming or Sunday tippling and be held individually responsible.

Clack went on to state that he knew Kelley didn't believe the rumor, but (not unlike today's claims of "fake news") "the only thing your words and methods clearly indicate is that you know exceedingly well where the faculty of misrepresentation can be most effectively exerted."[10]

On July 1, the Reverend Kelley finally responded with an open letter in the *Banner*, not to Clack but to the Board of Public Works. In an obvious attempt to placate Manny Shwab, the reverend complained that it was incorrect that his comments on Clack's association with "a well-known gentleman in this city were a criticism of private or official character."

> The ridiculousness of the position that my criticism was against the private character of a city official appears at once when a question is asked. Do not many of our highly esteemed citizens associate with Mr. Shwab? Has this association at any time been considered detrimental to their private character? I do not know Mr. Shwab personally, but understand he is an intelligent and companionable gentleman.... [I]t is hard for me to see how the most punctilious member of your board would regard it injurious to the private character of Capt. Clack to have social intercourse with Mr. Shwab.[11]

The scrutiny of the Clack/Shwab association was to continue throughout Clack's eleven-year tenure as chief of police (and most likely into his subsequent tenure as the first city judge). In 1894, the Nashville City Council conducted a months-long investigation into the police department's alleged neglect of enforcing the city's gambling and "Sunday tippling" (serving alcohol on Sunday) laws. The scrutiny came to a head when Clack demoted a Lieutenant Baker from office administrative work to "roundsman" (walking a beat). Clack claimed it was because Baker had an "arm ailment," couldn't

11. Temperance and Law Enforcement

write, and was having prisoners fill out their own paperwork. As Baker was in a position to order raids, the rumor mill had it that he was taken from this position to avoid raids that could prove uncomfortable for the high-profile whisky and gambling interests. Clack was accused of meeting frequently at "Shwab's liquor house" to get orders as well as cash payments.[12]

The city council wanted the Big Three—Kennedy, Stainback, and Nestor—investigated for pressuring Clack and his city police to ignore the liquor and gambling laws. City lawyer Claude Waller conducted the investigation "in that vigorous style which has characterized his course" and deposed many witnesses in the "well attended" public sessions, at which the audiences "were well repaid, as some very spicy testimony was brought out."[13]

During the May 30, 1894, session, board member J. L. Kennedy, who had been chairman, was questioned about his "Order Number One," which was supposedly created to enforce the tippling laws. Kennedy complained that the order was not enthusiastically carried out, and officers who attempted to do so were demoted, as Sergeant Baker had been. Kennedy did not believe the explanation for Baker's demotion. He called Clack before the board and the mayor for interrogation about the demotions and Clack's involvement with Shwab and the liquor interests. Kennedy stated he prepared a report "off what occurred" during the interrogation, but when he attempted to submit it, Clack "lost his temper" and complained that the report should not be made public, as it would be injurious to his reputation. Attorney Waller asked Kennedy to read the report aloud, and Clack interjected:

> **CLACK:** "Now wait just a minute!"
> **WALLER:** "Mr. Clack, do you have an objection to our knowing the results of this conference?"
> **CLACK:** "I most certainly do!"

Kennedy, ignoring Clack, proceeded to read the testimony from the report:

> **KENNEDY:** "Did you meet Henry Hudson, V.E. Shwab and others in Shwab's liquor house and discuss the selection of officers by the City Council?"
> **CLACK:** "I have never been in Shwab's house in this connection."

Manny Shwab and the George Dickel Company

At this point in the interrogation, board member Nestor interjected and complained that if they were going to charge Clack with something, they should do it "in the regular way."[14]

Kennedy stated that the police were employees of the board, and he and the board had a right to investigate their conduct.

Kennedy continued reading his interrogation of Clack, moving on to his alleged interference with the upcoming election for the board and his response to Order Number One.

> Q: "After the gambling resolution of November 14 was adopted, on which you made a report as to the difficulties towards having said order enforced, did you go to Shwab's and tell him that you would have the report published?"
> A: "I did not."
> Q: "Did you make known to him the contents of this report?"
> A: "I did not."
> Q: "Has Shwab any interest in any gambling house or saloon?"
> A: "I never heard that he had in my life."
> Q: "On November 28, when a certain order known as Order Number One was adopted by this board and given to you, why did you go to Shwab's whisky-house and return shortly afterwards and request the board to grant you a leave of absence, as you stated, your health was poor?"
> A: "I went to Shwab's to get a letter I had given to John [sic] Nestor."

At this time the letter was produced, addressed to the board. Kennedy continued:

> Q: "What efforts have you made to enforce the order?"
> A: "My reports show what efforts have been made."

Kennedy stated that no raids, except a few arrests for gambling, had been made since the order was issued.

> Q: "Have you removed men on request of Shwab?"
> A: "No, sir."

Waller then asked Kennedy about the Big Three's ongoing relationship with Clack and the lack of police raids. He stated that a list of gambling houses ("pool rooms") was formed and reviewed with Clack but that Stainback board member was anxious to have them suppressed. Clack reported that the difficulty in enforcement was

11. Temperance and Law Enforcement

because the rooms were "pocket rooms" and it was impossible to get evidence. These rooms had lookouts and "electric buzzers" that would warn participants when officers were approaching within blocks of the establishments. Kennedy stated that while chairman, he had "issued frequent orders which [he] expected to be enforced" and Clack may have been "a little conservative at one time, but no hold-up orders [had] ever been issued."[15]

Other officers were called up by Waller and questioned regarding whether Clack had ever done anything "directly or indirectly" to make them believe that he did not want the tippling and gambling laws enforced. When asked why he had not gone to a certain saloon, one officer stated he felt he was not to make himself "too obnoxious to that class of people.... A man who fools around them much can have it made right unpleasant for himself. I have never shirked duty, but do not want to be too smart. The signs of the times do not demand such heroic efforts on my part."

Waller continued questioning the officer:

Q: "Do you mean that the people do not want the laws enforced?"
A: "I never consulted the public."
Q: "When you took an oath as a policeman did you not swear to enforce the law?"
A: "No, sir. I took an oath to be obedient to the orders of the chief of police."
Q: "Do the lieutenants tell you to enforce the law?"
A: "Yes, sir."
Q: "Why don't you do it, then?"
A: "I do."
Q: "How do you do it?"
A: "I go into the saloons."
Q: "Do the police show any preference in raiding gambling houses?"
A: "We report houses to the lieutenants and they direct raids and say who shall be raided."
Q: "Did you tell me that the reason you did not arrest Johnson was because you were in debt and his arrest would cost you your head?"
A: "No, sir. I remember you asked me to come before the committee and tell about the workings of the police, but I said I did not want to have anything to do with it. I owed some money which I wanted to pay

and I feared if I came here I might tell something and my head would be chopped off."
Q: "What things could you tell?"
A: "I do not know what the committee wants to know. I said I might know some things."

Some "witnesses" were difficult to depose. Waller called a "collector" for different parties who was a night watchman at a restaurant and bar, the Utopia (Manny owned the building with Augusta Dickel). The committee was interested in how Rust had received certain information about a man in debt from whom he was attempting to collect.

Q: "To refresh your memory, do you know that you were interested in one T.L. Jones?"
A: "May have, don't remember."
Q: "You remember Jones?"
A: "Yes."
Q: "What interest did you have in him?"
A: "Can't say."
Q: "Why?"
A: "Don't want to."
Q: "Was he arrested?"
A: "It was rumored. But don't know where I got the information from."

The questioning went on in this way, eliciting some frustration on Waller's part.

Q: "Do you know you're under oath?"
A: "Yea, I remember that."
Q: "Did you ever see Jones?"
A: "I don't know. If I had, I wouldn't answer."
Q: "Is he white or black?"
A: "I suppose he is black."
Q. "Where did you know Jones?"
A: "Don't know."
Q: "Do you mean you refuse to answer?"
A: "Yes, that's it, just ain't going to tell."
Q: "Did you get that bond at the police station and give it to Bill Spain?"
A: "I refuse to answer."
Q: "Was it not gotten to use in having Baker removed?"
A: "I don't know. Did not say I had it. I had it, but don't know who I gave it to. I refuse to answer. I never gave it to Bill Spain."

Q: "Did you give the warrant and bond back?"
A: "Couldn't say."
Q: "Who saw you at the station-house?"
A: "Never said I went there."
Q: "Who told you not to answer?"
A: "Nobody."[16]

The investigation went on for another month, with testimonial details extensively covered almost daily by the *American* and the *Banner*, with the papers' editors spinning the information in opposite directions. The June 5 *Banner* highlighted testimony that "Climax gambler" John Williams was the brother of one of the "enforcing" officers, Charlie Williams, and there were (unsubstantiated) questions about information passing between the two. The *Banner* had previously referred to John as "proprietor of the Climax saloon and gambling house" and Baker testified that Officer Williams had told him his brother went "for a ride" with a prominent gambler who told him that Baker was being demoted for being a bit too aggressive.[17]

The Report Results

The committee's report was read aloud on June 15. It concluded that Baker's demotion was "an unholy scheme by lawless parties, by … certain members of the police force to frustrate law and order." Regarding each of the Big Three's involvement, Michael Nestor had erred in relying solely on Chief Clack's recommendation, while J. L. Kennedy's actions were "based upon a desire for the betterment of police service" (though his "judgment was greatly at fault" in relying on Clack's recommendation). George Stainback was faulted for his "reprehensible" action in relying on a bond—supposedly handwritten by Baker and given to him by a questionable source—as evidence of Baker's diminished ability to write. However, the committee concluded that each man had acted independently and not as part of a conspiracy to not enforce the laws. They recommended the restoration of Baker's former rank of lieutenant.

According to the committee, they "were unable to find a single instance" of the board trying to influence Clack not to enforce the liquor laws. But they chastised the "evident ease with which the police department and its Chief yield to the subterfuge of 'electric buttons' and 'lookouts,' and the lack of proper activity to address this by the mayor, Board of Public Works, and police officials."[18]

Councilman Sykes was incensed. "I had not intended to make any remarks," he said, but because a certain question was not addressed at all, he felt obligated to speak. He pointed out that during the months of the investigation, every time an allegation was made, those related were brought in to give testimony, "save one. Shwab." Sykes reminded the committee of claims that Clack had met with Manny Shwab and received $500, allegedly from the whisky interests to avoid police scrutiny. He felt that contention should have been addressed and stated, "I understand that Mr. Shwab, whose name was mentioned in connection with this matter, has always been ready and willing to testify."[19]

The committee's chairman confirmed that claims had been made that certain men had given Manny $500 to bribe Clack and the chief had asked for Shwab to be summoned as the committee's witness. However, the committee had insisted that Shwab would instead be Clack's witness, which the Chief refused. The committee and Clack ultimately agreed not to address this issue. The chairman added, "As to Mr. Shwab, the committee received a letter from him demanding that it summon Cartwright [one of his accusers] and others to testify.... [We] replied to this by telling Mr. Shwab that he could, if he so wished, come before the committee and give his testimony. He never came, and here the matter rests."

The report was adopted by a vote of eleven to eight.[20]

* * *

Clack wasn't the only law enforcement officer with whom Manny was associated. In January 1892, the federal government sued Manny, along with W.T. Hill, the sheriff of Davidson County, for the "penal sum" of $40,000 ($1.2 million today). Shwab was one of the county's five bondsmen who guaranteed the sheriff's performance of his duties. The government's complaint related to the escape from

11. Temperance and Law Enforcement

the county jail of Thomas C. Boalen, "a famous mail thief" who had been arrested for stealing checks from Nashville public mailboxes; he was caught by federal agents in Atlanta and returned to a Davidson County jail. The sheriff was accused of negligence in allowing the escape to occur. As with the abstract company lawsuit, this suit was said to be "without precedent."[21]

12

The Tennessee Election, 1894

In 1894, in addition to accusations of influencing law enforcement, Manny gained much unwanted attention for alleged political manipulations related to the state elections. Tennessee (as well as national) politics was entering a chaotic and frenetic period in which great chasms developed within the parties, like those of today, but at that time resulting from the issue of Prohibition, which would continue to be the dominating political force for decades. The newspaper coverage of this "chaos" is as interesting as it is educational.

On October 17, 1894, the Democratic Legislative Convention met in Nashville to select the candidates for state office, tapping J.C. Bradford as chairman. No speeches were to be made during the nominating process. After the fifth ballot was cast and the fifth man nominated, according to the *Banner*, J.B. Gordan declared (we can assume sarcastically), "I now move that as Maney [sic] Shwab has named five, he be allowed to name the balance."[1]

After the final selection of the Democratic ticket, there was pushback regarding the "methods" of nomination, so the conservative faction convened another gathering at the Ryman Tabernacle to nominate an alternative ticket. The October 24 *Banner* and the *American* covered the final day of this rogue convention, during which its selections for governor, state senate, and legislature candidates were announced and at which Manny was thoroughly roasted.

Nashville's two major papers were, for a century, strongly (and unapologetically) biased—the *American* (later the *Nashville Tennessean*) was Democratic, and the *Banner*, Republican. Following the conservative faction's nominations, the *American*'s lead in bold was "Selected a Ticket: Mongrel Political Meeting Completes Its Work."

12. The Tennessee Election, 1894

The paper stated that the leaders tried to outdo one another in their speeches, "vilifying the *American*": "They were sore, oh so sore, and a glance at their vehement gesticulations and their faces purple with rage as they delivered their philippics, showed they would have made it stronger if their vocabulary had just contained the words."[2] And what had so galled these political leaders? The subject was

> tossed backward and forward with furious energy, some of the players occasionally knocking a home run off the delivery of Victor Emanuel Shwab, whose alleged actions at the recent convention seemed to stick uncomfortably in their craw. Because of the *American*'s positive coverage of the "straight ticket," a "Mad Chairman" [complained] ... in a voice that shook and trembled with wrath, that the *American* was ... long connected with the machine.[3]

Captain Thomas G. Ryman, a powerful Prohibitionist steamboat captain and businessman (for whom the Ryman Auditorium of the Grand Ole Opry was named), was present at the second convention and stated that he had no qualms with the *American* even though the paper had been hard on him over the years. The *American* later quipped that "the ruling spirit" that night was Ryman, "who is less a Democrat than the Czar of Russia." The chairman called on a committee chair, Mr. Nolen, whose nominating committee had brought things to a halt for a time the previous day due to slow deliberations. In explanation, he stated:

> Had they been run by one man, like the late convention, they would have agreed in a half minute, but they had no Shwab. They didn't want to carry out the Shwab tactics. But he didn't blame Shwab, however, for controlling the Democrats if he could. But they had a right to select candidates as well as Shwab had, and the *American* ought not to get mad with them.... The fight was on, it was the people against Shwab. He [Nolen] was on the people's side.[4]

The *Banner*'s coverage added detail to the story, such as quoting Nolen:

> If I could boss the Democratic machinery of Davidson County I would do it. We may be Populites, Prohibitionists, Republicans, soreheads and kickers, but we have as much right to put out candidates as Mr. Shwab has. And the *American* ought not to get mad at us, since they did not get mad at Mr. Shwab.[5]

Manny Shwab and the George Dickel Company

A Mr. Whitman complained of "ring rule" and the "one[-]man convention" run by someone "who represented no district or ward, and was without creed or credentials."[6]

Another conventioneer stated that

> the Democratic ticket was not so particularly objectional ... but if one whisky head must nominate the Democratic ticket he would preserve his self-respect and not vote it. He had heard of one man not a member of the convention giving orders there which were obeyed, and that man was Shwab. It was a question when this thing of Shwab Rule would end. He believed it would be worse to allow a whisky head to control a convention than it would be to break up the work of a machine. The feeling of the men here to-night was, "I am as good as Shwab or any other man and I will not submit to be ruled by him." He appreciated the big Tammany in New York [a reference to Boss Tweed, the infamous political boss of New York's Tammany Hall and head of the state and city's Democratic machine] but couldn't stand a small one made up of one man: Shwab.[7]

The conventioneer then produced a paper originated by a "Mr. Jones" (an assumed name), which supposedly represented the platform and by-laws of the Democratic Convention. It was titled "The Shwab Democracy of Davidson County"; he read it, and, according to the *Banner*, it "was received by the crowd with considerable merriment."[8]

The *American* article ended with a note about each of the people quoted therein. Many were "Prohibitionists and Republicans" and one a "prominent leader of the A.P.A. [American Protective Association, an anti-Catholic, anti-immigrant secret society with over two million members in the 1890s]." Captain Ryman was described as "a steamboat man, Prohibitionist, and would-be political ward boss."[9] Manny's antagonists broke cleanly along the lines of Wet versus Dry. Perhaps, given his opposition, he might have thought of Jonathan Swift's quip that "when a true genius appears in the world, you may know him by this sign, that the dunces are all in a confederacy against him."[10]

And indeed the nomination process of both parties in Nashville in 1894 did appear to be peppered by a confederacy of dunces. The Republicans had also broken into two factions, the "Lilywhites" and the "Lampblacks," and nominated different tickets. The October 25 *American* (probably sarcastically) referred to the Lilywhite

12. The Tennessee Election, 1894

Republicans as containing "about all the brains in the Republican party in this county." The same day, the *Banner* added, "Yesterday the Lampblacks and Lilywhites came to the conclusion that their fires needed trimming and they went at it" and finally came to consensus on the ticket. The Lilywhite Republicans ultimately withdrew the platform nominated by their committee, as "there has been a ticket placed in the field by a mass-convention assembled at the Tabernacle."[11]

In the aftermath of the alternative Democratic convention, an editorial in the October 26 *American* defended Manny Shwab and bemoaned the hypocrisy of the debacle in the Tabernacle:

> When people put on a sanctimonious-better-than-thou countenance and broaden the phylacteries of their garments and go to the other side of the highway to shun political contamination they should themselves be free from criticism. Anyone less blind than a mole can see through the thinly veiled deceit.... It would seem that the gentlemen whose stomachs were so delicate that they were turned because Mr. Shwab, whom [sic] Mr. Jones said was a Republican, took part in the Democratic Convention and dictated certain Republicans and Democrats be nominated, would do otherwise ... [but they] did likewise, and must have thought the hair of the dog was good for the bite ... for they put two pronounced Republicans on the ticket, and the others were Populites, Prohibitionists and bolters [a runaway horse]. Not a single Simon-pure [genuine] Democrat did they select.
>
> Everyone knows that the Tabernacle ticket has no possible show for election and that its purpose was to have the Republican ticket prevail. These pseudo-Democrats pretend to be disgusted at Mr. Shwab and vociferously proclaim him to be a Republican and then themselves do more for the Republican party than Mr. Shwab ever did in his life. If he is a Republican, then they are his allies ... if he is a Democrat, then he is vastly better than they are.[12]

The gist was that this reaction was pettiness about the way the ticket had been chosen, but true Democrats would ignore the alternative ticket and "not be blinded by such a scheme."

The objection to Manny's political activities was explained by Colonel A.S. Colyar in a lengthy speech attended by six hundred or seven hundred at the Tabernacle on November 2, 1894. Colyar was a well-known figure in Tennessee who had blended his political and business activities since before the Civil War. A slaveholding Unionist before the war, but a Confederate colonel after secession, he had an unsuccessful run for governor after serving in the state legislature following the war. He was known for his support (and use) of the convict leasing program, presumably to make up for his loss of slaves.[13] According to Colyar, he wanted to wait to see who was nominated before making a statement.

> In order to ascertain if the people ... in some way and at some time manifested their disapproval of the power which had, for a good many years, absolutely dominated our county and municipal conventions, the substitution of the one-man power instead of the voice of the people would be the rule instead of the exception ... [it was a] question between yielding to this dominating influence making a final surrender—or making a protest. After this [nomination], I discussed at some length Mr. Shwab and his methods.[14]

Colyar went on to say that the Democratic "straight ticket" was composed of very good men—he had seen worse—but the trouble was the manner in which they were chosen. He said the *American* had erroneously claimed that Shwab did not name all of the ticket, that he actually entered his protest as to three:

> A protest is something a man does when his rights have been infringed upon. Shwab's right was to name the whole ticket.... Shwab sat in the room during the convention and sent out his little billets [notes] and the men fell in line. If this was the first time the people could stand it, but it had been going on for ten years and [I am] tired of it. [I am] tired of living in this enlightened city of nearly 100,000 inhabitants and seeing one whisky-head and one or two supports running the convention and then running the Legislature which they have elected.[15]

Colyar concluded by saying he wanted to correct an error of the *Banner* that misstated his comments about a Mr. Allison, who was alleged to have made Prohibition speeches in East Tennessee and who then insisted that someone "must go and tell Shwab that is not so." Colyar said that the message was not taken to Shwab. Apparently Mr. Allison was anxious about Manny's reaction to his activities.[16]

Colyar's speech was delivered in support of the APA, giving the organization credit for nominating an alternative ticket and breaking

12. The Tennessee Election, 1894

up Shwab's "ring and setting it behind the house." But then, according to Colyar, the ring had risen up and come through the back door. The machine needed "another lick, or maybe two, as it is said it takes three licks to kill a cat." The crowd cried, "It will get it."[17] But apparently the alleged ring did not get it, as each candidate on Manny's straight ticket, from governor down to "floater" congressman, prevailed.

The scrutiny and sometimes vehement criticism of Shwab's influence did not abate after this election, nor would it really recede for two more decades. The 1894 gubernatorial election was, if nothing else, controversial. The incumbent governor was Colonel Peter Turney, former chief justice of the Tennessee Supreme Court and, during the Civil War, member of the 1st Tennessee Regiment (along with Joseph Schwab). In his first term, Turney ended the convict release system, incensing Colonel Colyar. On December 12, the challenger, Republican Henry Clay Evans, was initially declared the winner by just 748 votes. Turney contested the vote on Christmas Day, and an investigative committee was formed. Three years earlier, a law had been passed in Tennessee (as it had in most Southern states) that required a poll tax be paid when voting; each county was to collect and produce receipts aligning with the county results. In April 1895, the investigative committee concluded that thirty-four Tennessee counties had unlawfully failed to collect and account for receipts, invalidating these votes, which resulted in a victory for Turney by 2,358 votes. The committee consisted of seven Democrats and five Republicans; Colyar was one of Evans' representatives. Foreshadowing attempts to challenge the results of the 2020 U.S. elections, the Democrat-controlled legislature had overturned the results due to voting irregularities.[18]

The Democratic Party was very much in control of Tennessee, but the party itself was strictly divided between Manny's now-dominant industrialist wing and the much more conservative neo-Confederate wing. A "mass meeting" was convened at the Tabernacle to protest the 1894 election results. Captain Ryman ended the meeting when, according to a letter in the *Banner* from "an anti-machine Democrat," a group of "rowdies" disrupted it and caused "great injury to the new seats." The writer worried about "the moral and political aspects of this noted event of the history of Nashville," declaring the election had been stolen. Ryman was said to have complained that if there was a killing at the Tabernacle, it would "impair its usefulness as a place of worship."[19]

About the disruption, an incensed Colyar stated:

> Three men, Jack Reeves (Chair of the Democratic Party), Maney [sic] Shwab and Billy Smith and their six lieutenants and their gang, broke up a meeting at the Tabernacle. It has been published three times that they called up their henchmen and placed them conveniently about in the hall and by concerted action drove law-abiding and peaceable citizens out of the building.... We are passing an era in our history, and if Reeves and Shwab and Smith are going to continue to boss things, you ought to know it and you shall rise up and say to these men, We are the Democratic party, not you.[20]

We shall never know exactly what happened, but it is difficult to imagine the chair of the Tennessee Democratic Party and the publicity-shy Shwab strong-arming one thousand people out of the Ryman Tabernacle.

Manny's activity did not abate following this incident. The House of Representatives convened in May. Representative Waddell complained of intense lobbying "by every State official, Coal Oil Inspector and other appointees of the Governor and Shwab working like bees upon members." An October note in the *American* opined, "*The Tribune*, the A.P.A. organ in Nashville, has opened its batteries on 'Shwab and

SAM JONES' HOT SHOT

Vociferous Applause as He Names One of Turney's Allies.

Special to The Chattanooga Times.

Nashville, April 14.—Sam Jones preached this afternoon on "Manliness," and in the course of his remarks mentioned the needs of manliness in politics, manliness to do the right thing regardless of what the bosses say.

He called Maney Schwab by name, and spoke of the influence he exercised over the legislature. An immense audience attended the services, and every reference to the political situation in Tennessee was vociferously applauded.

Evangelist Sam Jones calls out Manny for legislative influence. The fire-and-brimstone Jones was the most famous revivalist preacher of his day (*Chattanooga Times*, 1895).

12. The Tennessee Election, 1894

the whisky gang.' Shwab, however, is still doing business at the old stand."[21]

Evangelical Ire

Manny annoyed more than the politicians. Evangelical ire was evident in the April 14, 1895, sermon on "Manliness" by firebrand preacher Sam Jones before what was described as an immense audience. Preacher Jones took, according to the *Chattanooga Times*, a "hot shot" at Manny's influence over the legislature (to vociferous applause), complaining that politicians needed to be more manly in standing up to "the bosses."[22] Jones was the most famous evangelist of his time, once drawing a Nashville crowd at Eighth and Broad streets estimated to be in excess of ten thousand. He frequently packed Captain Ryman's Union Gospel Tabernacle (later the Ryman Auditorium).[23]

13

George Augustus Dickel, 1818–1894

At his home on June 11, 1894, eight years after his debilitating horse-riding accident, George Dickel passed away. Augusta, Manny, and other family members were at his side. The front page of the *Banner* carried Dickel's obituary with an image similar to one now used by Diageo on the products bearing his name.[1] Manny purchased plots in the Mt. Olivet Cemetery for Dickel's burial, where he would one day be joined by Augusta, the Banzers and the Shwabs. The Masons' Nashville Commandery No. 1 provided carriages and Templar pallbearers for the funeral of "Sir George A. Dickel."[2]

Dickel's faith in the future of GDC was apparently not rock solid. In addition to making it known that he wished his wife to sell their ownership following his death, he willed his entire estate to Augusta with written directions to sell. Manny, confident of the future value of the company, convinced Augusta to retain her ownership instead of selling it to him (he had previously purchased Salzkotter's shares). She followed his advice, and her faith in her brother-in-law was warranted: at her death, the IRS sought to tax her estate, managed by Manny, at $27 million in today's dollars. (That attempt would be another of Manny's diverse battles.)

Dickel's death occurred during the Nashville City Council investigation into the enforcement of the Sunday tippling laws. It is an interesting coincidence that immediately next to his obituary in the *Banner* was an article concerning multiple arrests that resulted in a number of saloons being shut down. There were seven arrests for Sunday tippling, more than on any Sunday for years, and the article stated, "[I]f it proves anything it goes to show that the police force is

13. George Augustus Dickel, 1818–1894

fully able to enforce the law against Sunday tippling notwithstanding the electric button and the ubiquitous lookout." The paper attributed the "vigilance of the force" directly to the ongoing investigation. It claimed that the arrests resulted from a "scheme" suggested by the *Banner*, though it had never been put into practice until then. The scheme consisted of watching customers enter the saloons and later arresting and summoning them as witnesses against the saloons. In perhaps another coincidence, neither the Climax nor the Silver Dollar was involved.[3]

MR. G. A. DICKEL DEAD.

The Well-Known Merchant Passes Quietly Away.

He Was a Prominent Mason and Had Lived Here More Than Fifty Years.

Mr. Geo. A. Dickel died at his home, two miles from the city, on the Dickerson Turupike, early this morning. Mr. Dickel had passed his three score and ten years, and for

GEORGE A. DICKEL.

George Dickel obituary (*Nashville Banner*, June 11, 1894).

14

Siblings

Throughout the 1890s, Manny wasn't the only Shwab gaining notice. His brothers Emile and Harry Clay Shwab were making their own waves. At the same time, his little sister Flora's musical career was blossoming: while at the Boston Conservatory and Columbia, she studied with and befriended the renowned composer and professor Edward MacDowell. Flora performed in Nashville, Boston, New York, and most likely Europe, and she also taught piano in several cities. Their stories provide insights into sides of late nineteenth- and early twentieth-century life apart from political battles.

Whist National Champions: Emile Shwab, 1854–1901

J. Emile Shwab, seven years younger than Manny, was listed in the Nashville city directories as a salesman and clerk at GDC. According to an 1896 *Knoxville Sentinel* article, he was a "noted large wholesale man."[1] But his heart was apparently elsewhere.

The card game whist (or bridge whist) was a wildly popular pastime that evolved into today's contract bridge. Whist was widely played in the eighteenth and nineteenth centuries and was so internationally popular in the 1890s that it could be called a national obsession in the United States and Great Britain. According to the *Banner*, virtually every "paper of importance gives space weekly to whist news, and ... that dispensed by the *Banner* is of itself sufficient to bestow distinction upon the paper."[2]

In 1895, Emile was the president of the State Association of Whist Clubs as well as of the Nashville Whist Club. His team of

14. Siblings

four—two from Knoxville and one from Shelbyville—would become a national force for four years. But in 1895, the rubes from the South—and Tennesseans, at that—were initially ignored as insignificant players for the national contests. Emile's team had defeated all state challengers to win the Biddle Cup, becoming the state champs and Tennessee's representatives for the American Whist League (AWL) national championship competition in Minneapolis.

The championship contest was evidently grueling. In the day's typical journalistic style, Minnesota's *Minneapolis Times* read:

> At midnight it was still anybody's game. A recess was called and taken and play resumed. [The teams] were late with their play, every card put down being handled as gingerly as a Venetian vase.... Three members of the Nashville team had never met each other previous to four days before the congress began. Mr. Branner is President of the Third National Bank of Knoxville, Mr. Cooper an attorney from Shelbyville and Mr. McClung a dealer in musical instruments. [Captain] Shwab is a Nashville business man. The team began its first play at Minneapolis Tuesday and continued to play with an average of three hours' sleep a night for five nights and days. Saturday night the battle to the death began, ending at 3 o'clock Sunday morning. Thirty[-]two hands were played. Mr. McClung was taken sick [and replaced] ... and Mr. Branner was prostrated [and replaced temporarily].[3]

Out of the two hundred contestants, the Nashville team was the only one from the South. They won.

The *Banner* traced the AWL trophy's historical journey around New Jersey, New York, Philadelphia, and Minnesota. It described the trophy as "a massive of [solid silver] engraved work about a foot high and almost as wide, with three embossed handles." The team members received pins that were a "crescent of gold set with a diamond and four pearls from the upper tip of which is suspended an ace of clubs with the league letters 'AWL' in gold on the three lobes of the ace." The paper claimed, "There are not four happier men in Nashville today, and [one cannot doubt] the other members of the whist club are almost as happy."[4] But, according to the national *Whist Journal*, which had a picture of the team on its cover, other teams were not happy.

> When play for the League trophy began ... had a prediction been made as to the result, we doubt whether any one of the main contestants or their

Manny Shwab and the George Dickel Company

National Champions—the Nashville Whist Club, left to right: D. McClung, M. Branner, S. Cooper and J. Emile Shwab, president (*Whist Journal*, 1895).

friends would have selected Nashville. They came unheralded and without any preliminary flourish of trumpets took the place assigned to them. [That] was reason enough for their being rated low, for a man is never presumed to know anything until he is believed to know everything. It was found that a club never heard of before ... had snatched the prize from the hands of all the old leaders. Then the wise ones put their heads together to give a satisfactory reason for the unexpected result, and, of course, they ... charged to luck the fortune that they were unwilling to credit to skill.... So far as Whist is concerned, the man who is lucky enough to always play the right card at the right time is a good one to back as a winner.... [T]he Nashville team evidently had the faculty of playing the right card at the right time in an extraordinarily severe test of mental and physical endurance. It was a fair match, fairly won, and the winners are entitled to full credit.[5]

For the next three years, Emile's teams would win many more championships, and he was elected the director of the Nashville Whist Club, entertaining the AWL executive committee members

14. Siblings

at the Nashville Club in Belle Meade on their visits to the city. (Manny was on the Nashville Club's board at the time.) Emile gained national acclaim for his whist expertise and wit. In 1899, New York's *Brooklyn Daily Eagle* stated, "There is a good deal of quiet humor in J.E. Shwab, a prominent member of the board of directors of the American Whist League and a loyal member of the Brooklyn Whist Club." It stated that in one match he had made "high score" in three out of four rounds, taking more tricks than any two others, and

The Championship Cup (*Nashville Banner*, June 25, 1895).

> [i]n one of the open events ... there came up to his table a tall, slab sided Hoosier, with long black whiskers and eye glasses. He had a most pompous and serious air and played every card as if the entire congress were watching him.... [T]his hayseed husbanded his ace of trumps, refusing to play it on a second round ... until on the last trick he came out with his ace of trumps with an emphatic slap on the table; whereupon Shwab quietly said: "My friend, do you want a check for that?" This old farmer was not the old visitor at the congress who smuggled home aces without advertising them as luggage.[6]

Little (or nothing) was mentioned in the papers about Emile's contributions to GDC until his July 14, 1901, obituary in the *Tennessean*, which described him as a "prominent and well-known citizen connected with the wholesale liquor firm of George A. Dickel & Co. since 1889." So Emile, married with no children, had moved from Ohio in 1889 to work with his brother. Emile's obituary in

Cincinnati's *American Israelite* indicated that he retained his Jewish faith.[7] Only forty-seven years old, he died after two years of failing health in 1901. The funeral was held at Manny's home.

Pennsylvania's P.T. Barnum: Harry Clay Shwab, 1852–1912

In the last decades before the advent of radio and silent films, visits to "theater halls" and museums represented a large part of the available entertainment. The venue offerings were enormously varied: operas, dancing bears, hypnotists, comedians, Shakespeare, "freak shows," orchestras, temperance rallies, burlesque, vaudeville, ventriloquists—virtually anything the theater managers and owners thought would fill seats. From the 1880s through the early years of the new century, Pennsylvania and New York had their own P.T. Barnum or Colonel Tom Parker shepherding the public into these venues: Manny's younger brother, Harry Clay Shwab. He was an acclaimed (and controversial) press agent, publicist, theater manager/owner, and promoter, renowned in Pittsburgh, New York City, and Brooklyn. In addition, Harry was one of the eight founders of the New York Friars Club, famous to this day for its celebrity roasts and its roster of entertainers.

Harry Clay Shwab (*Pittsburgh Press*, May 19, 1897).

Harry Shwab was listed in the 1860 Knoxville census

14. Siblings

as "Harry," age six, born in Tennessee. The 1870 Youngstown, Ohio, census lists Harry as an eighteen-year-old "clerk in store" and his father as a liquor dealer. But the young man had considerably higher aspirations than clerking in his dad's store. He was listed in the 1880 Pittsburgh city directory as a reporter. By the mid–1880s, he was well known in theatrical circles as a theater manager, press agent, promoter, and publicist. This writer found over sixty newspaper and magazine articles written between 1883 and 1906 about Harry's exploits in Pittsburgh and New York. His focus was, well, broad. He produced and promoted *Macbeth*; the Siberian Wild Man; the Jumbo Giant Brothers; Lily Langtry showing "her beautiful neck"; bookings at the Pittsburgh Opera House; the feeding of his pet monkey in public; four-year-old prodigy "Little Gertie ... who will answer any question from the audience"; and countless others. He apparently would promote any crowd-pleasing act, regardless of how outrageous or controversial. One event that would have gained Manny's disapproval was the appearance of temperance apostle Francis Murphy, who, according to the December 12, 1887, *Pittsburgh Daily Post*, drew "hundreds and hundreds" of his devotees, necessitating fifteen policemen to keep order.[8]

Harry's "exploits" were frequently covered in dramatic fashion by the papers; many (or most) of these stories were likely crafted by Harry to garner publicity. Entertainment venues sought publicity by placing outrageous stories in the local papers, often about the venues' associates rather than the acts themselves. As a newspaper man, Harry Shwab excelled at this tactic. More information on Harry and several of the entertaining stories can be found in the appendix, but as an example:

> In order to secure a box at the Bijou, a German barber from Allegheny made a "desperate effort" to place himself in the good graces of Shwab. He had heard the manager was looking for a bulldog which he procured, "with teeth like sharks and vinegary disposition." He went to the Bijou, where he asked a clerk, "Vell, vot shall I do mit der tog?" He was told to put it in Shwab's office (the manager having gone out to buy a monkey), and "for heaven's sake ... chain 'em up." The barber mistakenly let the dog loose in Shwab's partner's office, which the dog proceeded to tear apart. The partner suggested starving the dog into submission, but Clay [Harry,

going by Clay at the time] said that would be cruel and "when I was out West, I learned how to use the lasso. I'll just bring my cowboy knowledge into play." Climbing onto a ladder, he was able to subdue the creature and added him to the "collection of animals" in his office. The collection was said to include live rattlesnakes he was training to do a song and dance, half a dozen prairie dogs, a three-foot-long alligator, and a monkey from Ceylon. The paper stated that Clay had a "delight in caring for the dumb brutes" and would utilize his skills to tame the bulldog.[9]

Apparently Harry did buy a monkey. The September 21, 1890, *Pittsburgh Press* said that "at Davis' new Fifth Ave[.] museum it is worth 10 times the price of admission to see Harry Shwab feeding his pet monkey in the roof garden."[10]

Whereas the frequent "yarns" depicted Harry in ludicrous situations, he was apparently well respected in the theatrical business, as demonstrated by several benefits in his honor. In 1888, the *Pittsburgh Post* covered Harry's retirement from the Bijou. The paper expressed that "[t]o manager Shwab can much of the credit be given for lifting theaters of this city out of the dry rot of old fogyism." After starting as a press agent five years earlier for the Harris Museum in Cincinnati, he took house receipts from $16,000 to $28,000 in three years. He did so well that he was placed in charge of the Harris Museum, where he "boomed the house" using "his characteristic advertising methods." According to the *Post*, "the City of Hams" was thronging to see the "wonderful curiosities Shwab was painting so glowingly through the press, clearing $48,000 in his first year." The paper stated that Harry had few equals in theatrical circles and that it was hoped he would remain in the city and in the business.[11]

Harry's lifestyle may have caught up to him. An attack of "acute indigestion" in a theater in 1906, covered by New York and Pittsburgh papers, may have been something much worse. Harry Clay Shwab died in Nashville's City View Sanitarium on September 2, 1912.[12] His death certificate listed the cause as general paresis (also known as general paralysis of the insane) and syphilitic paresis (a severe neuropsychiatric disorder caused by late-stage syphilis that has gone untreated for years; it is often accompanied by delusions and severe dementia). The doctor stated on the certificate that the duration of the disease was six years, which coincides with Harry's collapse in

14. Siblings

1906. The carelessness of his death certificate indicates that Harry was not in good standing with the Shwab family. It lists him as seventy years old, with his date of birth "unknown" (he was born in 1852, making him sixty). His father's birthplace is shown as Ohio, and his mother's as England. Abraham Schwab, of course, was born in France, and according to census documentation, Annie was born in New York. In addition, her maiden name was listed as "unknown" (it was Dreyfous).[13] At least one thing was properly acknowledged: Harry's occupation was listed as "Theatrical Manager." His distant nephew, George Shwab IV, read a note from Manny to his brother, written on faintly lined paper, explaining that he was being left $1, as "you have drunk your inheritance." But apparently Manny purchased space in Mt. Olivet Cemetery for Harry. He and Flora are buried side by side with an impressive Shwab monument. However, Harry's birth year as shown is incorrect.

Concert Pianist: Flora Shwab, 1862–1925

Manny's sister Flora Shwab had an affinity for music and chose to train as a pianist. She studied with the renowned American composer Edward MacDowell and later taught piano in addition to achieving acclaim as a concert pianist in both the United States and Europe. (A detailed account of her life can be found in the appendix.

The details of Flora's early life are murky. She was born in the years surrounding the outbreak of the Civil War, and her childhood must have been fairly tumultuous given the family's smuggling activities and Nashville's occupation. By 1870, she, Harry Clay (Henry), and her parents had settled back in Youngstown, Ohio, where the family had previously lived and where Cecelia, Joseph, and Manny had been born. The family was again running their wine and liquor store, A. Schwab & Co. Flora's mother, Annie, died in 1871, and her father Abraham followed in March 1884.

After her father's death, and for the rest of her life, Flora traveled extensively and moved back and forth between Nashville, Louisville, Boston, and New York, teaching piano and performing concerts and recitals. Her association with Edward MacDowell (whose international reputation was quickly growing) and his wife, Marian, was both professional and personal. Louisville newspaper promotions and reviews describing Flora's November 29, 1910, concert of MacDowell's music touted her official authorization, by the composer himself, to interpret his compositions. "To be able to interpret worthily the pianoforte compositions of Edward MacDowell is to have sufficient reason for musical existence," notes one newspaper review of her performance. "To be authorized, as is Miss Flora Shwab," the review continues, "by the greatest of American composers to transmit his meanings and traditions, is to become some sort of prophet to students and lovers of piano."[14] MacDowell's reputation continued to grow years after his death (Nat King Cole and Elvis Presley both recorded versions of his "To a Wild Rose").

By 1914, Flora's career as a concert pianist seems to have been at its peak. In December of that year, Boston media, and especially the *Globe*, heavily promoted a performance she gave at Steinert Hall, which included several pieces written by MacDowell as well as other composers.[15] A decade later, in 1924, Flora was mentioned in Louisville and Nashville papers as being a resident of New York and living temporarily in Europe. Intimate letters written from Lausanne, Switzerland, to Marian MacDowell in 1924 and 1925 (currently in the Library of Congress) show that Flora was suffering deeply from depression and regret over not being with Manny when he died. In addition to reminiscing about their friendship, Flora touched on her mental health struggles and even her nephew George's desire for her to seek the professional assistance of a sanitarium. The latter proposition she found particularly unpalatable after her "experience last spring" (a possible reference to having spent some time in a sanitarium).[16]

On January 25, 1925, Flora Shwab took her own life at Lausanne's Hotel Belvedere. Her body was transported to Nashville and buried in a small Mt. Olivet plot, separate from the larger Shwab/Dickel plot, beside Harry, the sibling with whom she had grown up in Ohio.

15

1897–1898

Tennessee Centennial International Exposition

From May 1 through October 31, 1897, the Tennessee Centennial and International Exposition was held in Nashville's massive Centennial Park. A celebration (a year late) of Tennessee's 1796 entry into the union, this event was when President William McKinley pened the event from the White House by pressing a button that supposedly began the fair. He later visited the exposition in person. The exposition covered 265 acres with over 100 buildings at what was then the city's western edge. It had all the components of a World's Fair, with an enormous range of exhibits, highlighted by Nashville's own offering: a reproduction of the Parthenon (before "Music City," Nashville's nickname was "The Athens of the South") and Memphis' pyramid. The buildings housed exhibits covering such subjects as agriculture, government, history, and arts—there was a Negro Building and a lake with gondolas that exists today. Almost two million people attended with receipts of just under $30 million in today's dollars.[1]

Manny Shwab ventured into yet another business arena by gaining the "exclusive privilege of running the restaurant and café in the Club Building" of the exposition. The West Side Club House was elaborate and massive. When President McKinley visited the exposition, he and his entourage ate and sought "rest from the daily activities" there. In a letter on file with the Tennessee Archives, directed to the president of the West Side Driving Club, Major Thomas, Manny stated that he had paid $1,500 ($53,000 today) to have the exclusive right to run the restaurant for the "life of the Exposition." (The Driving Club owned rights to the club.) Manny promised to employ only the most efficient persons, that everything was to be "strictly first rate," and, significantly given his reputation, "I will not sell whiskey in the building." He went on to say the restaurant would be "conducted as well as Faucon's Restaurant in Nashville" (Faucon's was Nashville's crème de la crème of restaurants). Manny was to employ "gate keepers" to keep the place peaceful, who were "unobjectionable to the Committee." The five-man committee added to the end of his letter their acceptance "provided no intoxicants shall be sold, except those authorized by the charter and ordinance of the Centennial City."[2]

It can be assumed that two million visitors to a fair, almost anywhere, would consume a good amount of alcohol. But the sale of alcohol in the 265-acre park was illegal. Afterward, the Centennial Exposition Company believed Manny had made enormous profits off whisky and cigar sales due to the exposition and sued him

West Side Club (1897), Nashville's Tennessee Centennial Exposition, from the exposition's guidebook. Manny Shwab ran the exclusive club's restaurant after promising not to serve alcohol. The photograph was taken when President William McKinley dined there during his visit to the exposition (Tennessee State Library and Archives).

individually in Chancery Court to "recover those profits."³ In a clever turn, Manny "demurred," basically admitting the charge of selling alcohol but thumbing a "so what" nose at the claim. His position was that if such sales were criminal and illegal, as the bill showed, then "a recovery cannot be made on profits upon illegal sales." As to the sales of cigars, he also demurred, stating that the bill filed against him "did not show that a contract to sell or not to sell cigars existed."⁴

In October of the following year, the Davidson County Chancery Court Clerk and Master sold to Manny Shwab (joined in a committee by S.J. Keith and Judge E.H. East) the Centennial Park Club and one acre for $4,000 and the rest of the 265-acre park for $10,000.⁵ That agreement gave control of a huge amount of prime real estate at the fast-expanding western edge of the city. Manny built a grand Victorian home at 3100 West End Avenue, close to the center of the former exposition grounds, where he resided for over twenty years.

The Cumberland Telephone and Telegraph Company

Also in 1898, Shwab was actively pursuing with James E. Caldwell a monopoly of telephone and telegraph services in Tennessee and Kentucky. He was one of the drivers of the consolidation of Nashville's Great Southern Telephone & Telegraph Company with Kentucky's Cumberland Telephone and Telegraph Company. He served with six others on the executive committee and was a member of the board of the new company. Caldwell served as its president.

Reflecting their intended reach, the twelve-member board included E.M. Barton of Chicago, president of the Western Electric Company—at the time the largest manufacturer of electrical apparatus in the world—in addition to board members from Indiana, New York, Louisiana, and Ohio.⁶ After successful development of the territory, focusing on telephone toll lines and exchanges, they joined other regional communication companies in selling their shares to the Southern Bell Telephone and Telegraph Company—the future AT&T.

Manny Shwab and the George Dickel Company

A Lousy Whisky-Sucker

Colonel A. S. Colyar and others again went after Manny on August 15, 1898, when, according to the *Banner*, "The Voice of the People" was heard in a mass meeting of five to six hundred people held at the Masonic Temple. "Cheers, applause, and hisses resounded through the crowd as the speeches progressed." The complaints were that, once again, "the gamblers and Sunday tipplers have had their way in this city, manipulating and dictating affairs" by controlling the Public Works' Big Three in a forthcoming "wholesale decapitation of city officials," including the chief of police. Captain J. Hadley Clack had moved on to being city judge (Nashville's first), and it seems the new chief, perhaps appropriately named Sidebottom, was having some success "shutting down" the gamblers and Sunday tipplers. But he was in danger of being removed by the board, once again headed by J. L. Kennedy (who allegedly had been given $5,000 by the whisky men for his campaign). However, Sidebottom was pushing back. Colyar exclaimed that the arrival of Sidebottom was "like the dove came back to the ark. Every breakfast table was lighted up with smiling faces, every religious assembly met in holy worship with a new faith."[7] Praise the Lord, indeed.

The question was asked by Colyar as to the source of the significant changes in city management:

> Who is doing this? ... Then comes an eye-opener—the very nest egg of the present commotion, the moving spirit ... the boldest and most intelligently active man among them, indeed, the man who touches the button and rings the bell, and in a most gentlemanly way says to the Chief of Police, "There is going to be a change ... you can be Chief of Detectives." [R]eflect that this eye-opener as to what was contemplated came from the head man and the shrewdest of all the gamblers and that it was soon followed by the edict ... the gamblers have control. What is to become of this city if [men like] Maney [*sic*] Shwab, at the head of the Sunday tippling crowd, continue to run this city as they have been doing? Will the people stand it? ... If worst comes to the worst I may serve under Ike Johnson [allegedly the power behind gambling] but I will never serve under Shwab. I will die first. I am mad when I contemplate it. I feel like the grief-stricken Indian widow did. The news was brought to her that her husband had been gored to death by a neighbor's ox. She knew the ox and exclaimed: "I can't

stand this. My husband was a good man; he was a brave man; he went into the jungles and caught and tamed a wild elephant; he hunted lions and tigers in the Himalaya Mountains, and when the British came he fought in Singapore, and now what makes me mad is that he should be butted to death by a little, lousy bull calf."[8]

Poor Manny. That must have cut. He was certainly not lousy. But it got worse.

An ex-board member, Mr. Beasley, was asked to speak. He claimed that "a certain [police] Sergeant told Col. Colyar that he could do certain things, but his hands were tied." Beasley felt the sergeant must be compelled to say who was keeping him from doing his duty. When pressed, the sergeant claimed an officer "was doomed to go because he sees too much." He quoted another officer as saying when describing a partner, "Why, Bush, you know you and I have been drunk, and one time you were so drunk you tried to eat a raw goose and the blood ran all over your face." Beasley continued, "Who put these men in power? Maney [sic] Shwab.... [I]f there is not harmony in the police force it is because of the dirty, stinking, negro-hugging whisky-sucking—"; according to the *Banner*, "The rest of the speaker's remarks were drowned in the cheers and applause."[9] So, in addition to being a lousy bull calf, Manny was dirty, stinky, whisky sucking, and a Negro hugger.

A demand rose for Chairman Kennedy of the Public Works to take the stage, which he did, reluctantly, to hisses from the crowd, saying that he "came to listen, but the truth will prevail." So he pushed back hard, stating that he "had never done anything for money in a public way" or "betrayed the confidence of the people." As to Sidebottom, "There were good men, better than Sidebottom. Was the department to be made to fit one man?" Kennedy claimed no pressure from any "corrupt source" but suggested that "the excitement caused by the newspapers did cause a pressure." He said he had absolutely no knowledge of the funds raised to elect him and that he "owed the gamblers and tipplers nothing." According to Kennedy, the allegations that he was their friend were "held up" to defeat him. He volleyed that he had "heard of a fee being paid [meaning to Colyar and his supporters] in case that certain men were retained in office as the result of the mass-meeting."¹⁰

Colyar responded that "the infamous report" of him receiving money was started by a gang of liars. The meeting then devolved into hyperbolic accusations, such as that Judge Clack was "getting drunk and turning buggies over," was a liar, and had told the board that he "wanted them to wear silk hats and dress suits when the Cincinnati beer-suckers came down here." There followed complaints against specific officers: McKinney had been on the force twenty-one years and had never done anything "but draw his salary"; John Carter wanted "to give his coochee-coochie" (perhaps a reference to Thomas Edison's 1896 film short, *Coochee Coochee Dance*, starring Little Egypt); Mit Marshall was "mad because he had been told to enforce the law." A motion to adjourn was finally made, and Colyar "called Chief Sidebottom to come to the stage, which he did, and was introduced as the best-looking man on the stage, but who couldn't make a speech to save his life."¹¹

16

Full Ownership of the Cascade Hollow Distillery

As the daily pace of Manny Shwab's business ventures, relentless squeeze of the temperance forces, and caustic personal attacks in the papers increased, one can imagine that the short train rides through the bucolic Middle Tennessee countryside to the tiny village of Normandy and Cascade Hollow gave him much-needed solace and time to think. According to an interview in 1983 conducted by historian Kay Baker Gaston with Kie Davis' ninety-two-year-old son, Thurman Davis, whenever Manny made the trip to Normandy, Kie would pick him up in his horse and buggy for the ride to the Hollow. Gaston fondly recalls the interview, stating, "I remember that he was attired in slippers, pajamas, and a bathrobe, and had a housekeeper or sitter there with him. He seemed pleased that I was interested and was ready to tell his story. I was lucky to have gotten there in time."[1]

The distillery was a well-oiled machine by February 1898. Kie's formula, combined with his and Manny's management, had dramatically expanded Cascade Whisky's reputation, making it impossible to keep up with the demand. And demand was about to become much greater.

On February 15, 1898, the USS *Maine* was allegedly sunk by the Spanish in Havana Harbor; war was imminent. Economists and capitalists feared war would drag the U.S. economy back into the deep depression from which it was just emerging. Manny, like everyone else in the liquor business, was well aware that what depressed the nation often energized alcohol consumption. Soon, surging numbers of enlisted soldiers would be moving through Nashville on their way to San Francisco to await deployment to the Philippines, affording

Manny Shwab and the George Dickel Company

The tiny hamlet of Normandy near Cascade Hollow (painting courtesy of Ridley Wills II).

an opportunity to introduce them to Cascade. The whisky became a favorite and a staple on the West Coast.

However, increasing productivity was a challenge. The distillery already controlled virtually every aspect of the distilling process, no matter how trivial: growing the trees to produce the charcoal and barrels; farming the needed grains (or buying them locally); cooking the mash; distilling the whisky; warehousing during the aging process; bottling the whisky (which the company had started managing in 1891); designing and manufacturing the labels; producing the square, unfinished boxes, stamped with "Cascade Distillery" and "George A. Dickel & Company"; packing the bottles into the boxes and slapping on the labels that depicted a still with the copper worm; and marketing, selling, and distributing the now-famous product. And full accountability for this process was about to fall to Manny Shwab.

In March 1898, Kie Davis suffered a debilitating stroke. He was taken to Nashville but made no improvement. Manny took Kie to Battle Creek, Michigan, for treatment, but he died there on April 1. In Gaston's interview, Thurman said his brother Norman had been attending Vanderbilt University but returned to Cascade Hollow to

16. Full Ownership of the Cascade Hollow Distillery

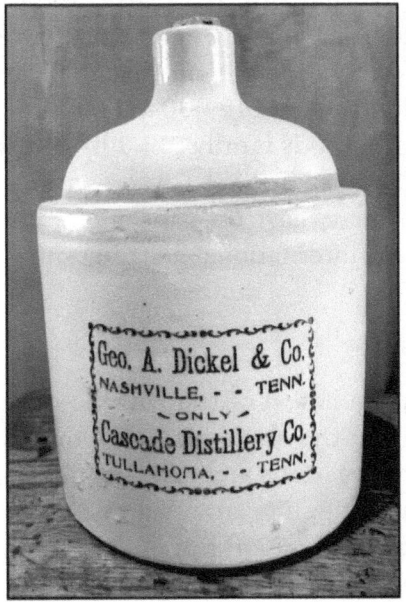

Cascade whisky bottles, jug, and pint bar glass. The jug and bottle on the top right date from before 1910, while distilling remained in Cascade Hollow near Normandy, Tennessee. The other bottles were made after the company's move due to Tennessee Prohibition to Hopkinsville and later to Louisville, Kentucky (bottles courtesy of George Shwab IV; jug and glass courtesy of author).

run the distillery in his father's place. However, he managed the distillery for only a short time. Norman Davis became "prominent in New York financial circles and held important government positions: Assistant Secretary to the U.S. Treasury and Special Ambassador to the Versailles Peace Conference, appointed by President Woodrow Wilson."[2]

The Davis family was obviously very close to the Shwabs. At the time of his father's death, Kie's son Paul was in Nashville. He soon completed the blending of the Shwab family with the primary participants in Cascade Hollow and GDC when he married Manny's daughter, Augusta (who was named after her aunt, Augusta Dickel). Paul later became president and then chairman of the board of Nashville's First American Bank. Manny obtained full ownership of the Cascade Hollow Distillery on February 15, 1899, after the Coffee County Chancery Court decided that the 260-acre distillery tract would be "valueless" to either party divided and that the Davises' one-third portion, valued by the court at $12,000–$18,000, was to be sold to Shwab. Manny paid the Davis family $12,000 ($400,000 today).[3] Later that year, he bought an additional 275 acres adjacent to the distillery. The resulting 535.3 acres gave the capacity for production that Manny sought to manage international distribution.[4]

The Humane Society

In 1898, Shwab served on the board of the Humane Society. In an almost laughable slap back at the Nashville City Council and Board of Public Works for their allegations and investigations of the police for not enforcing the Sunday tippling laws, Manny, serving on a committee of four, accused the Public Works of not enforcing the laws "relating to the prevention against the cruelty to animals." The board had fired the policeman who had been the humane officer in charge of investigating incidences of cruelty to animals, and who, according to the society, "devoted nearly all of his life to this." The board had added to his responsibilities "numbering houses," itself a full-time job. A brother-in-law of a board member then replaced the officer, allegedly due to poor performance. Manny's committee

16. Full Ownership of the Cascade Hollow Distillery

confronted the board with the ordinance passed in 1896 that stated the humane officer was to devote 100 percent of his time to investigating issues of cruelty to animals. That the intent of the ordinance was to dedicate an officer to those issues was admitted. It was also shown that the fired humane officer had sent out over 3,800 notices of incidences, but his responsibilities of house numbering had not left him time to properly follow up on the notices. He had often worked until midnight to try to cover his responsibilities. Since his dismissal, the Humane Society had notified the police of problems, but the station "failed to elicit any information as to the [new] officer's whereabouts." The society temporarily hired the fired officer but could pay him only $60 a month. Echoing the board's tippling investigation, the *American* stated that the Humane Society's fight was "to see the law enforced rigidly and to the letter."[5] Touché, Manny.

Prohibition Tick-Tock

The scrutiny of and allegations against Manny's behind-the-scenes political and law enforcement manipulations continued as the temperance movement slunk along. Since 1877, Tennessee laws had been expanding the "four-mile law" (prohibition of alcohol sales within four miles of a chartered rural school). In 1887, the restriction was expanded by the legislature to cover any country school, virtually banning the sale of liquor anywhere in rural Tennessee. In 1899, the restriction was extended to "newly incorporated" cities with populations of two thousand or less. Dozens of cities immediately rescinded their incorporated status and reapplied for new charters, thereby falling under the new restrictions. This situation resulted in the closing of any affected saloon.[6]

In 1901, the "Peeler Bill" was considered by the legislature to further expand the four-mile law to towns of five thousand or less, virtually banning the sale of liquor in all but the major urban areas: Nashville, Memphis, and Chattanooga. This persistent encroachment undoubtedly motivated Manny to leverage influence wherever possible. The bill was ultimately defeated amid accusations of

Manny Shwab and the George Dickel Company

corruption and bribes. A joint legislature committee was formed to formally "investigate charges of corrupt influence being used to defeat the Peeler [B]ill."[7] Fingers pointed at Manny.

The committee began deposing witnesses on February 16, 1901. The Reverend Ira Landrith was first to be interrogated. He stated that he and several others had gone to Nashville and confronted Senator D.M. Johnson of Smith County as to why he had voted against the bill after having allegedly told them he supported it. Landrith testified that the senator said he voted against the measure to save state revenue. The men told the senator he had been reported to have taken bribes and was "associating with saloon men." Regarding bribes, the senator allegedly exclaimed, "[I]f you believe that, there's the door!" and said that he could have made money, as he had been told he would be "cared for" if he opposed the bill, but he took no money. As for associating with liquor men, Johnson insisted that "it was by accident that he had sat next to Maney Shwab at the Press Banquet." The senator was pressed by the men for other reasons for voting against the bill, and, according to Landrith, he "did not care to state them."[8]

The February 28, 1901, *Nashville American*, covering the depositions, added the senator's explanation for "accidentally" sitting next to Shwab at the recent banquet. Johnson said he had initially declined an invitation to the event but changed his mind the night of the soiree. He was denied entrance as he tried to use another senator's nontransferable ticket. "As he was going up the steps to the banquet hall he met Shwab. He explained the situation to him and Mr. Shwab turned to the man on the door and told him to 'write out a ticket for Senator Johnson.' This was done and they sat together at the table."[9] Apparently Manny carried greater weight with the press than did the senator.

Allegations of corruption were made against individuals and organizations both for and against the bill. The next witness after Landrith was Dr. Hoss, the treasurer of the Anti-Saloon League. He testified that a senator told him he had been approached with bribes by both friends and opponents of the bill. He said he was aware that a "fund had been raised by a levy on the saloon men of the state."[10]

An article titled "Schwab Got It" in the February 23, 1901,

16. Full Ownership of the Cascade Hollow Distillery

Knoxville News Sentinel covered more testimony before the committee. James Hayes, an agent for Chattanooga's Hauck Brewing Company, testified that V.E. Shwab had telephoned him, stating that it was "necessary to raise a fund to secure legal advice," and he had sent him a check, payable to Shwab, for $100. He "supposed Mr. Shwab would attend to the matter [and] would render an account as to the use of the money." The interrogator asked, "Is Mr. Shwab regarded as an expert manager of legislation?" Hayes replied, "I don't know that he is." He was then asked whether he knew anyone he would "prefer to Mr. Shwab in undertaking to defeat legislation inimical to your interests?" Mr. Hayes pled ignorance on such matters.[11] George Shwab, as the cashier of GDC, did admit that his father had treated legislators and sent liquor to their homes and offices.

Following two months of investigation, the committee gave its final report on April 12. After covering the passage of a bill protecting quail in Knox County for five years, Knoxville's *Journal and Tribune* reported the committee's findings: "[Y]our committee has been able to unearth but one fact tending to show corruption—that of the raising of a fund to be used, as your committee believes, for improper purposes by the wholesale liquor dealers," to defeat the extension of the four-mile law. But there was no tangible evidence that any assembly member was guilty of "improper or corrupt conduct."[12] The paper added:

> Concerning the absence of V.E. Shwab in Florida during the session of the committee, it says:
> They are of the opinion that one especial witness who has been very active in the efforts to defeat the legislation above referred to has willfully absented himself from the limits of the state of Tennessee from the time the investigation began to the present time for the purpose of avoiding an appearance before the committee and testifying, your committee must further state, however, to be fair, that they are not aware that said witness is in possession of any fact that would shed light upon this investigation, but sufficient facts have developed to convince this committee that, if any corruption or other improper means was resorted to, this witness was cognizant of it and they therefore regard his continued and purposed absence with suspicion.[13]

A couple of weeks later, the *Chattanooga News*, referring to a *New York Herald* article on millionaires in Tennessee, ran an article

Manny Shwab and the George Dickel Company

headlined "How the Legislature Missed It by Failing to Get a Herald Report on Manny Shwab's Bank Account while in Session." The *Herald* had identified around thirty Tennessee millionaires (ten of them from Nashville). The *News* pointed out:

> It may be remarked in passing that it is a fortunate thing for at least one of the Nashville millionaires that the publication of the list was delayed until after the legislature adjourned. If the "lobsters" had known the size of Manny Shwab's roll, what they would have done to him would have been "a plenty."[14]

It is unknown what the committee would have done "a plenty" to the suspicious and elusive Mr. Shwab. Manny's efforts did serve to delay the inevitable. But in 1903, the Adams Bill extended the four-mile law to towns of five thousand incorporated after passage of the bill.

17

1900–1905

Family

The 1900 census shows a robust, obviously close Shwab family living at 221 Dickerson Pike. Fourteen occupants are listed: Victor, fifty-eight, and Emma, fifty; the four adult sons (Felix, twenty-seven; George, twenty-five; Buist, twenty-three; and Hugh, nineteen); the three daughters (Louise, fifteen; Augusta, thirteen; and Bessie, nine); and five servants (one "servant," Chany, is listed as ten years old, obviously a daughter of another servant). Augusta Dickel, sixty-two, is listed as a household "head" living next door at 222 Dickerson Pike.[1] Interviews confirm that Augusta ("Auntie") lived with the family, but the home configurations are unknown. The next year, after more than three decades on Dickerson Pike, the family moved to a grand Victorian home at 3100 West End Avenue, a major road extending from Broadway west of Nashville.

From the many defamatory newspaper accounts of Manny's character and nefarious influence, one would think Nashville society must have shunned the family as pariahs. But his business associations and blurbs in the papers' society sections prove otherwise. For example, in a reflection of days long gone, the December 12, 1901, *Tennessean* society page covered in detail "a beautifully arranged child's party for Miss Elizabeth Shwab [10 years old], entertaining in her West End home":

> Twenty young guests were present.... The afternoon was spent in the enjoyment of games and music. Pretty prizes were presented to give zests to the contests. In a chair game, Miss Sarah Bradford won the highest score and received the trophy, a bisque figurine. In the donkey contest Miss Bradford also made the best score and carried off ... a Brownie

Manny Shwab and the George Dickel Company

figure.... Miss Elizabeth Rhodes received a box of bon-bons and a doll as a consolation token. Miss Harriet Mason won a Dresden tea set.... A fish pond was provided also with souvenirs for every guest.

And what would the little ladies have for refreshment after such an arduous morning?

> Late in the afternoon a delicious menu was served. The table decorations were entirely in pink and white, the centerpiece being a large vase of La France roses on a centerpiece of drawn linen over pink satin. Loose pink roses also were scattered about on the cloth. The candles, candelabra shades and balls of spun candy were of the same color, and wicker baskets of candy tied with pink ribbon were souvenirs for each guest.

And the hostess' attire?

> Miss Shwab was a pretty and charming little hostess, her gown of white silk and mull being made over blue silk and tied with blue ribbons. She was assisted by Mrs. Shwab, Mrs. George A. Shwab, Mrs. Geo. A. Dickel and Miss Louise Shwab.[2]

One of the twenty guests (all members of Nashville's "high society" families), Louise Prichitt, would herself become a Mrs. Shwab in fifteen years when she married Buist Shwab.

Manny's whist wizard brother, Emile, passed away at the age of forty-seven on July 13, 1901. The obituary in the *Nashville American* stated that he was a "prominent and well-known citizen" who had moved from Louisville to Nashville and worked for GDC since 1889. Emile was married but had no children. The funeral was held at the V.E. Shwab home, and, indicating the family's move away from Judaism, services were conducted by a Presbyterian minister.[3] However, a possible indication that Emile and his wife, Bertha Wehle Shwab, retained their Jewish faith was notice of his death in Cincinnati's Jewish newspaper, *American Israelite*.[4] Emile had retired two years earlier due to illness, and the death certificate stated the cause of death was "paralysis." According to the Nashville paper, he had been in the city for twelve years, but his death certificate said he had resided in Nashville for twenty-five years. Also according to the certificate, Emile had been born in Knoxville, his father was from Lorraine, France, and his mother was from Philadelphia. (Annie's birthplace, according to various legal documents, ranged from New York to Germany to Philadelphia.)

17. 1900–1905

Nashville's 1903 city directory showed the Shwabs spreading out in downtown Nashville. It lists the "Shwab Building" at the corner of Church and Spruce streets (Eighth Avenue), George with GDC at 150 South Spruce, Hugh as "manager" on Market Street, Buist with the Cumberland Telephone and Telegraph on Broad Street, and Manny at GDC on Broad Street.[5] The Silver Dollar Saloon and the Church Street properties were at various times listed as the Shwab Building.

The July 19, 1903, *American* ran an article listing the "largest taxpayers" in Nashville for the year. It lamented that "the Cumberland Telephone & Telegraph Co. escapes with probably the smallest burden of any large corporation in the city of Nashville. This company, with a capital stock of millions, which is increasing in value constantly[,] gets off with $34,450," due to its headquarters being in Kentucky. Under "individual taxpayers to whose credit there are assessments of $50,000 or more" was an entry for Dickel and Shwab, $123,900 (almost $4 million in 2021 dollars).[6] Manny and Augusta Dickel may have been filing jointly, since Manny managed her affairs. Also in that year, indicative of legislative battles to come, the front page of the *Chattanooga Press* warned, "The anti-whiskey element seems to be on top in the legislature, [b]ut Maney [*sic*] Schwab has not yet opened his barrel."[7]

1905: Broadening Influence and Ongoing Notoriety

By 1905, Manny Shwab's name and influence were moving well beyond GDC and the "liquor interests," and he seemed to encounter opposition in each arena. He again found his name knocked about during the municipal elections for city officials: the Board of Public Works, mayor, and city attorney. But the machine politic accusations now focused on his work for the Cumberland Telephone and Telegraph Company, of which he had been a director since at least 1891.

On May 1, 1905, 1,800 people gathered to hear the candidates speak on Deaderick Street between Third and Fourth avenues. The tradition for open-air debates on public streets abided.

Manny Shwab and the George Dickel Company

Various speakers made their case, and, according to the *Banner*, "a clash occurred" when T.J. Bumpous stumped for a position on the board. It started with Bumpous opining, "The two greatest evils in the city to-day are the city machine politics emanating from the Board of Public Works, and the Cumberland Telephone Company. A few weeks ago you saw Senator Howse circulating a petition on Cherry Street." At this point, Senator Howse, who was in back of the speakers' stand, jumped up and, shaking his fist at Bumpous, said, "That is an infamous lie, you _____ ____ ____ _____ ___." Several of Howse's friends endeavored to persuade the senator to take his seat, but he repeated his charge against Bumpous several times, the latter pausing in his speech, unruffled by the interruption. Finally the senator consented to leave the stand, declaring as he went that "no ____ can tell a lie on me." Bumpous responded:

> I have a right to attack a man's public record. Maney [*sic*] Shwab of the Cumberland Telephone Company and Ed Barthell of the Tennessee Company got married overnight somehow, and you know the result. They practically controlled the Davidson County delegation in the Legislature, but they did not control the [nominating] convention which said that it wanted to reduce telephone rates.[8]

In an interview with the *Banner* after the speeches, Bumpous accused Manny and Barthell of meeting with Senator Howse as "the city machine" to control the Democratic nominating convention and the nominee's vote concerning regulation of telephone rates. In December of that year, James E. Caldwell, Manny, and the executive committee would successfully gain a "permanent" monopoly of Nashville's phone service for their Cumberland Telephone and Telegraph Company. Ingeniously, they convinced the city to grant them exclusivity by agreeing to take down all telephone poles in Nashville and running the cables in conduit underground. They would do this, pay the city 3 percent of their revenues, and keep their rates fixed (unless approved by the city council) as long as the city granted them exclusivity. The operations of Cumberland Telephone and Telegraph were moved to Nashville from Kentucky in 1888, and the company was purchased by Southern Bell Telephone and Telegraph Company in 1912 but continued to operate in the name of the Cumberland

17. 1900–1905

Telephone and Telegraph until 1926, when its name was changed to Southern Bell.[9]

A headline in the May 17, 1905, *American* read, "Enthusiastic Meeting—T. O. Morris refers to 'Maney' Shwab Owning the Legislature." The meeting, attended by hundreds on the corner of Church and Fifteenth Avenue, was again held to hear speeches for city official candidates. T.O. Morris was running for mayor against incumbent Democrat A.E. Williams. After stating that he was thankful for living and denigrating Senator Howse for "using improper language ... in the presence of ladies," Morris went after Manny:

> Maney [sic] Shwab, who owns the legislators of Tennessee, who has debauched more of your people than any living man, is fighting for A.E. Williams. Who are the professional politicians standing around supporting? Not Morris, but Williams. I ask your support. My hands are not tied by political rings.[10]

18

The Southern Electric Company and "A Harmless Shooting Affair"

The 1905 Nashville city directory contained nine Shwab entries: Victor E. on Broad; Augusta D., a student at Ward Seminary; the Shwab Building at Eighth Avenue and the NSE corner of Church; Elizabeth, a student at Ward; George A. at Eighth Avenue; Hugh, a clerk at 1511 Broad; Buist on Broad; Shwab School on Dickerson Pike; and Felix, the president of Southern Electrical Company (SEC).[1]

Felix (then a few years out of Harvard) and the SEC would soon become well known to Nashvillians for a variety of reasons. By 1905, the Cumberland Telephone and Telegraph Company (known simply as Cumberland) covered six states. Felix had been the manager of the New Orleans branch. In February, the company was being investigated by Tennessee's General Assembly for exorbitant rates and for managing as a monopoly. During a three-and-a-half-hour testimony on February 8, 1905, President James E. Caldwell stated that he was incensed and "humiliated" by the accusations of price gouging, claiming the company ran on the national average of around 7 percent profits, supported by "voluminous" income statements he submitted. Caldwell said that "if the charges of extortion were well grounded there would not have been room in the hall for the committee, as the public would crowd it to give their evidence." He colorfully added, according to the *American*, "the anti-telephone agitation reminded him of the wolves that hounded at night around his old Louisiana home, and it appeared there were hundreds of them.

18. The Southern Electric Company and "A Harmless ..."

Investigation showed there were only four or five, but they bunched their voices so as to sound like a legion."[2]

During his testimony, Caldwell stated that Cumberland had organized the Southern Electric Company, but it had been unprofitable, and Manny Shwab, an executive committee director, had purchased the SEC from Cumberland "for his son, and set the young man up in business, and he is now conducting it as a legitimate business venture."[3] Under Felix (and assuming Manny's directorship), the SEC offered a wide range of commercial products and services for electrical systems both locally and nationally. The company obtained large contracts from Nashville's Board of Public Works, such as a contract to run 140 miles of wire for Nashville's new electric-light plant. They won the contract over General Electric and others. In April 1902, SEC sold one hundred thousand locust-insulator pins to the Pacific States Telegraph Company in San Francisco ("which is the best developed telephone city in the world with about 23,000 subscribers"), with an order for another one hundred thousand.[4]

SEC was one of the earlier companies to sell cars to Nashvillians. An ad in the March 22, 1904, *American* appealed to "everyone interested in AUTOMOBILES," announcing "The 'Ramblers' are coming." The first carload of Ramblers, costing $750–$1,350, would arrive for inspection at the company's storehouse the following week.[5]

The SEC was quite successfully growing, prospering, and gaining acclaim under the Shwabs' management. But Manny was undoubtedly disappointed by another sort of publicity garnered by Felix on June 3, 1907, which became a heated political debate.

At the time, T. Dwight Webb was the treasurer of Cumberland. Apparently, Manny had asked him to "help out" Felix and the SEC by doing some bookkeeping and consulting. Webb was in the SEC office around 6:00 in the evening when an obviously intoxicated Felix, accompanied by his wife, Mary, stepped in and demanded $50. Webb, noting Felix's condition, declined but asked "if $25 would do." Felix pulled out a Wesson 32-caliber pistol. Mary shouted, "Don't shoot!" but Felix fired at Webb, who threw up his arms. The bullet

Southern Electric Company ad for Ramblers (*Nashville American*, March 1904).

grazed the bookkeeper just above the elbow and slapped into a massive iron safe in the corner.[6]

Patrolman J.W. Van Tien was assigned to the ward and was told Shwab had fired a shot. Illustrating the family's known business affiliations, the officer testified, "Thinking I could find Mr. Shwab at Geo. A. Dickel & Co., I went there immediately but was told I would find Mr. Shwab at the SEC." It was closed, so the police sent an officer

18. The Southern Electric Company and "A Harmless ...

to Felix's home, brought him in, and charged him with assault with a pistol and shooting in the city limits. Felix was released on his own recognizance. The next day, all charges were dropped. Papers throughout the state carried the story. According to the *Banner*:

> [R]umors were set flying. An investigation revealed the fact, however, that nothing had led up to the shooting, as there had been no feeling between the men and no misunderstanding over any business or other affairs. The affair, as stated, resulted from Mr. Shwab's condition and all parties concerned this morning seemed to regret it most heartily.[7]

Judge Baker of the city court stated that the city attorney had informed him that Webb refused to prosecute and he would dismiss the case. In addition, the charges for shooting in the city limits should be dismissed, as the shot fired was "accidental." "Judge Baker then asked Mr. Shwab if such were the case and he replied that it was, and then Judge Baker said he would dismiss the whole proceedings." Apparently the judge was convinced that Shwab's word was all that was needed. The *Banner* stated that when approached by a reporter, Felix said he did not care to respond, but

> [i]t was evident from his manner ... that he regretted the occurrence deeply and was heartily sorry for the part he had played.... Young Shwab is regarded as a genial, even-tempered man and his friends can only account for his rash act by the fact that he was drinking and not himself at the time. Both men are well known in Nashville's social and business world.[8]

Unfortunately, that was hardly the end of the matter. Whereas the June 4 *American* called it a "harmless shooting affair,"[9] according to the June 4 *Chattanooga Times*, Webb's "escape from death was narrow," the bullet came "tearing through the fleshy part of the arm and flattening itself against a big iron safe," and "the cause of the shooting is shrouded in mystery." The paper stated that Felix was "a son of V.E. Shwab, well known throughout Tennessee."[10] Much of the coverage seemed interested in an insignificant example of the times: Webb's hat. For example, the *Chattanooga Daily Times* stated that after being shot, Webb "secured his hat and went across Third Avenue ... and sent for Shwab's brother."[11] It is impossible to know, but perhaps Webb thought it best to consult with Felix's older brother and the son of his employer as to the next steps. The *Memphis*

Manny Shwab and the George Dickel Company

Commercial Appeal was at first more matter of fact, simply stating that Felix Shwab "recently shot Treasurer [T. Dwight] Webb." Ho hum.[12]

The aftermath of the affair, however, was more politically tinged. The June 5 *American* carried an editorial titled "What about It" with the following lead sentence: "It appears to make considerable difference whose ox is gored to Nashville." The point of the editorial was that the liquor interest controlled the police, the mayor's office, and "the Commission." Before discussing Felix, the article stated that a state officer had gone to the police "for aid in arresting a lot of men whom he said he knew were violating the law of the State against gambling." But the police claimed "they had nothing to do with that." The editorial went on to complain that the mayor and the chief of police had done nothing; perhaps "they all decided the Commission would exonerate anyway." The author then specifically mentioned Felix:

> Tuesday night, a reputable well-mannered citizen was shot while performing his accustomed duties in the office of an industrial enterprise. The police, after a time, heard about it and then scurried around to find the man that did the shooting.... [A] man by the name of Shwab was the gun user. When Shwab appeared, he was placed under arrest and then "released on his own recognizance ... without bond." Have the police power to release without bond a man who made, so far as they knew, a murderous assault on a citizen? ... [B]y what ordinance or statute do they get it? Or was it merely a courtesy to the man because of the name he bore?[13]

As an example, the article went on to a different case:

> Two little newsboys, loaded down with *Banners* for West Nashville waited at the Maxwell House corner for their car. The weight of their newspaper bags was so heavy they hung the bags on the spikes of the rail there. A policeman came along, hit the rail a violent blow with his club and said, "Move on! Get out of the way. You stop up the passway." Yet to get to these two boys the policeman passed five men standing close together, blocking the whole sidewalk and he never saw them. They must have been gamblers or whisky sellers, and therefore immune. It's a great Administration![14]

Another article in the *American*, dated June 7 and headlined "Non-Enforcement of Law," stated that the actions of the city

18. The Southern Electric Company and "A Harmless ...

attorney and the city judge in the case were "generally criticized" and asked:

> Did not the City Attorney and the Judge, in effect, set at naught laws of the State and city? What Mr. Webb wanted should have had no influence in determining a matter of such consequence.... Certainly Shwab was guilty of carrying a pistol in violation of law, but this does not seem to have occurred to Mr. McAllister [the city attorney] or Judge Baker.... What is the matter with the Criminal Judge, the Attorney General and the Sherriff? If it had been a poor white man or a negro who made the assault, who doubts but what he would have soon been on the way to the penitentiary?[15]

Judge Baker was incensed and refused to take this criticism in silence. In a lengthy letter "To the Editor of the *American*" carried in the June 8 paper, he complained of "the impression conveyed that I showed favoritism in this case by reason of the prominence and affluence of Mr. Shwab's family." He wanted "to state the facts exactly as they were." According to Baker, the assistant city attorney had informed him, on the day of the hearing, "that Mr. Webb regretted the whole occurrence, deemed it accidental, and was very unwilling to act as prosecutor." He asked the attorney what action he should take, and it was suggested that

> Mr. Shwab be fined for violating [the ordinance against] shooting within the city limits.... In the court room when the case was called I followed a practice which I found when I became City Judge and which I have uniformly adhered to in cases of laboring men and mechanics as well as those who possess more influence and prominence.[16]

Judge Baker dismissed the assault as well as the shooting case, relying "upon [the word of] Mr. Shwab and Mr. Shwab's attorney." He drew a distinction between the charge of assault and that of assault with intent, stating that since the charge was assault, "because of Mr. Shwab's prominence in the city I should not take the initiative and act as prosecutor in a simple assault case." Baker turned the tables on his critics by stating that he had dismissed similar cases "in the instances of laboring men ... without any criticism or comment from any source whatever." He went on to say that he had enforced the ordinances as he found them, regardless of what he might think of their policy and wisdom and regardless of the accused's position in society. "I challenge your paper or any individual to point out a single instance similar to this case in which the same procedure was not followed regardless of who the offender was [and in fact] the discharge of my official duties have rather been registered on the side of the unfortunate and destitute."[17]

Manny Goes Fishing

Shwab had attracted much lighter and more positive newspaper coverage in April of the same year. A weekly sporting column titled "Fins, Furs, and Feathers" touted "Mannie [sic] Shwab as a Fisherman." The article discussed a "strange incident" that occurred while Shwab and a friend were fishing for sea trout in Florida. Each fisherman got a bite at about the same time and simultaneously "yanked the fish. When they were reeling in each swore the other had tangled his line. When they had reeled in close, however, it was discovered that each had caught the same fish."

The article then turned to Manny's attire:

It is claimed by those who have seen him fish that it is worth while to take a peep at Mannie Shwab when he's after the finny tribe in Floridy [sic]. He dons a suit of old blue overalls, heavy shoes, a big straw hat and it would take several looks to be convinced that he was the same neat looking gentleman known to Nashville's business and social world. Mr. Shwab undoubtedly has the right idea about this fishing business, however. The man who wants to "dude up" when he's fishing generally gets the worst of it.[18]

19

The Killing of a Senator on Union Street

An incident on the streets of Nashville in 1908 finally tipped the political scale in favor of the Tennessee Drys. Edward Ward Carmack, a staunch Prohibitionist, was a former state representative, a one-time U.S. senator, and the editor for the new Prohibitionist daily, the *Nashville Tennessean*. He was also openly racist, nearly having Black civil rights journalist Ida B. Wells lynched after lambasting her in the paper and suggesting retaliation against her. In 1907, Carmack decided to run in the Democratic primary for governor. His once-close friend and employer, the owner of the *American* and a dedicated anti–Prohibitionist, Duncan Cooper, supported Carmack's opponent, Malcolm Patterson, who was narrowly reelected governor the next year. Carmack subsequently launched scathing attacks on Cooper in his paper and in temperance speeches at rallies.[1]

On November 8, 1908, Cooper and his son, Robin, were walking down Union Street when they saw Carmack, who lived on Seventh near the governor's residence, tipping his hat to a Mrs. Eastman. Cooper called out to him, and Carmack pulled a gun, apparently fearing an ambush. Cooper shouted, "You dastardly coward, hiding behind that woman, are you?" Robin stepped between the two men, and Carmack fired, the bullet going through Robin's necktie and into his shoulder. Robin drew his pistol and was walking toward Carmack when the latter shot again, with the bullet passing through Robin's left sleeve. In response, Robin fired three times. According to the coroner, he was a good shot. Any of the three bullets would have killed Carmack, who

Manny Shwab and the George Dickel Company

A Nashville streetcar with a Carmack speech announcement, circa 1907 (Tennessee State Library and Archives).

fell to the pavement, instantly becoming a potent martyr for the Drys.

Under the resulting wave of temperance propaganda, public opinion shifted in favor of Prohibition. Governor Patterson pardoned Duncan Cooper, who had been convicted of second-degree murder along with his son, after several failed appeals. Robin likewise received a court-appointed acquittal.[2] A statue of Carmack was erected at the Tennessee State Capitol; it was torn down by protestors in 2020 due to Carmack's racist history. According to an article in the University of Tennessee's *Library Development Review*, "[A]s Nashville distillery owner Victor Immanuel [*sic*] Shwab observed, 'When Cooper shot he killed Carmack, Patterson, [and] whiskey at the same time.'"[3]

19. The Killing of a Senator on Union Street

1909

The ripple effects of the Carmack shooting were dramatic. Tennessee state and local governments were, and had been for decades, strongly dominated by the Democratic Party. But the divisive and highly charged issue of Prohibition split the party in half. The daily political columnist for the Prohibitionist *Tennessean*, Frank W. Lewis, with great bias, covered the contentious political meetings and conventions of 1907–1909. In a December 8, 1909, column, Lewis accused the "saloon advocates" of the Democratic Party of colluding with like-minded Republicans (whose party had no hope of winning) and Black voters to elect the "regular Democratic [P]arty" candidates. He accused Governor Patterson and a Democratic powerbroker, John Cox, of spearheading this subterfuge:

> For the public ear they both cry out against the Republicans, but in their dark designs, trades, intrigues, schemes, manipulations, and traffic, they coddle and cajole the Republicans they can use. They induced poor Shwab to introduce his "[n-----] election bill" in the last legislature, and when caught in the act of promoting it, the whole Patterson gang forsook him, leaving him with the bag to hold. The infamous measure was theirs as much as it was Shwab's, but when it was called on its final passage by the state-widers, the liquor crowd made an effort to re-commit it, but the state-widers forced the light, bringing the bill to a vote, and not a living soul voted for it but poor Shwab. That crowd will put the [n-----] up and use him at election time and combine with the Republicans for advantage and all the while cry aloud against anybody else combining with the Republicans for any purpose whatever.[4]

It is not known exactly what was in the "infamous n----- election bill," but it may have been Manny's attempt to ensure Black access to the voting booth (Black voters were reliably anti–Prohibitionist). Unfortunately, as Manny had said, the "liquor crowd's" influence had been dealt as fatal a blow by Robin Cooper as had been Carmack. In January 1909, the legislature passed laws prohibiting liquor sales within four miles of a school as well as the manufacturing of liquor, effective January 1, 1910. Governor Patterson vetoed the laws, but the legislature overrode the vetoes. Enforcing the law, however, was to be another thing all together.

20

1909: The Largest Federal Seizure in History

By 1909, Cooper's bullet had indeed enabled the Drys to put the Tennessee liquor industry in a corner. More than any other single person, Manny Shwab had impeded the progress of Tennessee Prohibition, which had placed him in the movement's headlights. Since 1903, Manny had entrusted the operations of Cascade Hollow to his son George, and W.S. "Bill" Carroll had managed the plant for three years. The distillery was the alchemical result of Abraham Schwab's intrepid journey, Meier Salzkotter's sly persistence, "Uncle" George Dickel's "conversion" from bootmaker, Kie Davis' magic, and Manny's own transformation from boy smuggler to whatever he was now. He would keep pushing. Hard.

On April 1, 1909, following orders from U.S. Revenue Officer R.S. Sharp, deputy collectors Thomas Slapp and John Walker seized the Cascade Hollow Distillery in the largest federal seizure of any kind in the nation's history. This action came just days after the Tennessee legislature overrode Governor Patterson's veto of Bill No. 11, which banned the manufacture of alcohol in Tennessee, and just five months after the shooting of Edward Carmack. (The bill was not to go into effect until January 1, 1910.)[1]

News of the seizure hit front pages across the country, with headlines and coverage often reflecting the political bias of the paper while attesting to the event as "greater than that of any other seizure ever made by the federal authorities" of any kind: Atlanta: "Million Dollar Plant Held by Government"; Los Angeles: "Raid on Whisky"; Vicksburg, Mississippi: "Internal Revenue Grabs Cascade Plant"; Chicago: "Big Still Taken by U.S."; Memphis: "9,000 Barrels Liquor

20. 1909: The Largest Federal Seizure in History

Depiction of the Cascade distillery from company letterhead and ad in the *Nashville American* (May 9, 1909) shortly after the federal seizure of the distillery.

Seized.... Punishment Is Severe If Conviction"; Clarksville, Tennessee: "Whisky Valued at $1,000,000" ($30.4 million today); Barre, Vermont: "$1,000,000 Distillery Seized"; Chattanooga: "Chattanoogan's [sic] Think It Was Prompted by Politics"; Muldrow, Oklahoma: "Big Seizure of Whiskey"; Meadville, Pennsylvania: "The Cascade distillery is the most valuable property of the kind in the state"; Nashville (*Banner*): "Violation of Revenue Laws"; and Knoxville: "Sensation over Seizure of Distillery."

According to the federal agents, two internal revenue acts were allegedly violated: #3256, whereby if a person evaded the payment of the tax on any distilled spirits, they were to forfeit the spirits and pay double the amount of the tax evaded, and, more significantly, #3257:

> Whenever any person engaged in carrying on the business of a distiller defrauds ... the United States of the tax on spirits distilled by him ... he shall forfeit the distillery and distilling apparatus used by him and all distilled spirits and raw material ... and shall be fined not less than $500 nor more than $5,000 and be imprisoned not less than six months nor more than three years.

Manny Shwab and the George Dickel Company

There were approximately nine thousand barrels of whisky at the plant at the time—over five hundred thousand gallons of Cascade. Whisky in 1909 typically sold for $1.25 per quart, making the retail value of the seized Cascade $2,500,000 ($76 million today). In addition to the seized whisky, the distillery consisted of the plant, a granary, five warehouses, and six hundred acres of land.

The accused violation was for tax evasion that occurred due to the common practice known as "equalization of wantage." As whisky ages in barrels, evaporation naturally occurs. A typical barrel from this period had the capacity to hold approximately fifty gallons. When the whisky was first distilled and barreled, it was gauged by both the distillery and a government agent. The amount in the barrel was then stamped and dated. The government allowed for "outage" evaporation and leakage (for example, seven gallons from a barrel aged for four years). If a barrel was stamped as containing forty-seven gallons, then, when the whisky was removed four years later, the revenue officer would regulate the contents, and the distillery had to pay a tax on a minimum of forty gallons (in 1909, $1.10 per gallon) even if there were only thirty gallons remaining in the barrel. So in this case, the distiller would have to pay taxes on ten gallons that did not exist. If, however, the barrel contained forty-four gallons, the distillery was taxed on the total amount. Given this rule, distilleries commonly removed the amount in excess of forty gallons and placed it in barrels with excessive evaporation.

Manny moved fast. The seizure occurred on Thursday, April 1. Manny and several of his most influential friends—James E. Caldwell, F.O. Watts, Frank Lester, and others—executed a bond on Saturday, April 3, for $275,000 ($8.4 million today), and the government agreed to turn the distillery back over to Manny the following Monday. Under the bond, the owners and the signers of the bond would be held liable for the ultimate judgment amount.[2] Manny, George, Bill Carroll, and Cascade assistant manager Reynolds were arrested and indicted for "equalizing spirits in warehouses and removing spirits on which tax had not been paid."[3] Manny engaged attorneys John Vertrees and Frank Bond (the previous federal revenue collector) to pursue the case. The attorneys were quoted in several papers

20. 1909: The Largest Federal Seizure in History

as stating that any violations were "technical" and that the Shwabs "had implicit confidence" in Carroll and "repeatedly warned him to plumb the law."[4] According to the April 6 *American*, the plant was "again in the hands of its owner, V.E. Shwab, and the business of that concern is going on uninterrupted." To illustrate the tax burden already shouldered by the distillery and Cascade's significant economic impact on the state, the paper pointed out that "in four years the George Dickel Company has paid the Government approximately $1,120,000 [$34 million today] in taxes. This is about one-fourth of the entire amount paid by all the distillers in Middle and West Tennessee and has been an average of approximately $1,000 per day."[5]

Revenue collector R.S. Sharp was accused by many in the press (as well as Manny's attorneys) of being motivated by "political revenge." In an article titled "Liquor Men Declare Sharp Plays Politics," the *Chattanooga Times* quoted a prominent local liquor dealer as saying, "The wholesale liquor men and the distillers in Tennessee have on more than one occasion contributed to the campaign funds of the Democratic party, and for this reason Mr. Sharp seized the plant of one of the leading distillers and one of the soundest business concerns in the state."[6]

Not every paper was sympathetic, however. The April 8 *Baptist and Reflector* (Nashville), covering the seizure, stated, "We do not know what proof they have as to the violation of the revenue laws by the distillery. We presume, though, that it is ample. We hope that the violators of the law may be convicted and receive due punishment." The paper was quick to identify "Mannie [sic] Schwab; who for many years has been the leading liquor lobbyist in Tennessee."[7]

Throughout the spring and summer of 1909, Frank Bond would be stuck in Washington, D.C., attempting to settle the case with the government. The *Nashville Banner*, on July 12, 1909, opined that a compromise was imminent, as the Treasury Department had agreed to terms that were being considered by the U.S. attorney general. But it was pointed out that Collector Sharp strongly opposed the settlement and that he "stated his position quite plainly" to the revenue commissioner.[8] He apparently was insisting on the full payment of the original claim that the distillery and all product be turned over to the government; Cascade had agreed to pay the maximum fine of $5,000 with the exoneration of all the accused. The *Banner* on July 14 concluded that the Treasury Department considered the matter settled and had turned the case over to the Justice Department, where "it was stated ... [t]he Attorney General, Secretary of the Treasury and Commissioner of Internal Revenue have to 'get together' ... and they have not yet done so."[9]

So the case dragged on. According to the *American*'s "reliable information," a further investigation of the charges would be made by the Department of Justice. The revenue commissioner, the Department of Agriculture, and chief revenue collector all agreed to the settlement, but Sharp continued to vehemently protest, perhaps wanting to extract a pound of Manny's flesh (and most certainly to gain high-profile public notice).[10]

Finally, on August 11, 1909, a compromise was reached. The *Clarksville Leaf Chronicle* announced, "Cascade Case Compromised on Payment of $10,000 and All Costs—No Moral Turpitude on Part of Owners."[11] That same day, the *Chattanooga Times* and Mississippi's *Vicksburg Herald* ran an article from a D.C. correspondent, stating that the attorney general in Washington had fixed the sum of "$10,000 to obtain release of the seized spirits and immunity from prosecution for the wealthy distillers.... On account of the prominence of the Schwabs [sic] throughout the [S]outh, great interest was taken in the case."[12] Apparently, Manny just wanted the drama to end and agreed to double the settlement.

The case was settled, but not the animus between Bond and Sharp, who went after one another in the papers. Bond complained that Sharp "made a play like a baseball player posing for the grandstand." Referencing the fact that Sharp would not divulge to the Shwabs or their attorneys the nature of the indictments, claiming that the charges were "classified as a privileged secret service communication," Bond was quoted as saying:

> A great government, founded on equal and exact justice to all, denies the men being baited and badgered even so much as knowledge of the offense with which they were charged. Mr. V.E. Shwab, who has been the

20. 1909: The Largest Federal Seizure in History

particular target of slander and venom, has had no active participation in the management of the distillery near Tullahoma for years.[13]

In a front-page August 12 editorial, the *American*, in very loquacious fashion, went after Sharp and the insinuations against the Shwabs:

> Revenue Officer R.S. Sharp has succeeded in his partisan political play and shares with bigoted allies the realization of having cost somebody something.... The *American* has refrained from commenting on the Cascade case.... Now that an adjustment has been reached, it is not improper to comment on the verdict. Sharp's bitterness and malevolence, characteristic of the man since he has been in public life[,] has alone been satisfied. Mr. Sharp's animosity has not been fully accounted for. [P]olitically he espouses the great moral issue of Prohibition, chuckling over the discomfiture of his old-time enemy, Democracy, and her family divisions.... Sharp is a politician pure in tenacity if not simple in purpose. With the exception of about two years of monotonous commercialism, his life has been devoted to politics.... He has been a dominant, militant, rip-roaring, rampant Republican.... [I]t is whispered he now cherished ambition to become master instead of man. Sharp has had the call of the wild. There is a new man in the saddle, and he is riding for the Republican Gubernatorial nomination. Only politics has made a live question of the seizure of the Cascade distillery.... Sharp's spite has been gratified.
>
> Mr. V.E. Shwab and his son, George A. Shwab[,] have been closely identified with Nashville and her interests for the better portion of their lives. They are aggressive men who have succeeded in business while maintaining the confidence and respect of the community. That men of this character would risk their reputation and put in jeopardy nearly a million dollars in values in order to escape taxation on a few gallons of whisky is a proposition so preposterous as to have proven unworthy of consideration in the minds of any save Mr. Sharp and his sympathetic newspaper ally. The emotional excitability of the press agent in this instance has been especially gratified.
>
> In this particular case every precedent has been set aside in order that the revenue officer's personal ambition might be given recognition. Government officials admitted, following a full hearing, that the owners of the distillery had made no effort to defraud the Government, admitted that the Government had received every penny of tax to which the Government was entitled.[14]

The coverage was spun with as much bias as today's stories on Fox News and MSNBC. Tennessee's *Columbia Herald*, in an article headlined "Uncle Sam Takes Cool Ten Thousand in Cascade Case," emphasized the Shwabs having to pay double the original $5,000 agreement as reimbursement for "international revenue tax" that had been evaded through equalizing. It sang the praises of Sharp, who had rushed to D.C. to argue the flagrant infractions of the law by the Shwabs. The paper alluded to a story "making the rounds" that the parties "have been found guilty," having "connived at the illegal transaction of substituting spirits," and that the settlement was "anything but a 'clean bill of health'" for the Shwab business empire: "This case is considered one of the most serious that have come to attention of the government."[15]

Fallout from the Cascade case was to follow Sharp as he played Elliot Ness and aggressively pursued distillers and retail outlets throughout Tennessee. A conflict between Collector Sharp and other revenue officials arose as a result of the seizure of the Cascade Hollow Distillery. Other collectors accused him of being politically motivated. Sharp stated repeatedly that there was no political question involved in the Cascade case and ridiculed rumors that his activities were intended to secure the nomination for governor.[16]

Despite the remonstrations, the temperance Democrats were aligning with Republicans in support of Sharp. It was claimed that the Democratic wing of the coalitionists would not nominate a candidate for governor, leaving an open field for Sharp to be the Republican candidate with Democratic coalition support. According to the *American*, "The praise of Mr. Sharp is on the lips of every coalition Democrat. Mr. Sharp is a shrewd politician and it is said that he will have the endorsement of the Taft administration for Governor."[17]

Sharp was indeed in contention for the Republican nomination but withdrew when President William Taft tapped him to be the new chief post office inspector of the United States.

* * *

On a lighter note, Frank Lewis, in his November 10, 1909 column for the *Nashville Tennessean*, titled "Political," again turned his tongue-in-cheek attention to Manny and the efforts to conceal liquor distribution:

20. 1909: The Largest Federal Seizure in History

A distressing accident happened at Newsom Station Monday. A car door was accidentally torn off as a train rolled through the station, and out of the car, right in view of a gaping and meddlesome crowd rolled a barrel of gin addressed to Geo. A. Dickel & Co. (Cascade Shwab's wholesale liquor firm). Of course, accidents happen in the best regulated families. Nobody blames the railroad for it was purely accidental. The railroad company was trying to deliver the goods without anybody finding it out, but an accident happened which exposed the liquor firm.

Cascade Shwab has the profound sympathy of his many friends in his deep affliction.

Moral: Don't ship liquor in rail cars that are going to have their doors torn off.[18]

* * *

In November 1909, for $110,000, Manny and J.J. Gray purchased 2,700 iron-ore-rich acres near Nashville in Hickman County. The property contained features appealing to the fisherman in Manny. The November 26 *Nashville Tennessean* contained a detailed description:

> About a fourth of the tract consists of fine farming land, the remainder of well wooded timber land. Piney River, one of the most beautiful streams in the State, and long a favorite resort of fishermen from Nashville, courses through this property. On its bank lies the attractive little village of Pinewood, adorned with handsome elms, maple and cedar trees giving it quite an English appearance. A large cotton mill, at one time run by water power and operated by some 250 girls of the neighborhood[,] was for many years the chief feature of commercial interest, the cotton yarns made there and marketed in Nashville and elsewhere bearing a high reputation.[19]

Gray had prospected the tract and discovered "large bodies of brown ore" only a few miles from the well-established Nunnelly Mines. That ore produced the highest-quality "Tennessee boiler plate iron of ancient fame," used by the Warner Iron Company. However, a rail spur would need to be constructed to bring the ore out. The Nashville, Chattanooga & St. Louis Railway (of which Shwab was a director) had extended its service to nearby Dickson, so it was assumed that the company would construct the spur. The paper also noted that the railroad owners had long believed "the car wheels made for the Chattanooga Railroad should have a liberal proportion of this iron [from Nunnelly ore]. Their toughness and lasting quality justified [this] requirement." The *Tennessean* article continued:

> If it is found in the working that this deposit equals the Nunnelly Mines in depth and richness, this purchase, by experienced and financially strong parties and the immediate opening up of such a large body of ore of fine quality so near to consuming furnaces and within such convenient reach of Nashville stove and other foundries, will mean very much to Nashville as a manufacturing city.[20]

The next year, Manny sold a thousand of the Pinewood acres for $55,000. Five hundred of the purchased acres were farmland, and five hundred were in timber. The remaining land contained one of the richest ore deposits in the state. Manny also retained the mineral rights to the sold property, thereby cutting in half the price he paid.[21] The Pinewood Ore Company was chartered with George Shwab as president and Hugh Shwab as treasurer. The 1911 city directory listed George as president and treasurer of the company.

With the passing of Prohibition legislation casting a long shadow on the future of GDC, accompanied by the seizure of the Cascade distillery and Manny's many other enterprises, 1909 proved to be an impactful year for the Shwabs. But the year came to a happy close and further consolidation for the GDC family. On December 16, Kie's son, Paul McLin Davis, married Augusta Shwab. The ceremony was solemnized at the home of the bride's parents in the presence of several hundred relatives and friends. The occasion was impressive, complete with an orchestra, and the home was festooned, in honor of the season, in a color scheme of white and green. Much was made in the papers of the decorations, flowers, hanging friezes, palms and "luxuriant foliage plants," and, of course, "A large and costly collection of wedding gifts was received by the young couple."[22]

21

Distilling, Prohibition, and Shifting Plans

Since the Tennessee legislature's prohibition of the manufacturing of alcohol, GDC (now under George's direct supervision) placed advertisements and notices across the country hyping the superiority of Cascade whisky and assuring the public that nothing was to change due to the new laws. The company engaged the D'Arcy advertising agency (GDC and Coca-Cola among their largest and earliest accounts) to ensure the most creative, far-reaching, and effective results. A brilliant advertisement, run in May 1909, included a beautiful rendering of the distillery with the heading in all caps: "CASCADE'S BEST COMPLIMENT." On the left side of the ad, a telegram was depicted from the *American* to R.H. Watkins, a D.C. correspondent, asking the name of a brand recently referred to by a "government food expert" who had stated that of all the whiskies he knew, "a well known Tennessee brand was THE BEST AND MOST HONEST." The reply from D.C. was carried on the opposite side: "The Tennessee Whiskey referred to in my dispatches of May 6th is CASCADE Brand." In between the two telegrams, headed "TENNESSEE JOY WATER IS BEST," was more detail. The D.C. "food sharp" was an expert who was testifying before the solicitor general on the question "What is whisky?" when he made the statement. The dispatch went on to complain that former president Theodore Roosevelt "was unable to distinguish between blended goods and straight whisky" but had taken with him on a trip "five casks of a popular club brand as an antidote for the tsetse fly bite."

The distillery is impressively depicted in the ad like a classic Currier and Ives print, with the Cascade falls tumbling down into

Full-page Sunday ad appearing a few weeks after the federal seizure of the distillery. The ad claims that, in testimony before the U.S. solicitor general in Washington, a government witness declared Cascade the "best and most honest" whisky (*Nashville American*, May 9, 1909).

21. Distilling, Prohibition, and Shifting Plans

and through a small village of ten two-story buildings. The scene is that of a plant in bustling operation, with black charcoal smoke billowing from the distillery building as men on horse-drawn carts bring produce and product to and from various buildings and workers move contents from wagons into the warehouses.[1]

As attention focused on the Tennessee distillers' predicament, the papers covered rumored plans. The May 9, 1909, *American* ran an article with the headline "Where Liquor Men Will Go, Dickel & Co. Halting Between Opinions." For most of the distillers who would move and then ship product back to Tennessee and elsewhere, the likely cities in states unaffected by statewide Prohibition laws were Evansville, Indiana ("seems to be the favorite"); St. Louis, Missouri; Cincinnati, Ohio; and Louisville and Paducah, Kentucky. The paper, focusing on GDC, opined that the dealers would hold "their present trade, and work up new business.... [T]he original package business will probably be very decidedly on the increase instead of decrease." At that time, the Shwabs had not decided where to move operations when the new law went into effect. St. Louis was being considered, as the company was looking into the likelihood of Missouri passing statewide laws; Louisville was the second choice. Some possible alternatives to distilling being discussed for dealers were to sell soft drinks (bring your own to mix), to develop restaurants, or to go out of business. According to the paper, the Climax Saloon had "not decided as to what they will do." There was also speculation "that St. Louis would probably be the home of Jack Daniel's #7."[2]

By Christmas, reality had set in. And yet the December 24 *American* reflected continued resistance with the headline "Think It Is Temporary.... Manufacturers' Bill is to be tested in courts." Referring to Cascade as "the largest plant of its kind in Tennessee," the subheading read, "The Cascade Distillery Announces Temporary Suspension of Manufacture at the Big Plant—Brewery to Make Beerette and Soft Drinks." The company's size is apparent in the explanation of the plan:

> Night and day the stock has been increased until all their bonded warehouses are taxed to their capacity and carry many thousand barrels. The Cascade people said yesterday they would temporarily suspend operation

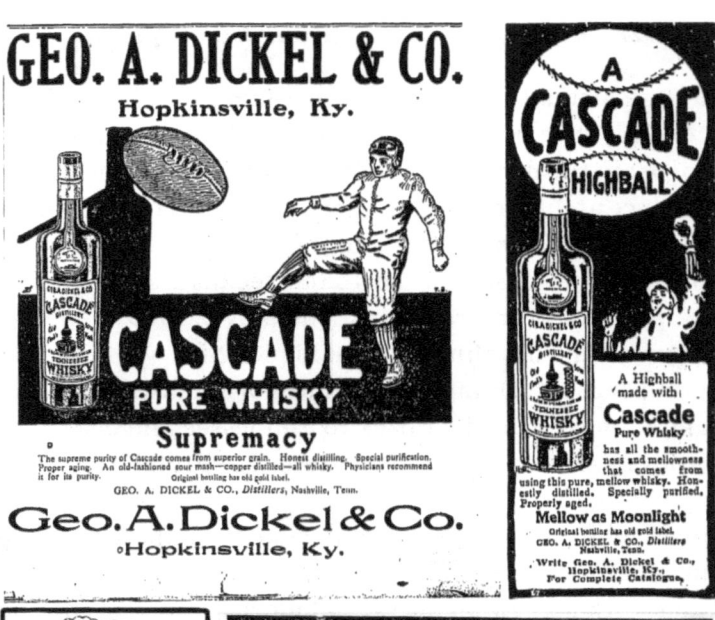
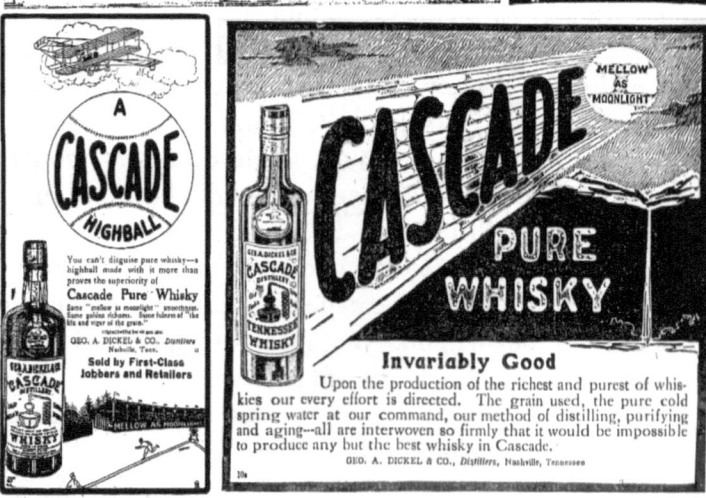

In the early 1900s, GDC and the D'Arcy agency placed playful and innovative ads in sports pages around the country tied to the athletic seasons that tapped into new innovations. Clockwise, starting at the top left: a football player kicking through Cascade-bottle goalposts (*Nashville Tennessean*, November 24, 1909); ad in the sports page hawking a highball made with Cascade and showing a baseball player catching a fly ball (*Nashville Tennessean*, June 10, 1910); moonlight bathing a bottle of Cascade (*Nashville American*, April 6, 1909); another highball ad showing a biplane flying overhead (*Washington Post*, April 24, 1913).

As Prohibition loomed, with limited distribution outlets, GDC and D'Arcy reacted creatively. Clockwise from top left: a national ad stating that Cascade would be shipped directly to the consumer, express paid, to the nearest railroad station—the boxes would be marked with "nothing of any kind" to indicate the contents (*Chattanooga Daily Times*, December 8, 1909); a national ad reassuring readers that, despite Cascade having to move operations to Kentucky, the whisky would be shipped as always and that its "superior quality ... *cannot* be affected by legislation" (*Fort Worth Star-Telegram*, April 1, 1909); a national ad claiming that physicians prescribe Cascade in sick rooms because it is pure and full of the "life and vigor of the grain" (*Nashville American*, February 4, 1909); a matchbook hawking Cascade in Honolulu, circa 1910 (author's collection).

As Prohibition pressed forward, D'Arcy and GDC leaned into the old tagline "Mellow as Moonlight." For their newspaper ads, they leveraged the eye-catching contrast of nighttime imagery. Clockwise from the top left: a moonlit country scene featuring "nature—honesty—time" (author's collection); a dark ad calling Cascade "Bottled Sunshine" (*St. Louis Globe Democrat*, January 19, 1909); "Nature's finest" being observed by moonlight by a farmer finishing a day of harvesting (author's collection); Cascade's promised "bouquet" is fulfilled (*St. Louis Globe Democrat*, January 16, 1909).

21. Distilling, Prohibition, and Shifting Plans

at the distillery, and were glad of the opportunity to shut down at this time as they contemplated such additions and improvements as would have made temporary cessation inevitable anyway. They have provided against every contingency. Their present stock will supply the trade for many years if it be found necessary to suspend distilling in the State permanently.... They will be prepared to continue the manufacture in other territory.

The warehouse in Hopkinsville [Kentucky], the office in Nashville, the various branch houses throughout the country, and the present force of traveling men will remain intact, and the entire selling organization will continue as at present. The distillery employees at Normandy, to the number of forty, will alone be affected. On account of the high price of grain and uncertainty in Tennessee, all the manufacturers appear satisfied to suspend at this time. They appear confident the confiscation of their property will be finally avoided, and that the courts will eventually declare the manufacturers' bill void.[3]

By March 1910, GDC's address was Hopkinsville, Kentucky, as well as Nashville, and the company's approach was evident in its advertising. Like today's medical marijuana laws, many states would allow whisky to be sold for medicinal purposes. An ad run in March stated, "Physicians everywhere recommend Cascade for medicinal purposes because of its purity and quality" and "Cascade by Mail ... If you can't get Cascade Pure Whisky in your town we will supply you direct.... All shipments made in securely packed boxes—nothing on the box to indicate the contents." D'Arcy was also getting more clever with the Cascade ads. Capitalizing on the country's baseball obsession, one ad hawked "A CASCADE HIGHBALL" boldly printed on a baseball with a player leaping up to catch it.

After distilling at Cascade Hollow for as long as possible, GDC moved production to Louisville, where the whisky would be produced under the Stitzel Distillery (Pappy Van Winkle, president). George moved to Louisville to run operations along with his brother Hugh.

22

That Reif Letter
Legislators Flee to Alabama

The Shwabs continued the fight to repeal the statewide Prohibition laws throughout 1910 and 1911. Their efforts were brought to the public's attention when a letter between liquor interests in Chattanooga and Memphis was published in a front-page article by the *Nashville Tennessean* on the last day of 1910. The article carried the headline "Reveals Plans of Liquor Men," followed by "Geo. Shwab Has Secured Six Republican Votes for Them, and That, With These, He Considers They Are Now Safe in Both Branches." The letter was from Charles Reif, president of the Chattanooga Brewing Company, to J.W. Schorr of the Memphis Tennessee Brewing Company. Reif related that George Shwab had come to him, stating that it was "absolutely necessary that we 'cinch' the lower house" of representatives and that he had "made arrangements by which we get six Republican votes.... I think we are now safe in both branches.... It, of course, required immediate money." Reif went on to say that unless Schorr helped, he and George would be out $1,250 apiece, as George had already paid out $2,500 and "it appears we will possibly have to get up something in the neighborhood of ten or twelve thousand dollars [$350,000 today] ... to cinch matters during the entire session." Reif admonished Schorr to destroy the letter "by all means." He ended the message by saying that if Schorr needed more information, he should write George: "He is the cleanest cut fellow I have ever seen, and he is certainly hustling."[1] The publication of the letter launched an all-out Tennessee political crisis that would last over a year, with issues being contested as hotly in the press as in the legislature.

22. That Reif Letter

The December 31, 1910, *Banner* responded with front-page coverage, including an interview with George subheaded "Mr. Shwab's Statement" and "Almost Sole Topic of Politicians about Hotel Lobbies To-day." The article described conflict between "regular Democrats" (traditional, anti–Prohibition) and independent Democrats (that is, "Fusionists" and Drys), with the former "laughing over the matter." The Drys, however, charged that the regulars' efforts were in the form of promises of important committee places under the regular organization that would carry with them additional financial emoluments provided for the additional service rendered.[2]

The article said that George directed the reporter to the "writer of the letter" and

> the statement that he was exceedingly anxious that the manufactures act passed two years ago should be repealed was correct. He said that they had large interests in distillery property, made under the law, and that the act was unjust and oppressive and that he believed now that there had been two years of reflection and experience, all fair-minded persons in the Legislature would see the unreasonableness and injustice of that law. He said if there was anything he could do in proper way to bring about its repeal he would certainly do it, but that the idea had been not to appeal to any particular class, but to the judgment and sense of fair play of the Legislature, and that when it was organized he did propose, if allowed to do so, to have the case of the distillers fully presented to such committees as might be appointed to hear them, and that this was the extent of his efforts.[3]

As for Reif himself, his secretary said he was in Ohio, but she had looked through the company files and Reif's private files and could not find a copy of such a letter. But as more accusations of a slush fund to bribe legislators were made, the letter became the subject of renewed interest and was reprinted in papers along with new allegations. Interestingly, as the temperature rose, except for the Reif letter, George Shwab was not referred to directly, only as a "well known liquor dealer."

The rumors became direct allegations on April 12, 1911, when the *Banner* headline exclaimed, "High-Handed Corruption Alleged in Election Bill Fight.... Member or Members Have Been

Manny Shwab and the George Dickel Company

Fixed—Money Furnished by Well Known Liquor Dealer." According to the paper, there was

> abundant evidence to indicate that the "fixing process" was put into full plan last night and that enough members who needed "fixing" have been secured to pass the bill.... The current report is that a well-known large liquor dealer agreed to furnish the money, that over twenty thousand dollars was placed in the hands of [a] ... go between who is handling this corruption fund, and placing it where it accomplishes the end in view.[4]

On April 12, a preliminary motion of an election bill was passed by the Tennessee legislature with an outcry from the Fusionists, the Prohibitionist Democrats who now (and in the future) aligned with the Republicans. They referred to it as the "liquor-election bill." Their complaint was that, suspiciously, three Republicans and two Independents who had previously voted with the Fusionists now voted with the regular Democrats. The bill would increase the number of election commissioners from three to seven, giving the regulars an advantage in their attempt to revise the liquor manufacturing and local Prohibition laws throughout the state. Prohibition advocates feared the liquor interest would then have full control of the elections and could appoint every county election commissioner in the state. In response, thirty-four members left the state that day and convened in Decatur, Alabama, in order to deny a quorum needed to finally pass the bill. The April 14, 1911, *Memphis Commercial Appeal* read:

> The expressed determination of the runaway members to remain away as long as necessary is met by the position of the "regulars" who ... faced the situation with the assertion that they would hold the present session two years and not budge an inch.... This would mean that the whole public machinery of the state would be clogged so long as the present situation exists.[5]

Perhaps not coincidentally, on April 15, the Davidson County Grand Jury returned criminal indictments against Manny and George, "manufacturers of Cascade whisky," for "tippling without license." They made bond of $500 each.[6]

The April 29 *Banner* claimed on its front page that the "Reif Letter Again Is Interesting" and explained that a proposed investigation

22. That Reif Letter

of the alleged corruption by the legislature could not begin until they again had a quorum. The report described the Democrats as "unterrified." The paper stated that many believed the Reif letter "proved positively" the existence of the slush fund and then again ran the entire letter. Afterward, it explained, "[U]nder this law, it is asserted the whisky people would dominate the constitutional convention." It was feared that "the gubernatorial plum, the treasuryship and other offices ... are being dangled before the eyes of weak-kneed Regulars ... to keep them in line."[7]

The April 28 *Knoxville Sentinel* headline read, "Tennessee Legislative Situation Approaches Revolutionary Stage." A Republican representative, J.Q. McDonald (described as "one of the Alabama division of the legislature"), claimed in an affidavit that on December 31, 1910, "Judge" E.C. Goodpasture had offered him $1,500 to vote with the regular Democrats on contests for speaker, election, and liquor legislation.[8] The April 28 *Banner* reported that Goodpasture admitted to having "urged" McDonald to align with the regulars but denied offering a bribe. However, McDonald produced alleged written proof, which he claimed was signed in "the washroom at the Maxwell [Hotel]":

Nashville, Tenn.,
December 31, 1910

I, E.C. Goodpasture do hereby agree to pay to J.Q. McDonald $1,500, provided said McDonald votes for the "Regular" Democrats or a majority of the said Democrats on all questions coming before the Legislature.

(Signed) E.C. Goodpasture

The Fusionists were, of course, elated, while the regulars were irate, reasonably pointing out that although Goodpasture was known to drink, no man would be drunk enough to document such a thing. McDonald described earlier meetings with Goodpasture, who allegedly promised him $5,000 but later lowered the amount to $1,500, saying that he would give McDonald $500 for each of three votes (one being the repeal of the temperance law) and that Goodpasture would be getting $500 for his efforts. The representative stated that he had not come forth earlier for "fraternal reasons" but now felt obligated to "show the methods used by the whisky machine in Tennessee and [to] corrupt young manhood of the state." Goodpasture denied ever signing or writing the note.⁹

Papers throughout the state rolled up their sleeves and dove headlong into the fight. An editorial in the May 1 *Tennessean* referred to a letter written by a candidate for the house speakership, Jesse C. Beesley (referred to by the editor as "Jesse Cascade Beesley"). The representative charged that the Prohibitionist McDonald had hypocritically and illegally ordered whisky during the session, and it was filled (without charge) and was being held by the local liquor firm. The paper urged Beesley to call out the local liquor dealer and hinted that the liquor interests had supported his campaign, as opposed to its being self-funded as he reported.¹⁰

The May 1 Knoxville *Journal* reprinted "That Reif Letter," claiming it "proved positively" that a slush fund existed that was rumored to be used to bribe politicians in favor of the liquor interests. But a volley came in the form of accusations of another slush fund, this time created by the Fusionists to "influence" legislation.¹¹

In April, an article in the *Chattanooga Times* headlined "Fusionist Slush Fund" was run along with names of subscribers to the fund. The *Tennessean* took exception to the *Times'* claims in a May 3 article headed with "Denounces Story as Entirely a Fabrication," subheaded "Chattanooga Paper Probably Got Its Wires Crossed." The article included a letter from the president of the Anti-Saloon League, who demanded a retraction, claiming the purpose of the fund was to "assist the officers of the law in the suppression of crime and enforcement of law, chiefly the anti-liquor laws," an objective "of which no honest, law-abiding *Christian* man need be ashamed."¹² The next day, the *Tennessean* editorialized against the legislators who claimed to be Prohibitionists and yet voted for the election bill:

> The self-denominated temperance advocates who are supporters of the liquor-election bill are divided into two classes—namely the arrant hypocrite and the mutton-headed ignoramuses.... [T]he man who is sincere in both his support of the bill and opposition to liquor rule has an inherited affliction which cannot be cured and for which he should be pitied, and not censured.¹³

22. That Reif Letter

By June 26, the Fusionist retreat to Alabama was apparently over, as the Legislature had a quorum to pass a resolution (#57) for an investigation into the slush-fund allegations as well as into new allegations from a lower house representative, J.S. Cooper. Cooper claimed that he knew or "had reason to believe" that eight members of the Legislature had been offered from $500 to $1,000 to vote for the election bill which would have opened the door for the repeal of the temperance laws."[14] In July, Governor Ben Hooper vetoed the joint resolution for the investigation, stating that there was "not sufficient time" for conducting the claims.[15] Interestingly, on the same day that it passed #57, the House passed a bill, on first reading, to give a pension to all Confederate soldiers who surrendered at Vicksburg in July 1863.

* * *

While his family's aggressive fight to repeal the anti-liquor laws continued through 1912 and 1913, with an additional push to enable the sale of liquor in major urban areas, Manny Shwab was becoming more embedded in Nashville's financial, social, and charitable circles. In January 1912, he was elected to the board of the First Savings Bank & Trust, once again with James E. Caldwell, and both men were elected to the board of the Fourth and First National Bank (the latter claiming in advertisements to have "resources" of $16,500,000, which would be almost half a billion dollars today). Manny was also elected director of the Nashville Golf and Country Club during its proposed move from Harding Road to Belle Meade, forming the new Belle Meade Country Club. Those plans would have to await the Nashville Railway & Light Company's extension of the West End line to Belle Meade (Manny was a director of the company).[16]

In March 1912, the "elopement ... of two young persons prominent in Nashville society" was announced in Tennessee papers. According to the Knoxville *Journal*, "The young woman was Miss Bessie Shwab, daughter of one of the wealthiest men in Tennessee, and the groom was Benjamin E. Tate."[17]

The 1911–1912 winter weather was apparently brutal, resulting in scores of applications for assistance from those "suffering among

Manny Shwab and the George Dickel Company

the poor of Nashville." In January, Fannie Battle of the United Charities (and famed social reformer and spy for the Confederate Army) confirmed that "the car load of coal donated to the poor by Mr. V.E. Shwab through the *Banner* was being distributed."[18]

Manny continued to be vilified by the Prohibitionists in the newspapers. An editorial in the July 8, 1913, *Banner* took direct aim at him:

> The whisky ring has for fifty years furnished the campaign money for the Democratic party. This is a notorious fact. The leaders in the party know it and have known it for these many years, even if the rank and file did not know it (and we don't believe they did). Maney [sic] Shwab, the incarnated quintessence of the whisky power in Tennessee, booted and spurred, whip in hand, with the lordly air of a conquering hero, used to strut like a cock-partridge in mating time across the stage of Tennessee politics and give orders to the legislators each of whom had a gallon jug of Shwab's whisky in his room at the hotel. Of course it is so.[19]

23

Manny and Boss Crump
Liquor by the Drink

A special and highly contentious legislative session of both houses was called by Governor Hooper in October 1913. He initially called for the session to consider only law enforcement measures and a bill on funding, but it turned into what the Knoxville *Journal* termed a "battle royal."[1] Two extra bills were introduced—one prohibited the shipping of liquor into Tennessee from another state (or from county to county), while the other was "the Nuisance Bill." The latter would "declare a saloon, gambling den, bawdy house or any other business the conduct of which is a violation of the law, a public nuisance." Any business could be closed by five qualified voters (electors) in an effort to get around public officials who were seen as ignoring the activity.[2] This ploy was analogous to the 2021 Texas anti-abortion laws giving private citizens the right to directly sue, for monetary gain, providers who were not following the law.

The thirty-nine-year-old mayor of Memphis, E.H. "Boss" Crump, was in Nashville to fight and alter the legislation. Crump would be a major figure in Tennessee politics for the next twenty years in similar fashion to Manny for the previous thirty. He wanted to enable liquor to be sold in eleven of twenty-nine wards in Memphis, so he slyly had a substitute nuisance bill introduced first, specific to Memphis, that would exclude the eleven wards and contain the clause "repealing all laws in conflict with it." This change could kill the four-mile law for the entire state. Crump appealed to Manny for support. Since there was a rule that once an issue was voted on, a similar bill could not be introduced that session, Manny was all for it, as it would enable liquor to be sold in the larger cities. A legislative

Manny Shwab and the George Dickel Company

AFTER THE BATTLE ON CAPITOL HILL

Illustration depicting "John Barleycorn" and the liquor interests being slain by the extra session of the state legislature when passing the "Nuisance Bill." This bill resulted in Manny Shwab and over 150 Nashville liquor dealers pleading guilty to grand jury indictments (*Nashville Banner*, October 17, 1913).

clerk, Mr. Cason, was rumored to have agreed that, when calling on a role vote, he would not call on eight Fusionists who were also fire marshals (it was against the rules for anyone to have two paying state jobs at the same time).[3] Crump and Sheriff Cate (his Memphis sheriff and campaign manager) were hard at work "aiding and abetting in the fight." According to the Knoxville *Journal*:

> Backing up Mayor Crump and his henchmen was V.E. Shwab, the wealthiest whiskey man in Tennessee, the owner of Cascade and the Gibraltar of the whiskey interests in Tennessee. While heretofore Mr. Shwab has seen fit to entrust the lobbying business to men representing him, he found the

23. Manny and Boss Crump

issue of sufficient importance today to be on the ground himself. He was seen to talk with various members of the house and senate on the floor of the Maxwell lobby this morning.... Some little excitement went the round in whispers this morning when it got started that the whiskey interests are threatening the weak-kneed fellows.[4]

As an indication of how tense the situation in Nashville was, the Bristol *Courier* declared, "The Tennessee Legislature has been in session and nobody has been killed, not even Boss Crump."[5]

The whiskey lobbyists knew they were going to lose, so they were pushing for a filibuster, as they had successfully done in the January session, to prevent the bills from being voted on "or threaten dire consequences to those who have accepted 'courtesies' from them." But it proved a losing battle. The three "jug bills" passed, prohibiting shipment of liquor to Tennessee from other states and between counties and allowing any five citizens to shut down saloons and gambling halls when local enforcement refused to act (the Nuisance Act). The Democrats' filibuster was successful only in keeping one bill, the Removal Act, from a vote. This bill would have allowed any citizen to sue to remove county or city officials from office who were deemed derelict in their duty.[6]

On October 14, 1913, the *Tennessean* exuberantly announced, "John Barleycorn Knocked Out in Second Round," declaring "Nashville Nearly Arid" and that criminal court Judge A.B. Neil had closed more than two hundred saloons. "John Barleycorn" was a reference to the well-known fictional character who was the personification of barley and alcoholic beverages, originally depicted in a traditional Scottish folk song; Robert Burns had written a rendition of the song, and the name was used as the title of Jack London's autobiographical novel dealing with his love of drinking and his battles with alcoholism. Over 150 Nashville liquor dealers pleaded guilty to grand jury indictments. The judge ordered that "no intoxicating liquor shall be sold across their bars in the form of drinks, that their saloons shall not be kept open on Sunday nor after midnight, that no gambling devices shall be operated on their premises, and that no lewd women shall be permitted to loiter about their places of business." Enforcing the latter order would surely be interesting.[7]

Manny Shwab and the George Dickel Company

The Anti-Saloon League, through the Tennessee Attorney General, Frank Thompson, quickly wielded their new weapon, the Nuisance Act. Thompson filed two injunction bills on June 12, 1914, against thirty-one soft-drink-stand proprietors and the owners of the buildings they occupied, shutting down the businesses by nightfall. Many Nashville saloons had converted to soft-drink stands, allowing customers to flavor their soft drinks as they wished (and presumably selling more than soft drinks). The business operators, building owners, and "imbibing public" were now restrained from entering the soft-drink stands for any purpose. Large placards were "conspicuously exhibited on the front doors.... The stocks and fixtures in the places ... [were] to be sold in a legal way as far as possible, and that part of the business which cannot be legally disposed of [was] to be destroyed."[8]

The thirty-one bills were filed by attorneys for the Anti-Saloon League and the attorney general. The *Tennessean* stated that the league "for the past four weeks has been active in securing evidence against the soft drink dealers." Each bill stated that the business had been "conducting, maintaining, carrying on or engaging in the sale of intoxication liquors [and] is declared a public nuisance" and that each had "a bar and bar fixtures and a stock of intoxicating liquors." The injunctions issued included the property owners. Augusta Dickel and Manny Shwab were caught up in the net. Among the list of "the men proceeded against under the nuisance law" were "William Luigart, 727 Church Street (Bohemia), Mrs. Augusta Dickel, V.E. and E.B. Shwab, owners." (Apparently, in addition to his other saloons, Manny owned the high-profile Bohemia saloon building.) They were accompanied by many others, including Nashville notables such as the owners of the Maxwell House bar, as well as Percy and Edwin Warner, Lem Motlow, and William Gerst.[9]

Liquor licenses expired on June 30, 1914, but circumstances prompted a July 1 rush to obtain new licenses to sell liquor "at retail"—by druggists. According to the July 2, 1914, *Banner*, among the list of applications "are found the names of some of the leading drug establishments of the city. All of them are careful to explain that they are taking out the licenses absolutely for medicinal purposes."

23. Manny and Boss Crump

(As with medical marijuana today, one could still get liquor by the drink, by doctor's orders.) It was stated that "very few" licenses were taken out "for the purpose of selling liquor over the bar—if the chance ever again comes to sell in the good old way." There were, however, licenses being applied for by clubs and fraternal orders that "intend to take advantage of their nature" for selling liquor to their members. There was a forest of lodges, such as the Elks, Beavers, and Eagles, along with social clubs such as the Nashville Golf and Country Club (later the Belle Meade Country Club) plus V.E. Schwab [sic], 201–203 Second Avenue North, wholesale liquor dealer.[10]

* * *

Another depiction of John Barleycorn's demise, this time by the "Four Mile Law" (*Nashville Tennessean*, October 14, 1913).

Manny Shwab and the George Dickel Company

Manny was sixty-seven in 1914. His business focus had decidedly moved from GDC to real estate, banking, railroads, lighting, mining, and power. The distilling of Cascade whisky continued at Cascade Hollow as long as possible until operations had to be moved out of state. Manny formed an alliance with the Stitzel Distillery in Louisville, where distilling and operations with the original formula were managed by his sons George and Hugh. While GDC was still highly profitable and demand for Cascade ever growing and continuously exceeding supply, state, local, and national politics had clearly shifted due to the relentless efforts of the temperance movement and the Anti-Saloon League. It was clear to Manny that his efforts would not succeed in the long term. Distilling continued until 1917, when Prohibition was passed in Kentucky. George moved back to Nashville, but Hugh remained in Kentucky, where he found great success in banking. On June 14, 1917, Manny sold the Cascade Hollow Distillery to the Highland Company, W.R. Marshall, and M.R. Campbell for $5,249.[11] That amount was far less than what he had paid for it, but his return on the investment in the distillery was certainly satisfactory.

In December 1917, due to the US entry into World War I earlier in the year, President Woodrow Wilson signed a proclamation forbidding brewers to brew beverages with more than 2.75 percent alcohol by volume. The Eighteenth Amendment was ratified in January 1919, banning the manufacture, transportation, and sale of intoxicating liquors.

24

Nashville's Largest Office Buildings
Dueling Newspapers

Manny Shwab's interest in central Nashville real estate and architectural aesthetics, as exemplified by the Climax and the Silver Dollar, was publicized in 1912 and 1914. The front page of the January 19, 1912, *Nashville Tennessean* carried a large picture of the Castner-Knott Building on Church Street with the heading "Imposing Nashville Business House Is Sold."

Manny purchased the building, located at the corner of Church and Seventh, for "$265,000 cash" ($7.5 million today). At the time, the Castner-Knott Dry Goods Company had occupied the building for fifteen years. It was described as "one of the handsomest department store buildings in the [S]outh.... The structure is five stories high and has a very large basement. It is built of white glazed brick and has plate glass windows on both Church and Seventh." The department store was one of the first to move to Church Street, which had since become a popular retail street with many new "handsome buildings." Regarding the wisdom of the investment, the *Tennessean* opined, "Although the price paid seems large at first thought, the investment was a good one, and only a few years will see property in this locality sell for an advance in value of at least one-third the present price." Because of this sale, 1912 realty sales exceeded any previous year in Nashville's history.[1] It represented the largest sale in years, with the exception of the property for the Peabody College for Teachers.[2]

Another imposing project was covered in an article headlined "New Structure Will Be Modern" in the *Tennessean* on April 26,

Manny Shwab and the George Dickel Company

IMPOSING NASHVILLE BUSINESS HOUSE IS SOLD

The Castner-Knott Building, purchased by Shwab in 1912 and sold by the Shwab family in the early 1990s. This purchase represented one of the largest real estate sales in years (*Nashville Tennessean*, January 19, 1912).

1914. Plans were being drawn up for a new building on Shwab's property at the corner of Eighth Avenue and Church Street (one block from Castner-Knott) at a cost of $250,000 ($7 million today). The writer's description highlights "modern" architectural innovations of the time:

> The new five-story building to be erected by V.E. Shwab ... for which Marr & Holman are now drawing plans, will be ... ahead of any building of its kind in the country, with the exception of the large buildings of the [N]orthern cities. Provision has been made for twelve stores on the ground floor which are to front Eighth [A]venue. The corner of the basement on Eighth [A]venue will be leased by a well-known grocery firm. A feature of

24. Nashville's Largest Office Buildings

this store will be tile floors with [woodwork] and walls of white enamel. There will be a refrigerating system installed.

The basement corner on the boulevard will be occupied by a barber shop and Turkish bathrooms. There will also be pool and billiard rooms.... The stores on the main floor will all be equipped with electric elevators and will have a second story. A number of well-known firms have leased the stores.

The building ... will contain 120,000 square feet. The three upper floors will be occupied by doctor's offices and about forty of the city's leading professional men have already signed leases for suites. A novel feature will be compressed air [air conditioning] which is to be furnished to each office. There will be a pneumatic calling system.... [W]hen an automobile is desired, the notice can be sent from the office to the attendant.... [H]e will then call the car from the parking space along the boulevard and upon arrival at the door of the car the caller will be notified. [The entrances] will be protected from bad weather by heavy bronze marquees. This is quite an innovation in the equipment of an office building and should prove a very attractive feature.

The floors of the corridors will be of cork, preventing noise[,] while the offices floors are to be of quartered oak, which is to match the other woodwork. The floors in the toilets and operating rooms [of the doctors' suites] will be of sanitary composition and the walls will be wainscoted with white tile. On the top floor, the offices will receive additional light from skylights, which will be over some of the rooms to be occupied by dentists. Two high-speed electric elevators will be installed.

The new building is to be constructed with a steel skeleton and re-enforced concrete floors. The outside walls will be of cream terra cotta, and the three street sides of the first floor will be entirely of plate glass show windows.... [I]t is to be completed by January 1, 1916.[3]

The *Banner* highlighted the building's location: "[It] has long been said that this was one of the most desirable locations in the city and especially has this been the case since Eighth Avenue took such a sudden and decided leap in importance."[4]

But regardless of Manny's diverse interests and influences, his reputation with some sectors of Tennessee as a "debaucherer" of society persisted. The August 6, 1915, *Memphis Commercial Appeal* covered a "mass" Nashville town meeting. The *Appeal*'s article ran in the *Banner* that same day. Interestingly, the article took a shot at both of Nashville's major papers, as well as Nashvillians themselves, by pointing to the disparity of coverage by the *Banner* and *Tennessean*.

Manny Shwab and the George Dickel Company

The subject and writing style warrant direct quoting:

> There were two very interesting stories of a mass-meeting held Saturday night in Nashville. One ... in the *Tennessean* ... and the other in the *Banner*. The stories are interesting because they are so different. Nashville is a great town for clubs of various sorts. There are business men's clubs, commercial clubs, church clubs, bridge clubs, and they do say there are some very fine poker clubs in Nashville, not to speak of the locker clubs.
>
> Representatives of these various organizations gathered in a mass-meeting. They were to discuss ways and means to put Nashville on a higher plane. Incidentally, a few fellows were there to jockey for the inside rail for their political leaders. The Hon. Frank Bond was there. When the meeting got going, Frank began to boil inwardly like a hog-scalding water when the hot iron is thrown in. He took a fearful crack at Senator Lea.
>
> But the *Tennessean* does tell how that Senator Lea finally appeared and swept all before him. [He] threw his banner far into the ranks of the enemy and cleaved his way toward it. In an oratorical effort he passed everybody like a pay car passes a tramp. It is notated in the columns of the *Tennessean* that he made Frank Bond look like thirty cents. He knocked Frank to the floor when he accused him of once having tried a lawsuit for one Mannie Shwab [during the seizure of the Cascade Hollow Distillery]. Frank said he had tried a lawsuit for Shwab and Shwab at that time was engaged in legitimate business, but thenceforward the *Tennessean*, in its report, did call Frank the "distiller lawyer."

It would seem that association with liquor (in the form of Manny Shwab) was not publicly considered legitimate by either side of the political spectrum.

As to the disparity of coverage, the *Appeal*, giving much credit to the education of its readers, pointed out that the *Tennessean* felt that Senator Lea "was like another Caesar on the Lupercal, with McConnico [a Lea supporter] doing a Marc Antony glide in front of him." Lea's opponent, Bond, "didn't get much of an ovation." By contrast, the *Banner* "intimates that Lea strutted in there like a peacock, but that some of the opposition plucked his tail feathers." The *Banner* estimated that 80 percent of the audience was against Lea. The *Appeal* went further, pointing to the *Banner*'s headline, "Ovation for Maj. Stahlman"—the paper's publisher, who had his letter read to the audience. The *Appeal* concluded:

> Now, somebody is wrong; somebody has seen double. There was no audience in Nashville that will ovate Luke Lea and Maj. E. Stahlman in the

24. Nashville's Largest Office Buildings

same meeting. Applying the newspaper test of ascertaining what is approximately true from reading the newspaper accounts ... the [M]ajor's crowd had rather the better of Luke's crowd. It is an amazing thing that the people of Nashville cannot agree upon a half a dozen honest men who could for a time take over the affairs of their city.[5]

* * *

Manny continued to increase his business influence and real estate transactions in 1916. He and two longtime associates, F.O. Watts and Walter Stokes, had previously purchased three-fourths interest in the control of a steel bridge crossing the Cumberland River at Carthage, Tennessee. It was the only "high bridge" crossing the Cumberland in the state east of Nashville and was said to be a great convenience and benefit to the people of the area. They sold their interest in January 1916.[6] Later that year, on October 10, Manny was elected to the board of at least a third railroad, the Nashville & Decatur Railway Company.[7] Also in October, the Memphis *Appeal* covered his reelection as director and executive director of the finance committee for the Nashville, Chattanooga & St. Louis Railway.[8]

But Manny, along with his family, was starting to ease into a more relaxed lifestyle. In 1909, Manny's daughters, Louise (who was living in Columbus, Ohio) and Bess, had vacationed in the resort village of Charlevoix, Michigan. To escape the summer heat and, according to the family, the threat of accompanying diseases such as typhoid and measles, Charlevoix was to become the summer home for the Shwab family (and remains such for one family member, even to this day). Bess' letters concerning the resort and its Belvedere Hotel and Club are a delightful reflection of the times. "Ah yes, I remember it well," wrote Bess, reminiscing about her first stay at the Belvedere. While there, she "received an invitation from Nashville to attend another meeting and social event of the Army. All was planned for my departure but it was not to be! The night before I was to leave a black cat appeared on the porch and walked by my door. Horrors, the trip was off, OF COURSE.... The Belvedere Hotel was so gay ... so popular!"[9] Best to honor that black cat at all costs, of course.

All that winter, the girls begged, both in letters and in person,

Manny Shwab and the George Dickel Company

for Manny and Emma to visit Charlevoix. In her book, *The Belvedere Club*, on the early days of the resort area, Elizabeth Ives discussed the Shwabs:

> Whether it was the glowing letters or the prospect of a glowering Nashville summer, we shall never know, but early one sultry morning two private cars bearing Shwabs of various shapes, sizes, and married names steamed out of the old Union Station in Nashville bound for Charlevoix. Due to the precarious health of Mrs. George Dickel, Mr. Shwab's sister[-in-law] for whom the rigors of travel were hazardous, Mr. Shwab chartered two private coaches ... from the N & C & St. Louis line. One car was used for family and guests and the other for servants who attended their needs. Mrs. Dickel stood the trip in fine shape ... and the coaches arrived in all their comfort right at the front door of the Belvedere Club at the little [r]ailway station used exclusively by Club visitors [such as frequent visitor August Busch, founder of Anheuser-Busch].[10]

The Shwabs retreated to the Michigan resort each summer through 1913, when, according to Bess,

> The following summer saw my parents buying the cottage at the top of the hill, "The Fairview." By this time, [Charlevoix] had completely sold itself to all of us, especially my father. He now bought three cottages: one ... was given to my brother, George Shwab.... My sister, Louise, was given the stucco house on the corner. I was given the cottage facing the park.[11]

On September 16, 1916, the Shwabs' beloved "Auntie" Augusta Dickel, wife of George Dickel and sister of Emma, passed away in her own Charlevoix cottage. According to a *Banner* obituary headed "Death Comes to Mrs. Dickel," she had been there since June, and "her health has been failing since the middle of July. Her death was not expected, however, and the news comes as a shock to her many friends in Nashville." Manny, Emma, Felix and his wife, Bess, and Louise were all with her.[12]

25

The Final Game
U.S. Supreme Court: Shwab v. Doyle

Augusta's death launched Manny on his last adventure and battle, one that would take six years to finally resolve in front of the U.S. Supreme Court. Mrs. Dickel had been wise not to heed her husband's wish that, following his death, she sell her holdings in GDC. Manny had persuaded Augusta to retain her shares, and he craftily managed various investments and real estate transactions for her in addition to GDC. At her death, her estate was worth (in today's dollars) quite a bit more than $25,000,000. Her will gives great insight into the closeness, trust, and absolute faith the family members had for one another. After Augusta bequeaths $5,000 to each of her nieces and nephews ($127,000 today), she states in her will:

> I am a member of the firm of George A Dickel & Company, but have had no part in conducting its affairs. I have entrusted the matter exclusively to my partners. In the event of my death before the death of my partner and brother-in-law, V.E. Shwab, I will and direct that the business of the partnership shall be wound up and settled, or it shall continue as heretofore, accordingly as V.E. Shwab shall decide and determine.
>
> I have a valuable estate, and no near relatives other than my sister Emma B. Shwab and her children, and they are all dear to me. I wish them to receive and enjoy the benefit of my estate. My brother-in-law ... and I have long been jointly interested in business affairs and I have great confidence in his judgment. He and ... Emma ... and I have considered the disposition of our estates and agreed to what ... will be best. Accordingly, and to that end, I give and bequeath ... all my property ... of every kind, wherever situated, real, personal and mixed, to my brother-in-law.... My sister will understand why it is I have bequeathed nothing to her. She has an abundance and will know my affection for her.[1]

Manny Shwab and the George Dickel Company

According to Supreme Court records from *Shwab v. Doyle, Collector of Internal Revenue* (argued on April 17, 1922), Augusta "assigned stocks and bonds of the declared value of $1,000,000 to the Detroit Trust Company," and "a power of delegating and selling or exchanging all securities was given to Shwab."[2]

Augusta Dickel died in September 1916. At this time, Congress was anticipating entering the war in Europe and in need of methods to finance it. Seven days before Augusta's death, Congress passed a new "Estate Tax Act" stipulating that "a tax [was] to be imposed upon the transfer of the net estate on every decedent dying after the passage of the act." Manny was subsequently hit with a $56,548.41 bill ($2,500,000 today), the equivalent of $357,000 tax per day since Augusta's death. He did not want to pay it. So, he sued the federal government. His positions were, according to the suit:

> (1) The deed of the securities to the Trust Company took effect more than a year before the enactment of the act—meaning it took effect immediately, not in possession or enjoyment at or after the death of Mrs. Dickel.
>
> (2) The words in the Act "in contemplation of death" do not refer to that general expectation of death which every mortal entertains, but rather the apprehension which arises from some existing condition of body or some impending peril.
>
> (3) If Mrs. Dickel, when she made the trust deed, was not in that apprehension arising from that condition of body or of an impending peril, it was not made in contemplation of death within the meaning of the act of Congress.
>
> (4) Mrs. Dickel having made the deed before the act of Congress was passed, her purpose was not to defeat or evade the federal Revenue Law.

Manny also argued that the act did not impose a tax on the deed to the Detroit Trust Company, and that if it were taxed, it "would be the taking of private property for public use without just compensation, contrary to the Fifth Amendment for the Constitution."

The game was afoot. Since Augusta was a citizen of Charlevoix, Manny's first suit was brought against the collector of internal revenue in the District Court of Michigan. He engaged a local Michigan lawyer and an attorney acquaintance from Nashville, John Vertrees. The court ruled against all of Manny's contentions "according to law," except the clever argument concerning whether the transfer

25. The Final Game

was made "in contemplation of death." The court wanted a jury to decide that point. But the jury also ruled against Manny.

He appealed to the Sixth Circuit Court of Appeals, which also, in a ten-page decision, ruled against him on December 10, 1920. Finally, he appealed to the U.S. Supreme Court, arguing that the law was being applied retroactively, against which, according to precedent, there was "absolute prohibition" and "condemnation" as being punitive. In this case, "there could have been no foresight or contemplation" of the tax when the trust was established, and therefore the "Act of September 8, 1916, is within the condemnation." In 1918 (perhaps in response to Manny's claims that the act did not specify that it could be enforced retroactively), Congress passed another estate act, which stated that an estate established in contemplation of death within twenty-five years of death was subject to taxation. The defense stated that the intention of the act was for clarification.[3]

On May 1, 1922, the Supreme Court ruled in Manny's favor, reversing the lower courts' judgments. Justice Joseph McKenna, in his decision delivery, said that the Court regarded "the act of 1918 rather the declaration of a new purpose not the explanation of an old one," and if Congress had intended it to be so, "it should have declared it." Manny was, in today's dollars, $2,500,000 richer. The precedent-setting case continues to be cited.[4]

Manny had expended a great deal of sweat and equity for this lucrative victory. But a testament to his willingness to fight any perceived unfairness, whether it concerned $2,000,000 or $200, was his lawsuit in the Davidson County Chancery Court in March 1917 "to recover $280 in taxes paid under protest." Manny had purchased many Nashville properties in Emma's and Augusta's names and was protesting the board of equalization's decision to raise the assessment of buildings in Augusta's name at 618 and 620 Church Street from $205,000 in 1916 to $225,000 in 1917 without notice. He found out about the new assessment when he went to pay the tax. The law required notice of a change in taxation assessment. In December, he filed another suit against the city of Nashville for "wrongfully back assessing" his personal property as a citizen of Nashville for the years of 1915–1917. His complaint asserted that "though, for some years

Manny Shwab and the George Dickel Company

past, he and his family have during certain parts of the year, resided in the city of Nashville, his domicile, home, and voting place" was in the country and had been since 1877. (He had not sold his and Dickel's Dickerson Pike property.) The assessment was for $900.[5]

* * *

The die was cast. In early 1917, Governor Thomas C. Rye signed the "bone-dry bill" into law, completing the Prohibitionist campaign in Tennessee. This legislation outlawed the receipt or possession of liquor and prohibited the transportation of liquor into or out of the state. The February 6 *Banner* front page proclaimed, "Passage of 'Bone Dry' Law Takes Liquor Firms to Other States, Dickel Co. to Louisville.... Building on Second Avenue [a three-story building] Sold to E.A. Hall for $11,000." Wholesalers had until July 1 to dispose of their existing stock; after that, it would be illegal even to store liquor in Tennessee. The article read, "The firm of George A. Dickel & Co., one of the largest in the United States, has arranged to move to Louisville and will go about March 1."[6] The article incorrectly stated that Hugh and Buist Shwab, "who have been managers of the wholesale concern[,] will leave for Louisville." In fact, Buist would not go to Louisville. George had been in charge of the company with Hugh. They had been living in Louisville, directing the production of Cascade with the Stitzel Distillery, which was led by President "Pappy" Van Winkle.

According to Harry Kroll in his *Bluegrass, Belles, and Bourbon*, Van Winkle had acquired controlling interest in Stitzel in 1908 with a partner. In an interview, Van Winkle, quite the whiskey authority, stated that they attempted to produce "the great Cascade whiskey" until 1917, and "They will tell you its like has not been seen since Prohibition." The book adds that Stitzel was one of only four distilleries licensed by the Internal Revenue Service to produce whiskey for medicinal purposes during Prohibition.[7] Van Winkle whiskeys today command prices in the thousands of dollars. Perhaps they stole away the Cascade recipe and have perfected it at last.

The *Banner* article from February 1917 went on to state that Jack Daniel's was to move to St. Louis, with Lem Motlow as "head of this house," and Charles Nelson's Greenbrier Distillery "will not establish

25. The Final Game

any new business in any other state. The house is now closing out its stock ... and this house will go out of business." Other, "smaller ... wholesale concerns were also being affected."[8] The Shwabs would continue to produce the popular Cascade whisky until the ratification of the Eighteenth Amendment in 1919, initiating the tumultuous era of national Prohibition. They may have continued to distill and sell it "medicinally," but there is no public record of that.

In 1937, after Prohibition ended, the family met at Buist Shwab's Nashville home on Jackson Boulevard, and, according to Buist's wife, Louise (the author's grandmother), the consensus was that it "just wasn't socially acceptable" to revive the business, so they sold it to Schenley Industries for $100,000 (only about $2,000,000 in today's dollars). It was said by family members that Schenley produced "rot gut" and never took advantage of the reputation Cascade had achieved.

War

Citing the resumption of submarine attacks on passenger and merchant ships in the Mediterranean and North Atlantic, Congress declared war on Germany in April 1917. Manny's father was technically Alsatian, but George Dickel, as well as Emma and Augusta's family, the Banzers, had been German immigrants. During World War I, Buist Shwab joined the quartermaster's corps as a captain. The emotional conflict within the family can only be imagined. Little is recorded about Manny Shwab's specific involvement in the war effort, but it must have been significant and public, as "Aid in War Effort" was one subhead of an obituary. The text read:

> Mr. Shwab was descended from a family of Alsatians, and when the U.S. declared war on Germany, he was anxious that the fight should be carried on to a finish, and it was due to his efforts and to his means largely that the bond issues in Middle Tennessee were financed so rapidly, as he invested heavily in government securities from his private fortune and through the various financial institutions with which he was officially connected. While Mrs. Shwab was of German parentage, his interest was not abated, and after the war he contributed in a substantial way to the relief of her family who had remained in Germany.[9]

Manny Shwab and the George Dickel Company

The Tennessee newspapers from 1918 to 1924 were full of social notices concerning the Shwabs: trips overseas; Felix's son Paul Eldridge ("Jack") being declared "Nashville's Genius," as he studied sculpture and modeling at the Beaux Arts in the New York, at Columbia College, and for several years in Paris in the 1920s (there is a permanent endowment in his name with the Department of Art at Vanderbilt University); marriages; parties; equestrian events (according to George Shwab IV, events at George Sr.'s farm would become the popular annual event the Steeplechase), and so forth. But with the exception of board directorships and legal defenses of his holdings, Manny was no longer in the front and center of Tennessee business or politics.

In 1922, Manny suffered a stroke that resulted in partial paralysis and a reduction in management and new acquisitions. On November 2, 1924, Victor Emmanuel Shwab passed away from pneumonia in his home surrounded by family. His obituary was front-page news in Tennessee papers, running over to two columns, stating that he "was generally reputed to be the city's wealthiest resident" and that he oversaw his affairs until contracting pneumonia. The papers singled out his directorship and holdings of the Nashville, Chattanooga & St. Louis Railway, the Nashville Railway & Light Company, the Cumberland Telephone and Telegraph Company (as an "originator"), and the Fourth and First National Banks and declared his "War Record Notable." The papers also listed his many close friends who had "risen to eminent prominence" and "local industrialist and

Profile photograph of Manny Shwab, circa 1910 (Shwab family collection).

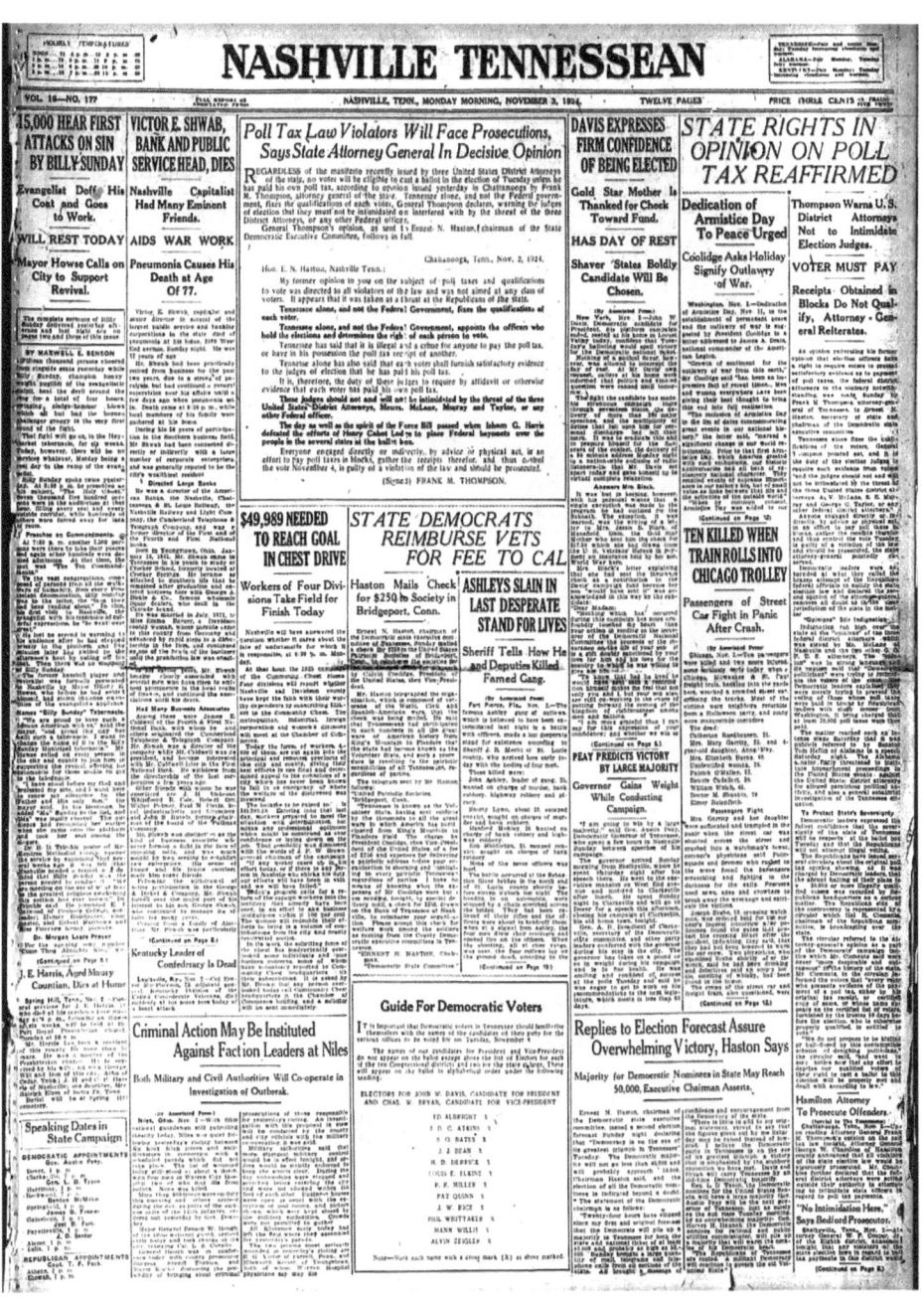

Shwab's front-page *Nashville Tennessean* obituary (November 3, 1924).

Manny Shwab and the George Dickel Company

Shwab/Dickel monument, Mt. Olivet Cemetery, Nashville, Tennessee.

financier associates." Included, of course, were James E. Caldwell as well as John Runnells (chairman of the board of the Pullman Company), Walter Palmer, and Paul Davis, who had made a name for himself in banking. Mention was likewise made of Manny's ownership of George A. Dickel & Co., "famous wholesaler liquor dealers, who dealt in the Cascade brand."

The *Tennessean*, which during the Prohibition battles had often demonized Manny, stated, "Mr. Shwab won distinction as the kind of business associate who never forsook a fight in the face of opposing odds, and was much sought by men seeking to establish new enterprises. His sense of humor and his innate courtesy made him many friends." Abraham would have been proud of his son. The papers

25. The Final Game

CASCADE DISTILLERY BURNS AS OWNER DIES

NORMANDY, Tenn., Nov. 5.—The famous Cascade distillery, founded a half century ago by Victor E. Shwab, who died Sunday night in Nashville, was burned here last night. It was ignited by forest fires.

Cascade whisky, formerly made at the distillery, was advertised as being "mellow as moonlight" and attained an international reputation.

Forest fires in this vicinity were still burning fiercely. Squads of men worked all last night in an attempt to check the flames.

Chattanooga Times, "Cascade Distillery Burns as Owner Dies" (November 6, 1924). Papers all over the country and Canada carried the story of the distillery being destroyed by a forest fire the day Manny was buried.

referenced Manny's numerous valuable real estate holdings, Democratic political sentiment, and wartime fundraising efforts, as well as the one thing Abraham would not have supported: his membership in the Vine Street Christian Church.[10]

Manny was buried in the Mt. Olivet plot he had purchased for George Dickel and the Banzers, with Emma laid to rest by his side two years later. Augusta Dickel was buried next to George Dickel. Manny's brother from Philadelphia, Harry Clay Shwab, and his sister, Flora, were also buried in Mt. Olivet with their own imposing monument (undoubtedly erected by Manny).

Manny Shwab and the George Dickel Company

In what could be called dramatic justice and exquisite synchronicity, on the afternoon of November 6, as Manny was being buried, the Cascade Hollow Distillery was destroyed by forest fires during "a fierce gale that fanned the flames." The irony was not lost on papers throughout the United States and Canada, from Vancouver, Calgary, and Montreal to Maine, New York, and Alabama, with articles containing headlines like "Cascade Burns as Owner Dies," stating, "Squads of men worked all last night ... to check the flames" in an effort to save the "far-famed plant."[11] One Massachusetts paper noted that Cascade whisky had "attained international repute as living up to its advertised quality"—that of being "mellow as moonlight."[12]

In perhaps the last statewide newspaper mention of Manny Shwab, the September 2, 1925, *Knoxville Journal* stated that V.E. Shwab, a Nashville capitalist, had paid $14,730 in income tax for 1924 ($230,000 in today's dollars), the most identified by a Nashvillian.[13]

Epilogue

So that was the end of the story. Prohibition won and the distillery burned as Manny was buried. Shwab involvement with George A. Dickel & Co. ended with a family vote in 1937 to sell to Schenley Industries (which did rebuild the distillery in Cascade Hollow in 1958). "The famous Cascade whisky" faded away, and the company's reputation became an "also ran" in the whiskey arena while Jack Daniel's rose to world domination. But there is a new chapter being written (here, just an epilogue). A whiskey phoenix is rising out of the ashes of Cascade Hollow.

In 2019, exactly one hundred years after shutting down production, *Whiskey Advocate* declared thirteen-year-old George Dickel Bottled in Bond Tennessee whisky the number-one whisky in the world. Something good was obviously happening in the Hollow. In 2018, Nicole Austin, a chemical engineer who got her start in New York City at a small distillery (Kings County), became distiller and general manager for the George Dickel company. In the fall of 2022, two articles appeared in the *Tennessean* covering Austin and her bottled in bond whisky. I was struck by her use of words that seemed out of place when describing distilling. But they could have been lifted from dozens of Dickel & Co. and Cascade ads from 1859 through 1917, including words like *trust, honesty, values, integrity, transparency,* and *authenticity*. Austin stated that "your first release as a distiller is going to set a tone about what kind of values you have."[1] The whisky of the year was that first release. Pretty impressive.

So I reached out to Austin, and she spoke with me on January 18, 2023. I asked her what values her first release had projected. Her insistence that it be bonded represented one. "Bottled in Bond" is a

Epilogue

rigid set of U.S. government rules from 1897, which includes being produced in a single distillation season by a single distillery, aged for a minimum of four years, and being 100 proof (50 percent alcohol). The original intent was assurance of quality, and, as incentive, the government granted tax breaks for compliance. Ms. Austin said it would enable people to judge her product on an "apples to apples" basis and guarantee its quality.[2]

But that first release had been aged for thirteen years, far beyond the four mandated by law. She said that was a bit "cheeky," but "people didn't think of Dickel as what it was—we *are* one of the great whiskies and we *do* belong next to the great bourbons." And she wanted it to be priced fairly so people would drink it instead of keeping it as a trophy bottle. The retail price was $34.[3]

She stated in the *Tennessean* that her "only talent is math" but that she always wanted to be an artist of some kind.[4]

I asked her what part of distilling was math and what part art. She said that at first, "I thought it was math and engineering—that I could engineer my way through. But ten years later, I see that it is mysterious and complex." She emphasized that the ingredients "come out of the ground." One must consider weather, soils, and so on; "engineering is helpful, but it's so complex; I appreciate that there is so much that we don't know." She went on to say that if things are "off kilter," figuring out why is the artistry. "You just try to make it more and more perfect."[5]

There was another artist a long time ago, distilling with the same water from the same cascade on the same soil. He wanted his product to be more perfect, so he took his art into the night, under the full moon, and distilled a whisky "as mellow as moonlight." Maybe Austin should give Kie Davis' alchemy a try. One hundred years ago, Manny and Kie's product was on top. After all, according to Pappy Van Winkle, Cascade's like "has not been seen since Prohibition." For the time, that accolade from Pappy was about as close an anointment to being the No. 1 whiskey as one could get. It's pretty cool that a century later, Cascade Hollow is back on top.

Appendix

Harry Clay Shwab, 1852–1912

Little is known about the early life of Manny's brother, Harry Shwab, other than his birth in Tennessee in 1852 and his work at his father's Youngstown, Ohio, wine and liquor store, Schwab & Co., in 1870. He was listed in the 1880 Pittsburgh city directory as a reporter.

To say that Harry was transient in his residences and positions is an understatement. His address and job changed in virtually each of the Pittsburgh city directories from 1880 to 1900, in which he was usually listed as a manager or press agent for a theater or museum. He often had positions tied to the theatrical season. He managed and co-owned several well-known Pittsburgh theaters and museums, notably the Opera House, the Bijou Theater, and the extravagant Schenley Casino. An 1887 article in the *Pittsburgh Daily Post* covering his purchase of the Bijou for $10,000 described him as an old newspaper man,[1] and a June 1895 *Post* article stated that Harry ran a labor paper in Youngstown, Ohio, "long years ago."[2]

In 1896, the *Post* covered "A Benefit to Popular Men." The event was held in honor of Harry C. Shwab and one other theatrical man at the New Grand Opera House. The bill was "an extraordinary presentation of Hoyt's masterpiece 'A Trip to Chinatown' by the original cast in the famous run of 656 nights in New York." Hoyt, its author, was to be in attendance to direct the entertainment.[3]

The next year, the *Pittsburgh Press* announced another testimonial to Harry, signed by over 150 men who "wished to do the testimonial" for yet another of his retirements. The article began, "Harry Shwab, the genial Harry, general manager of Harry Davis'

Appendix

multitudinous enterprises," was to have a benefit at the New Grand. "If there is any one man connected with the theatrical profession who is [more] deserving of a testimonial of appreciation from the citizens of Pittsburgh than is Harry Shwab, that man has not been as yet discovered." After other praises, the article went on to say that "it behooves not only his friends, but the general public, to see that the testimonial is in the fullest sense of the word a 'howling success.'"[4]

The September 12, 1897, *Press* covered Harry's moving on to greater things. He was headed to Chicago to meet with David Henderson about joining his many enterprises throughout the country, perhaps being based in Philadelphia, the company's headquarters. "Mr. Shwab has an enviable record as a manager and his name has ever been synonymous with success in every theatrical enterprise with which he has been identified."[5]

However, by July 1898 Harry was back in Pittsburgh serving as press representative for the Avenue Theater and Grand Opera House. Covering the new position, the *Post* declared Harry "one of the best known theatrical men in the country," who "built up" the two theaters when he previously worked there. A *Press* article stated that before this appointment, Harry had "been figuring with some leading capitalists" to purchase the struggling Duquesne Theater, and he "had another scheme" to open another museum.[6]

By 1902, Harry was living in New York. In May, the *Pittsburgh Weekly Gazette* ran a story about attempts to forge his signature on complimentary tickets for several local Pittsburgh theaters while he was in New York. The article stated that many recognized his well-known signature, describing it as going "diagonally across paper in great oblique jerks, each running to about a third of the page, regardless of its being a business letter sheet or a bank check."[7]

In 1905, Harry was returning to New York after his travel with a successful play, *The Earl of Pawtucket*. Apparently the production was moving west, and Harry stated that he was okay traveling "on the right side of the map" but was not interested in touring on the other side of the country.[8]

On April 14, 1906, the *Evening World* and the *Sun* (both in New York), as well as the *Pittsburgh Press*, covered Harry's collapse in the

Appendix

lobby of the Gilsey House. It was initially thought to be a stroke of paralysis. He was taken to a private hospital, where a doctor stated that his ailment was acute indigestion. However, it is difficult to see how acute indigestion could appear as a stroke of paralysis, and future events would belie the diagnosis.[9]

But by July 1, 1906, the apparently recovered Harry was back in action. The front page of the *Brooklyn Citizen* ran an article titled "Goes Abroad for Gorilla." Harry was quoted as saying, as he climbed up the gangplank of the *Cedric*, that he was not going abroad for his health but to bring back a gorilla for the Bostic show. In typical Harry fashion, "he raised his voice until every newspaper man on the waterfront" could hear: "This gorilla is the most remarkable specimen of its kind ever captured." The animal was said to stand 5'9" in his stocking feet (stockings said to be needed because his feet had been injured when captured). The paper declared, "[T]hus spake Harry C. Shwab, the dean of press agents."[10]

A May 1908 *New York Tribune* article answering the question "Who are the Friars?" listed Harry as one of the eight founders and original members of the Friars Club, famous today for its annual "roasts" of celebrities.[11] It is a private club now based between Park and Madison avenues in New York City. The initial idea was for influential Broadway press agents to exchange lists of people fraudulently receiving complimentary passes to shows, reflecting Harry's Pittsburgh experiences.[12] The club, meeting frequently at Browne's Chop House, almost immediately began its tribute dinners or "Friars Frolics." Within three years, it had dramatically grown to include agents from all over the world as well as the "most prominent men in the theatrical and amusement world."[13]

They began the annual "Frolic" in 1907 and declared to make it a distinct and historical affair each year.[14] Mission accomplished. Will Rogers and Irving Berlin (who wrote "Alexander's Ragtime Band" for the event) participated in 1911; over the years, Frank Sinatra, Larry King, Jerry Lewis, and Ed Sullivan would serve as officers of the club.[15] Toasts became "Roasts" of celebrities from a variety of niches—including, infamously, the 2004 skewering of the nation's future Commander-in-Chief, Donald Trump.[16]

Appendix

The 1906 attack of "acute indigestion" may in fact have been something much worse. Harry Clay Shwab died in Nashville on September 2, 1912. According to his death certificate, the cause of death was general paresis and syphilitic paresis.

Harry Yarns

There are dozens of examples in the press of exotic, farfetched stories featuring Harry, almost weekly in 1888 and 1895–1897. Newspaper theatrical sections often were titled "stage tales" or "yarns." What follows is a sampling of the more outrageous stories.

Harry's Gussie

An April 1888 article in the "Tales of the Stage" section of the *Pittsburgh Post*, titled "A New Story on Shwab," opened by describing a "pensive look in Manager H. Clay Shwab's eyes." According to the article, he "had been wearing buttonhole boquets [sic], gorgeous raiment, and had his drooping poetic mustache carefully waxed." The article included a letter he had supposedly received. It began, "My Idol…. I have long worshipped you from a distance. Since I first saw you my heart has been torn by the throes of an overmastering, wild, delirious love." The letter went on to say the writer was twenty years old and considered beautiful, her father was wealthy, and she was worth $150,000 on her own. She would call on him "some afternoon." The letter was signed "Gussie."

The paper stated that Harry had decided to "sacrifice himself" and waited anxiously day after day until finally it was announced that a "veiled lady" awaited him in his office. He bought a "boutonniere of lilies" and ran to his office to meet his visitor. After his exclamation, "You are Miss Gussie, I suppose," the paper quoted her reply: "Shure an' its Gushie yer lookin' tur. Yis I'm Gushie and it's the foine gintlemin down be the dure tould me to till yez so, will yez buy some apples, sur?" She drew aside her veil—she was seventy years old and a modest apple woman. The article concluded by revealing that Harry "beat a retreat down the back stairs" and "was no longer a dude."

Appendix

Boxing a Mountain of Himalayan Flesh

The March 10, 1888, *Pittsburgh Daily Post* covered a "comic scene down in the green room of the Bijou." Two men were described as "mountains of flesh—regular Himalays [sic] of adipose tissue." One of them, Paul Dresser, suggested the theater staff play a joke on the other man, Fatty Stewart. Dresser said Stewart thought of himself as a boxer—he even had to talk Stewart out of fighting Jack Dempsey—but wouldn't it be funny if Harry put on boxing gloves and offered to fight him? Harry exclaimed, "But I don't know anything about boxing!" Dresser said, "That don't make any difference," because Stewart really was a "regular greeny" and would collapse after one or two punches. "It will be a great gag." It was said to be "working like a charm" until, after a few "prods" by Harry, Stewart "let out a blood curdling yell and projected his 325 pounds toward Shwab," crushing him "worse than a hydraulic press." When Harry got up, he "gazed at Dresser with a sad, reproachful look and said: 'Say, boys, the cigars are on me.'"

The Story of the "Gul-Gul"

According to the *Pittsburgh Daily Post* of March 24, 1888, Harry Shwab was asked by a patron for two good tickets and a "Gul-Gul." The "brunette Adonis" replied that they were exceedingly accommodating at the Bijou, and he would certainly oblige the stranger. (The Adonis quip is evidence that the mostly bald Harry had written the account. He referred to himself as the "brunette beauty" in another rendition of this story.) Unfortunately, Harry had no idea what a Gul-Gul was, even after consulting six friends and the dictionary. So, in an act of desperation, he bought a silk cushion, a bottle of cologne, a bouquet of flowers, and an umbrella and put them on the man's seat. Harry and his partner anxiously watched as the patron took his seat; smiling, he smelled the flowers and dabbed on the cologne, but he then called for Manager Shwab to come to him. He asked Harry why there wasn't a Gul-Gul for him and whether he even knew what one was. Harry admitted his ignorance. The patron explained that a Gul-Gul was what "we call a spittoon down in Texas." Harry immediately brought one to him.

Appendix

Twenty-Eight Panes of Glass

On March 27, 1895, the *Pittsburgh Press* reported "gossip" connected with a play showing at the New Grand Opera House, *The Fatal Card*. A scene in this play called for an explosion that took "an entire afternoon to arrange" as a wall with several windows was blown up and twenty-eight panes of glass were shattered onto the stage. After a rehearsal, Harry and a manager were looking at the scene, and the manager commented that it would "cost the New Grand considerable money to furnish the glass."

"Not much," said Mr. Shwab.

"How is that?"

"Well, you see, Davis ... also owns the museum and he contracts to furnish the freaks with board."

"But of what value is broken glass?"

"We give it to the glass eater."

The Eagle and the Maltese Cat

In May 1888, the *Pittsburgh Daily Post* informed readers of a live eagle that was "let loose" in Harry's office. It chanced that a favorite Maltese cat of his was reclining on a rug in the office at this time. The feline sprang for the bird. The two engaged in a "desperate combat ... the fur and feathers flew at a lively rate while the air was filled with discordant squalls and piercing yells and howls." The cat managed to escape, and "at last accounts the eagle had undisturbed possession of the premises."[17]

No Boys or Bums

In March 1895, Harry needed one hundred people for a play, *War of Wealth*, and he notified his "captain of supers" to round them up, admonishing him not to bring in "boys or bums." However, Harry was dissatisfied with the result—a "crowd that couldn't ... deceive the audience into believing the whole hundred could raise the price of a beer." He fired both the super and the throng, which riotously circled the theater of Fifth Avenue. The police stormed their position, and the crowd dispersed.[18]

Appendix

Harry and the Posers

In the 1890s, a unique and fairly short-lived form of entertainment called for attractive actors and actresses to perform as "posers," posturing motionlessly in sometimes elaborate scenes as if in a photograph or painting, known as "tableau vivant" (living pictures). The most famous poser was Lily Langtry, "The Jersey Lily," an actress and a mistress to the Prince of Wales—the future Edward VII—and other nobles, as well as the first celebrity to endorse a commercial product (Pears Soap). She performed in Harry's Opera House.

In April 1895, as reported in the *Pittsburgh Press*, a dispute arose when Harry engaged a "world famous" poser, Catherine Beach (who was the model for the State of Nevada statue), to appear in "The Living Bronze Statues" exhibit at the Opera House. Another poser, Lillian Lewis, who was appearing in *Cleopatra*, refused to appear in the living bronze exhibit with "the marvelously beautiful" Miss Beach. According to the paper, her objections also concerned the "character" of the exhibit. Harry assured the public that the concerns were based on an erroneous report and that "the pictures are works of art in the strictest acceptation of the term and entirely free from any immoral tendency."[19]

Legal Advice and Malted Milk

A tin was often noticed by the many theatrical men "who, no matter how they may wander among downtown theaters, always come home to Shwab sometime before midnight." Harry explained that one of his managers, a man named Davis, had opened a nursery associated with the theater, a "loafing place for babies," and that he might be regretting it. The children frequently got colds, and Davis would run to the druggist and buy anything recommended—and there were many cures recommended. Harry's staff had taken to "easing [Davis] of his purse and money" before letting him go downtown, as he would spend it all on these "cures." Apparently this tendency was well known, as, when Davis met with his lawyer, Willis McCook, the attorney pulled out a tin and told Davis that "Horlick's powder is the best." Davis bought it and "sped away" to Harry with the new, surefire cure that

Appendix

"never fails to work." On inspection, it turned out to be malted milk, which Harry declared was now called "Legal Advice."[20]

The Siberian Wildman

The *American Magazine*, "one of America's leading investigative magazines," was published (under several names) from 1876 to 1906, when three editors left *McClure's* to relaunch and rename the publication, which then ran continuously until 1956. Many notable authors were contributors, including Sir Arthur Conan Doyle, F. Scott Fitzgerald, and H.G. Wells. The magazine's focus was human interest stories, social issues, and fiction.[21] Maurice Brown Kirby's 1908 story about Harry, "The Siberian Wildman," may have qualified as all three.

The story begins with an 1881 letter addressed to Harry at 281 Bowery, New York, from J. Isman York. The writer had heard that Harry, through Harris' Dime Museum, was looking for a "Rushin Anarkist." He included a photo and described himself as being covered with hair, having incredibly long "whiskurs," and "I don't think you ever seen enybody uglier."

Harry replied that he wasn't interested in Isman being a Russian anarchist, "but we should like to place you on exhibition in a cage as a Wildman," and, based on the photo, if "properly managed and exploited, you would be a success." Isman replied that he would be "no wildman at eny price," as he "hav respect for my relatives," but still wanted to be a Russian anarchist. He later thought better of the situation and wrote that for $25 a week, he would like to be a Wildman.

According to the article's author, Kirby, the "letters are genuine" and had passed through the U.S. Mail, adding that the transaction was "more or less typical for Harry who was a manager and press agent [who] is still living and a familiar figure on Broadway" (the story from 1881 appeared in 1908). He wrote that the museum's owner, Harris, had hired Harry Shwab from the city editor's desk of the *Pittsburgh Leader* and "set him at work, inventing and 'planting'" stories that would drive people into the museum. So the story is at least partially based in reality. According to Kirby, when Isman arrived in Pittsburgh, Harry hired a "four-horsed dray" to drive through the city streets every day carrying a large iron cage

Appendix

with a huge sign reading, "EXTRA! EXTRA! EXTRA! This is a facsimile of the cage in which the ferocious, untamed SAVAGE SIBERIAN WILDMAN" would be exhibited at the museum. Harry also created a pamphlet that was a "marvelous history" of the Wildman's terrific deeds and distributed "no less than one hundred thousand" copies on the streets and vestibules.

Harry dyed Isman mahogany brown, clamped a brass ring in his nose and gave him "immense earrings and wide bracelets." Manacles were attached to his ankles, and he was chained to the animal cage. A mob stormed the box office of the museum on the opening date; "Shwab ... complacently smiled at the result of his clever work." Isman, yelling, would run along the bars and rattle his chains and rings. During each show, the museum's "lecturer" claimed the Wildman had been captured in Siberia after a chase of two years costing $10,000 and that he had "the heart of a hyena, the mind of a wolf and the soul of Satan himself." The museum made an offer of $500 in gold to "the man, woman or child ... who will enter the cage with the Siberian Wildman and exit—ALIVE!"

Isman began to believe the fabricated history and grew proud and overbearing, once trying "to bite off the nose of his creator" (Harry) after having received "some unpleasant orders." Harry gave him a black eye. Apparently Isman's attitude and fame annoyed the museum's other attractions, including the "large, buxom, and jealous bearded lady" and her "knotty-muscled husband Abdul Adia O'Brien." One day a heated argument ensued, with Isman raining insults on the bearded lady. O'Brien then entered the fray; "one sweep of his heavy paw and the savage denizen of the forest was stretched on the floor." O'Brien was fired and became determined to get even. At a bar, he partnered with an African American man who was endowed "with pig-iron muscles in his arms and back and a neck as thick as a young hickory tree."

One day, after the museum's customary announcement of $500 in gold for entering the cage, O'Brien's enormous confederate shouted that he would take the offer. The lecturer was incredulous. "What?" he exclaimed. "Do you wish to commit suicide, to fly in the face of certain death, to be torn to pieces before our very eyes?" In

Appendix

spite of the lecturer's (and later Harry's) insistence that it would be suicide for him to try, the man insisted they follow through with the offer. Looking for any way out, Harry said he would not permit it without a letter from the mayor of Pittsburgh, William McCallum, that released the museum from all liability from the man's relatives. The man said he would get the letter, but Harry went to the mayor first to explain the situation. The mayor, who knew Harry from his newspaper work, indicated that he would help to prevent the confrontation. However, on the front page of the evening paper was an announcement that the mayor had granted the license. Apparently, the mayor, "who possessed a well-developed sense of humor," wanted to see how Harry would "side step" the issue.

Harris and Harry were in a panic. Reporters descended on the museum, and Harry calmly stated that the event would take place "next Monday promptly at four o'clock." "What do you expect?" asked a reporter. "The [man] will be killed," he "asserted with an air of finality." This was on Tuesday. Massive crowds attended each day's show, and each day Harry told Harris he had not found a way out. Museum employees suggested ghoulish ways to thwart the aggressor, but "Mr. Shwab bravely turned a deaf ear." He was still in a quandary on Monday morning. Harris fled to New York, telling Harry to get out of it as best as he could.

The moment arrived with a highly excited crowd in attendance. "The Wildman had lost all interest in his art. He jangled the chains wearily like a broken-spirited convict on his way to the scaffold." At a quarter to four, the lecturer was trying to figure out what to say about the challenger's absence, as he knew a secret: Harry had made arrangements to kidnap and keep him "quietly imprisoned for a fortnight." As the lecturer practiced his speech, he was disheartened by the sound of a familiar voice: "Ah'm here." The lecturer hurried to Harry.

LECTURER: "That Black man's here."
HARRY: "Yes."
LECTURER: "To claim the reward."
HARRY: "Yes."
LECTURER: "Well, what shall we do about it?"

Appendix

HARRY: "Nothing. Tell them what you please. Tell them we are not responsible for anything that happens."
LECTURER: "But—"
HARRY: "'But' nothing. Do as I say."

At the appointed hour, as the lecturer "wet his lips to speak, the ticking clock sounded like heavy machinery." As the audience listened, he read the mayor's letter releasing all employees of any resulting liability. The lecturer repeatedly warned "Robert Parker" (we learned his name from the mayor's letter) that he was going to be killed. Parker insisted, but as he began to enter the cage, "a big, determined-looking man forced himself through the crowd, like a bull going through a flock of sheep, and cried dramatically, 'Robert Parker, STOP!'"

ROBERT PARKER: "What's dat?"
MAN: "You can't go in that cage!"
ROBERT PARKER: "Why?"
MAN: "Because you'll be killed."
ROBERT PARKER: "S'pose Ah am killed. What's dat to you?"
MAN: "It's this to me."

The man pulled back his coat's lapel and displayed a police officer's shield. He was the chief of police and was arresting Parker for a robbery in Allegheny the week before. The chief declared, "When the law gets through with you, you can do as you please about this Wildman. But until then, you're mine," and hustled him out of the museum.

The story concluded, "Of course, [Parker] had committed no crime and of course he was not wanted; but Harry Shwab and [the policeman] were good old friends and Shwab had successfully appealed to his pal in the hour of his necessity."[22]

Flora Shwab, 1862–1925

Like her parents and older siblings, Harry's sister, Flora Shwab, seems to have possessed both an industriousness and a headstrong nature that would dictate the course of her life, for good or for bad. Pursuing a career in music, she achieved academic success at the highest level, studying with the renowned American composer Edward MacDowell at both the Boston Conservatory (now Boston

Appendix

Conservatory at Berklee) and Columbia University while maintaining an active career as a piano teacher in Boston, Massachusetts; Louisville, Kentucky; and perhaps Youngstown, Ohio, as well.

There is some confusion surrounding the circumstances of Flora's birth. According to a handwritten amendment she recorded in her passport, issued August 21, 1924, her brother V.E. "Manny" Shwab felt confident that she was born in Nashville, on Gay Street, in 1858. Flora believed her older brother and legally amended the document. However, according to this same amendment, Flora lived her entire life believing that she was born in 1862.[23] It is unlikely that Flora could make such a mistake, as it would mean that at age fourteen, for instance, she would have believed herself to be just ten. Additionally, the 1860 census shows Abraham, Annie, Joseph, Manny, Emile, Harry, Cecelia, and Meier Salzkotter living in Knoxville, without Flora.[24] However, Manny was terminally ill at the time that the amendment was made, and it is a testament to the faith and respect that Flora had for her older brother, with whom she had a very close relationship, that she would defer to his opinion regarding her own age. Most likely, her birth took place in Nashville in 1862. She was the youngest of six children.

The details of Flora's early life are murky. Following the turbulent war years, she apparently settled with her parents and older brother, Henry (Harry) Clay, around Youngstown. Flora was most likely raised in the Jewish faith, since her father was an integral member of Youngstown's Jewish community. Harry worked in a shop with Abraham briefly before moving to Pittsburgh to begin his remarkable career as a theater manager.

Annie Schwab died on October 23, 1871, and Flora likely took care of her father after her mother's death.[25] At the age of eighteen, she appears in the 1880 census as a schoolteacher (most likely of piano).[26] At that point, Abraham and herself were the only people remaining in the household. Flora was with her father when he died at the Tod House in Youngstown on March 24, 1884.[27]

By September 1889, Flora moved to Nashville, having already graduated from the Boston Conservatory. The September 7 edition of the *Nashville Tennessean* from that year notes that she returned

Appendix

to the city after studying at the conservatory with Edward MacDowell, suggesting that she had previously spent time in Nashville.[28] This may have occurred after Abraham's death and before her move to Boston. At some point she must have spent a substantial amount of time in Nashville and around Manny, given their closeness in later years. Flora's residency in the city was short lived, though, as she returned to Boston and began advertising piano lessons in, at the latest, 1891.[29] She would offer piano lessons in Boston until at least 1897.[30]

By 1903, after spending a few years as a piano teacher in Louisville, Kentucky, Flora enrolled in music classes at Columbia University in New York City.[31] There, she again studied with MacDowell, and while the extent of her academic work at Columbia remains unknown, she became familiar enough with MacDowell's teaching and role within the music department to write a letter adamantly defending his competence during his final year at the university. She complimented the rigor of his classes and his passion and creativity as a lecturer, especially noting his music history lectures. MacDowell resigned in February 1904 following a disagreement with the university's president. Within a few years, his mental health declined significantly, and he would die in 1908.

Because MacDowell was a well-known composer, his resignation was of public interest, and Flora may have felt obligated to support her teacher, who was also the husband of her close friend, fellow pianist Marian MacDowell. Marian would go on to become an arts philanthropist after Edward's resignation. She founded the MacDowell Colony (now called simply MacDowell), an artists' residency and workshop that she ran for twenty-five years; it remains a vital resource for artists working in all fields. Marian saved Flora's letters praising her husband's work at Columbia, and today they exist in two nearly identical, handwritten copies held by the Library of Congress. Marian's papers also include a deeply personal letter from Flora written just before the latter's death in January 1925, which testifies to their long and intimate friendship.[32] However, the precise details of Flora's professional relationship with Edward MacDowell remain more elusive.

Appendix

Between 1891 and 1894, advertisements listing Flora as a piano teacher ran in the *Boston Evening Transcript* adjacent to advertisements for piano composition lessons by Edward.[33] Flora's advertisements championed her as "recommended by E.A. MacDowell, to whom all inquiries may be addressed." Even by 1897, when the MacDowells had already moved to New York, advertisements for Flora's piano lessons still stated that she "refers to Mr. E.A. MacDowell," suggesting some type of professional association.[34]

Flora and the MacDowells' relationship predates Edward's greatest successes of the latter 1890s and early twentieth century, making it even more probable that Edward and Flora (like Marian and Flora) were very close friends. Flora and the MacDowells may even have summered together in 1893, when both Flora and Edward ran newspaper advertisements listing the resumption of their respective music lessons on October 1.[35] The formal nature of Flora's letters vouching for Edward's professional faculties (as evidenced by the lack of addressee, tone, and the existence of two handwritten copies) may indicate that Flora meant to avoid personal matters like the longevity of their relationship.

From 1899 until 1903, Flora taught piano lessons and performed concerts in Louisville, Kentucky, where she must have moved following the MacDowells' departure for New York in 1896. During this period Flora became a fixture of Louisville's artistic and musical culture. She was an active and charter member of the city's Musical Art Society[36] and performed regular piano recitals as part of the Louisville Woman's Club's "Concerts for Young People" series. Flora joined a number of Shwabs in Louisville, including her nephews George and Hugh, along with their families. An 1899 advertisement for piano lessons explains that Flora had returned to Louisville, suggesting that she had previously resided in the city—perhaps immediately following her father's death and around the time that she was also in Nashville, having family in both cities.[37]

She gave her first well-publicized public performance in Louisville at the city's Galt House on April 10, 1900, wherein she played music by Beethoven, Chopin, Mendelssohn, and Schumann, as well as MacDowell. The performance was advertised as her first in

Appendix

town since returning from Europe; however, the details of that trip remain unknown.[38] Although this was her first full concert since her return, Flora had already performed in a "musical meeting" of the art department of the Woman's Club in December 1899, where she was listed among "Louisville's best musicians."[39] Clearly an avid traveler, Flora spent the summer of 1902 in California.[40] An October 1903 bulletin in Louisville's *Courier-Journal* explains that she had then traveled to New York, "where she ... remain[ed] for several months studying music under Edward MacDowell."[41] (If she entered Columbia University in October 1903, she could not have studied long with MacDowell, as he resigned the following February. Likely, her most formative experiences as his pupil took place in Boston, rather than during her time at Columbia.)

Flora returned to Louisville to perform in 1910. Newspaper promotions and reviews describing concerts given by Flora, performing MacDowell's music, highlighted her close relationship with the MacDowells and official authorization, by Edward himself, to interpret his compositions.[42] In the years following his death, MacDowell's fame increased, and Flora seems to have benefited from this prestigious association. A promotion published in connection with a November 1910 concert explained that Flora, who was "once one of the leading pianists in the city and contributed in many ways to its musical life ... in her present tour [was] ... interpreting some of the most beautiful works of the American composer who ranks before all nations as one of the great ones of the earth." This promotion then elaborated on Flora's relationship with the MacDowells: "It is with Miss Shwab almost a sacred pilgrimage, for she has been friend and counselor as well as pupil to Edward MacDowell and his wonderful wife."[43] Clearly, MacDowell's reputation had strengthened substantially by this point, and Flora recognized the growing market for his music. The newspaper's reference to Flora's "present tour" suggests that during this period of her life, following her time in New York in 1903 and perhaps early 1904, she traveled and performed music in various locations, at least to some extent.

By the mid-1910s, Flora had achieved some renown as a concert pianist. A lukewarm but overall favorable review of her December 8,

Appendix

1914, performance of piano music principally by MacDowell at Boston's Steinert Hall appeared in the *Boston Globe* the following day.[44] In addition to numerous pieces by MacDowell, the concert included traditional compositions by Bach, Chopin, and Schumann as well as more contemporary music, such as pieces by Debussy. The *Globe* promoted this performance significantly, even referring to Flora as MacDowell's "assistant" in a December 6 listing.[45] A November 15 listing in the same *Globe* column explained that Flora "was for several years a pupil of MacDowell's, and after that for some time a collaborator."[46]

Following her 1914 performance in Boston, little concerning Flora's pursuits can be ascertained. Given her and the Shwab family's penchant for traveling, she may not have had a permanent residence for at least some of this period. However, when she is again mentioned in Louisville and Nashville newspapers in 1924, she is described as a resident of New York and temporarily living in Switzerland.[47] Flora likely spent most of the years between 1903 and 1924 in New York, aside from travels. In March 1924, she visited the family of her nephew Hugh in Louisville.[48]

In September, she traveled to Lausanne, Switzerland. Her correspondence with Marian MacDowell indicates that Flora deeply regretted being abroad when her brother, Manny (with whom she was extremely close), passed away on November 2, 1924. Flora was staying at Lausanne's Hotel Belvedere when, in an undated letter from late 1924 or early 1925, she wrote to Marian, reflecting on their long friendship, her struggles with depression, and even her nephew George's desire for her to seek professional assistance. Whether Flora had previously spent time in a mental health facility of some type is unknown; however, it seems that her suffering had been ongoing by this point. Flora stated in this letter that she had "no home and no place to go." She also provided some insight into her close relationship with Manny: "The thought that my brother is gone is a constant sense of loss for he had affection for me and I had much for him."[49]

Manny's passing and the end of his emotional (and likely financial) support was, perhaps, too much for Flora to bear. On January 25, at around 5:00 in the morning, following what may have

Appendix

been a difficult decade in which, seemingly, her musical career had declined, she took her own life at the Hotel Belvedere. Her body was transported to Nashville and buried in a small family plot beside her brother Harry, the sibling to whom she was closest in age (and who also lived with her in Ohio during his youth). Why these two members of the family were buried in a separate plot in a city where they spent little time remains unclear but surely relates to the efforts of either Manny (who seems to have provided support for his sister during her life) or George (who oversaw the return of his aunt's body to the United States), or most likely both.[50] The gravesite and Shwab headstone that Flora shares with Harry must have been arranged prior to or just after the latter's death, over a decade earlier in 1912.

Chapter Notes

Introduction

1. "Owners Now in Charge," *Nashville American*, April 6, 1909, p. 5.
2. Harry Kroll, *Bluegrass, Belles, and Bourbon* (New York: A.S. Barnes, 1967), p. 208.

Chapter 1

1. "Victor E. Shwab, Bank and Public Service Head, Dies," *Nashville Tennessean*, November 3, 1924, p. 1.
2. John Fitch, *Annals of the Army of the Cumberland* (Philadelphia: J. Lippincott & Co., 1864), pp. 489–98.
3. Vicki Caron, "Alsace," in *Antisemitism: A Historical Encyclopedia of Prejudice and Persecution*, Vol. 1, edited by Richard Levy (Santa Barbara, CA: ABC-CLIO, 2005), pp. 13–16; Vicki Caron, *Between France and Germany: The Jews of Alsace-Lorraine, 1871–1918* (Stanford, CA: Stanford University Press, 1988).
4. *Early History of Temple Beth El, Knoxville, Tennessee* (Temple Beth El internal history).
5. U.S. Census Bureau, 1850, Louisville, Kentucky; 1870, Youngstown, Ohio.
6. *The Universal Jewish Encyclopedia*, https://www.jewishencyclopedia.com, p. 102.
7. Nashville City Directory, 1853–1854.
8. "State vs. A. Schwab," *Knoxville Register*, November 12, 1857, p. 2.
9. Tennessee Acts of 1813 (66) and 1832 (69), http://genealogytrails.com/tenn/slavelaws.html.
10. Testimony of officers H. B. Smith; Carloss; Turolman, State of Tennessee Supreme Court, August 8, 1857.
11. *Ibid.*
12. *Ibid.*
13. *Ibid.*

Chapter 2

1. U.S. Census Bureau, 1850, Louisville, Kentucky; 1870, Youngstown, Ohio.
2. "Knoxville's First Passenger Train Arrived in 1855". *Knox News*, June 25, 2016, knoxnews.com/story/life/2016/06/25/knoxvilles-first-passenger-train-arrived-in-1855.
3. William MacArthur, "Knoxville's History: An Interpretation," in *Knoxville: Crossroads of the New South*, edited by Lucile Deaderick (Knoxville: East Tennessee Historical Society, 1978), p. 23.
4. U.S. Census Bureau, 1870, Youngstown, Ohio.
5. Wendy Lowe Besmann, *A Separate Circle: Jewish Life in Knoxville, Tennessee* (Knoxville: University of Tennessee Press, 2001), p. 10.
6. Testimony of detectives Charles Wood and Edmund Schlemann, City of Philadelphia Police records, September 29, 1859.
7. *Ibid.*
8. Knox County Archives, East Tennessee Historical Society, April 24, 1860.

Chapter 3

1. W. Calvin Dickinson, "Temperance," October 8, 2017, https://tennesseeencyclopedia.net/entries/temperance/.

Chapter Notes

2. W. G. Brownlow, "Ramsey Drawn Out of Overton by a Soaped Pig," *Tri-Weekly Whig*, August 9, 1859, p. 1.
3. *Early History of Temple Beth El, Knoxville, Tennessee* (Temple Beth El internal history).
4. "Fire in Knoxville," *Nashville Republican Banner*, April 7, 1860, p. 1.
5. Brownlow, *Tri-Weekly Whig*, January 1860, p. 1.

Chapter 4

1. Edwin Drake, *The Annals of the Army of Tennessee* (Whitefish, MT: Kessinger Publishing, LLC, reprint 2007).
2. "Military Burial," *Knoxville Daily Register*, March 12, 1862, p. 3.
3. *Early History of Temple Beth El, Knoxville, Tennessee* (Temple Beth El internal history).
4. *New York Times*, "The Occupation of Nashville," March 2, 1862.
5. John Fitch, *Annals of the Army of the Cumberland* (Philadelphia: J. Lippincott & Co., 1864), pp. 489–98.
6. *Ibid.*
7. *Ibid.*
8. *Ibid.*
9. "Alton Military Prison Site," American Battlefield Trust, https://www.battlefields.org/visit/heritage-sites/alton-military-prison-site.
10. Fitch, *Annals of the Army of the Cumberland*, pp. 489–98.
11. Erin Blakemore, "During the Civil War, Gen. Ulysses Grant Began Expelling Southern Jews—Until Lincoln Stepped In," July 23, 2019, https://www.history.com/news/ulysses-grant-expulsion-jews-civil-war.

Chapter 5

1. Kay Baker Gaston, letter from Parson Bremer, 1983.
2. *Ibid.*
3. Kay Baker Gaston, "George Dickel Tennessee Sour Mash Whiskey," *Tennessee Historical Quarterly* (Fall 1998), p. 152.
4. "Mammoth Pears," *Nashville Union and American*, August 25, 1871, p. 4.
5. Chris Chamberlain, *Nashville Beer: A Heady History of Music City Brewing* (Charleston, SC: History Press, 2014), pp. 6–9.
6. "Off for Europe," *Nashville Union and American*, May 22, 1870, p. 4.
7. "Lost," *Daily American*, May 22, 1885, p. 3.
8. Nashville City Directories, 1859, 1860, 1866.
9. "Circuit Court of the United States," *Nashville Union and American*, May 15, 1867, p. 3.
10. Minutes of Davidson County Chancery Court, Book N, 38, 1864.
11. U.S. Census Bureau, 1870, Youngstown, Ohio.
12. "Died," *Nashville Tennessean*, October 5, 1872, p. 4.
13. "Statue a Reminder of Life Stories Left Untold," *Tennessean*, February 15, 2004, p. B1.

Chapter 6

1. "Temperance Movement in Tennessee," Tennessee State Library and Archives, https://sharetngov.tnsosfiles.com/tsla/exhibits/prohibition/temperance.htm.
2. "Wholesale Liquor Trade," *Nashville Union and American*, March 14, 1875, p. 5.
3. *Ibid.*
4. "Imported in Bond," *Nashville Union and American*, November 8, 1872, p. 4.
5. "South Nashville Brewery," *Nashville Tennessean*, May 19, 1871, p. 2.
6. "Destructive Fire," *Nashville Tennessean*, August 14, 1874, p. 4.
7. By 1875, Meier had moved to Vine Street from College Street, where he lived through 1880. The 1880 census indicates the Shwab/Dickel household was robust, as resident in the home were George (sixty-two) and Augusta (forty), Emma (thirty) and Manny (thirty-three), their four sons, and a cook.

Chapter 7

1. "The Toll-Gate Tragedy," *Nashville Union and American*, June 2, 1877.

Chapter Notes

2. Ibid.
3. Ibid.
4. Ibid.
5. "Hooper Tragedy," *Daily American*, June 28, 1877, p. 4.

Chapter 8

1. "Yesterday's Fire," *Daily American*, May 18, 1881, p. 4.
2. "Nashville's Big Fire," *Nashville Banner*, May 17, 1881, p. 1.
3. "Yesterday's Fire."
4. "George A. Dickel & Co," *Daily American*, May 18, 1881, p. 4.
5. "Reform," *Nashville Banner*, October 6, 1883, p. 4.
6. "Nashville, Tenn.," *New York Times*, October 12, 1883, p. 1.
7. "The Death Call," *Pittsburgh Post-Gazette*, March 25, 1884, p. 4.
8. "Personal," *Daily American*, March 26, 1884, p. 5.
9. "Editorial," *Nashville Banner*, February 20, 1885, p. 5.
10. "A Distressing Accident," *Daily American*, August 29, 1885, p. 4.
11. "Damage Suits," *Nashville Banner*, September 23, 1886, p. 3.
12. "The Courts," *Daily American*, October 13, 1886, p. 8; Minutes, Davidson County Circuit Court, December 23, 1886.
13. "Wines and Liquors," *Daily American*, August 11, 1889, p. 3.
14. "For Sale," *Daily American*, November 18, 1886, p. 3.
15. "Real Estate," *Daily American*, January 12, 1887, p. 5.
16. Wayne Witt, "Climax Is Gone ... Memories Linger," *Tennessean Magazine*, July 8, 1973, pp. 10–11.
17. Ibid.
18. Thomas P. Lowery, *The Story the Soldiers Wouldn't Tell: Sex in the Civil War* (Philadelphia: Stackpole Books, reprint 2012), p. 83.
19. Ibid., 77.
20. Ibid., 78.
21. Ibid., 79.
22. Ibid., 79–80.
23. James Boyd Jones, "A Tale of Two Cities Civil: The Hidden Battle Against Venereal Disease in Civil War Nashville and Memphis," *Civil War History* 31, no. 3 (1985), p. 276.
24. Lowery, *The Story the Soldiers Wouldn't Tell*, 82.
25. Ibid., 81.
26. Ibid., 83.
27. "Died," *Daily American*, August 4, 1891, p. 3.
28. "A Confessed Murderer," *Daily American*, August 3, 1891, p. 5.

Chapter 9

1. Kay Baker Gaston, "George Dickel Tennessee Sour Mash Whiskey," *Tennessee Historical Quarterly* (Fall 1998), p. 162.
2. Jerry Wayne Cook, *Historic Normandy, Bedford County, Tennessee* (Normandy, TN: Cook, 1976), p. 16.
3. Kay Baker Gaston, "Note from Barton to Wright," *Tennessee Historical Quarterly* (Fall 1998), p. 158.
4. Ibid.
5. Ibid., p. 160.
6. Kay Baker Gaston, "M. B. Sims and Wife to V.E. Shwab," Coffee County Deed Book, W, 14, March 1888, 267, p. 166.
7. "Tennessee Whiskies," *Nashville Banner*, December 14, 1889, p. 4.
8. Ibid.
9. Ibid.
10. Ibid.
11. Ibid.
12. Author's email with Nicole Austin, general manager/distiller, Cascade Hollow Distillery, January 18, 2023.

Chapter 10

1. "Real Estate Transfers," *Daily American*, June 16, 1889, p. 7.
2. "Sold by Trimble & Co.," *Nashville Banner*, May 9, 1890, p. 8.
3. "Limited Local Items," *Daily American*, November 12, 1890, p. 5.
4. "Value of a Title," *Memphis Commercial Appeal*, May 1, 1890, p. 1.
5. Tennessee Supreme Court finding, 1891.
6. Peter Turney, "Liability of Abstract

Chapter Notes

Companies for Defective Abstracts," *Daily American*, December 15, 1890, p. 6.
  7. Author's interview with Ridley Wills, December 9, 2022.
  8. "Pleasing Entertainment Given by the Seventeenth District School," *The Nashville American*, May 22, 1898 p. 7.
  9. "Bought $40,000," *Nashville Banner*, April 28, 1892, p. 1.
  10. "Cascade Distillery," *Daily American*, March 3, 1891, p. 8.
  11. "Growing Commerce," *Daily American*, September 21, 1890, p. 5.
  12. "The Situation Dry," *Nashville Banner*, January 16, 1892.
  13. "Dear Buck," *Knoxville Journal*, January 18, 1892.
  14. "Society," *Nashville Tennessean*, September 7, 1889, p. 2.
  15. "Postal Improvement," *Nashville Banner*, October 7, 1891, p. 6.
  16. "Circuit Court," *Daily American*, March 7, 1890, p. 5.
  17. "Montgomery Bell," *Nashville Tennessean*, January 19, 1890, p. 7; "Society," *Nashville Tennessean*, August 16, 1890, p. 5.

Chapter 11

  1. "Captain J. Hadley Clack," *Nashville Banner*, January 18, 1904, p. 2.
  2. "Capt. J. Hadley Clack, Chief of Police, Nashville" *Daily American*, May 14, 1893, p. 11.
  3. "Clubbed by Clack," *Nashville Banner*, September 27, 1893, p. 1.
  4. "Our Press Censorship," *Lucifer the Light-Bearer* (Valley Falls, KS), September 1, 1893, p. 3; "Clubbed by Clack."
  5. "Clubbed by Clack."
  6. "Capt. J. Hadley Clack, Chief of Police, Nashville" *Daily American*, May 14, 1893, p. 11.
  7. "Capt. Clack to Dr. Kelley," *Nashville Banner*, June 24, 1893.
  8. *Ibid.*
  9. *Ibid.*
  10. *Ibid.*
  11. "Dr. D.C. Kelley," *Nashville Banner*, July 1, 1893, p. 4.
  12. "Still at It," *Nashville Banner*, May 30, 1894, p. 1.
  13. *Ibid.*
  14. *Ibid.*
  15. *Ibid.*
  16. *Ibid.*
  17. "The Investigation," *Nashville Banner*, June 5, 1894, p. 2.
  18. "The Report," *Nashville Banner*, June 16, 1894, p. 12.
  19. *Ibid.*
  20. *Ibid.*
  21. "The Sheriff Sued," *Daily American*, January 30, 1892, p. 5.

Chapter 12

  1. "The Ticket Named," *Nashville Banner*, October 18, 1894, p. 6.
  2. "Selected a Ticket," *Nashville American*, October 24, 1894, p. 5.
  3. *Ibid.*
  4. *Ibid.*
  5. "The Ticket Named," *Nashville Banner*, October 24, 1894, p. 6.
  6. *Ibid.*
  7. *Ibid.*
  8. *Ibid.*
  9. "Selected a Ticket," p. 5.
  10. Jonathan Swift, *Thoughts on Various Subjects, Moral and Diverting* (1706; independently republished, 2019).
  11. "Lily Whites Act," *Nashville American*, October 25, 1894, p. 5; "Political Matters," *Nashville Banner*, October 25, 1894, p. 5.
  12. "A Political Masquerade," *Nashville American*, October 26, 1894, p. 4.
  13. James B. Jones, Jr., "Arthur St. Clair Colyar," https://tennesseeencyclopedia.net/entries/arthur-st-clair-colyar.
  14. "At the Tabernacle," *Nashville Banner*, November 3, 1894, p. 3.
  15. *Ibid.*
  16. *Ibid.*
  17. *Ibid.*
  18. J. Eugene Lewis, "The Tennessee Gubernatorial Campaign and Election of 1894," *Tennessee Historical Quarterly* 13, issue 3 (September 1, 1954), p. 224.
  19. "Last Week's Outrage," *Nashville Banner*, April 11, 1895, p. 4.
  20. "Democrats," *Nashville Banner*, April 15, 1895, p. 4.
  21. "The Tribune," *Nashville American*, October 1, 1895, p. 4.

Chapter Notes

22. "Sam Jones' Hot Shot," *Chattanooga Daily Times*, April 15, 1895.
23. Kenneth Fieth, "Samuel Jones," October 8, 2017, https://tennesseeencyclopedia.net/entries/samuel-jones/.

Chapter 13

1. "Mr. G.A. Dickel Dead," *Nashville Banner*, June 11, 1894, p. 1.
2. "Asylum of Nashville Commandery No. 1," *Daily American*, June 13, 1894, p. 3.
3. "Made Seven Arrests," *Nashville Banner*, June 11, 1894, p. 1.

Chapter 14

1. "Cpt. Shwab in Town," *Knoxville Sentinel*, February 24, 1896, p. 1.
2. "A Splendid Whist Victory," *Nashville Banner*, June 25, 1895, p. 8.
3. "Fergus Falls Finally," *Minneapolis Times*, June 23, 1895, p. 8.
4. "The Challenge Trophy Cup," *Nashville Banner*, June 25, 1895, p. 8.
5. "The Champion Nashville Team," *Whist Journal* 5, no. 52 (September 1895), p. 40.
6. "There Is a Good Deal of Humor," *Brooklyn Daily Eagle*, August 13, 1899, p. 18.
7. "Louisville, Kentucky," *American Israelite*, July 18, 1901, p. 3.
8. "A Rousing Welcome Home," *Pittsburgh Daily Post*, December 12, 1887, p. 2.
9. "How Manager Shwab Is Getting Along with His Pup," *Pittsburgh Daily Post*, February 11, 1888, p. 9.
10. *Pittsburg Press*, Sept 21, 1890, p. 3
11. "Shwab's Retirement from the Bijou Theater," *Pittsburg Post*, May 5, 1888, p. 5.
12. "Harry Shwab In Hospital", *The Evening World* (New York), Apr. 14, 1906, p 6.
13. Harry C. Shwab, Standard Certificate of Death, County of Davidson, State of Tennessee Sept 2, 1912.
14. "Music and the Drama," *Courier-Journal*, November 29, 1910, p. 6.
15. "Recital by Miss Shwab," *Boston Globe*, December 6, 1914, p. 36; "The Day's Concerts," *Boston Globe*, December 9, 1914, p. 12.
16. Flora Shwab to Marian MacDowell, undated, box/folder 49, Papers of Marian Nevins MacDowell, Edward and Marian MacDowell Collection, Special Collections, Music Division, Library of Congress, Washington, D.C. This letter must date from between Manny's death on November 2, 1924, and Flora's own death on January 25, 1925.

Chapter 15

1. "Tennessee Centennial Exposition," Tennessee Virtual Archive (TeVA), https://teva.contentdm.oclc.org/customizations/global/pages/collections/centennial/centennial.html.
2. "Letter to the West Side Driving Club," Tennessee Archives.
3. "Demurrers," *Nashville American*, January 25, 1898, p. 5.
4. *Ibid.*
5. "Clerk and Master Weaver," *Journal and Tribune*, October 18, 1899, p. 1.
6. "Board of Directors Meet," *Nashville American*, March 5, 1898, p. 5.
7. "The Voice of the People," *Nashville Banner*, August 16, 1898, p. 3.
8. *Ibid.*
9. *Ibid.*
10. *Ibid.*
11. *Ibid.*

Chapter 16

1. Author's interview with Kay Baker Gaston, May 13, 2022.
2. *Ibid.*
3. County Court Minutes, February Term 1899, Coffee County, Tennessee, pp. 235–38.
4. Coffee County Deed Book 5, p. 396; Deed Book 6, p. 103; Deed Book 7, p. 255.
5. "After the Board," *Nashville American*, December 13, 1898, p. 5.
6. W. Calvin Dickinson, "Temperance," October 8, 2017, https://tennesseeencyclopedia.net/entries/temperance/.
7. "Bribery Investigation," *Chattanooga Daily Times*, February 17, 1901, p. 5.

Chapter Notes

8. *Ibid.*
9. "At the Press Banquet," *Nashville American*, February 28, 1901, p. 3.
10. "Bribery Investigation," p. 5.
11. "Schwab Got It," *Knoxville News Sentinel*, February 23, 1901, p. 1.
12. "Committee Which Investigates Charges," *Journal and Tribune*, April 13, 1901, p. 1.
13. *Ibid.*
14. "Tennessee Millionaires: How the Legislature Missed It by Failing to Get a Herald Report on Manny Shwab's Bank Account while in Session," *Chattanooga News*, May 1, 1901, p. 8.

Chapter 17

1. U.S. 12th Census, Nashville, Tennessee, 1900.
2. "Miss Shwab Entertains," *Nashville Tennessean*, December 12, 1901, p. 8.
3. "Emile Shwab," *Nashville American*, July 14, 1901, p. 2.
4. "Louisville, Kentucky," *American Israelite*, July 18, 1901, p. 3.
5. Nashville City Directory, 1903.
6. "Largest Taxpayers," *Nashville American*, July 19, 1903, p. 9.
7. "The Anti-Whiskey Element," *Chattanooga Press*, January 16, 1903, p. 4.
8. "Campaign in Full Blast," *Nashville Banner*, May 2, 1905, p. 12.
9. Stock certificate: Cumberland Telephone and Telegraph Company (Became Bell South) Henderson, Kentucky, 1884, https://scripophily.net/cumberland-telephone-and-telegraph-company-became-bell-south-henderson-kentucky-1884/.
10. "Last of Campaign ... Enthusiastic Meeting," *Nashville American*, May 17, 1905, p. 9.

Chapter 18

1. Nashville City Directory, 1905.
2. "Cumberland's Head," *Nashville American*, March 1, 1905, p. 3.
3. *Ibid.*
4. "Southern Electrical Company Makes Sale," *Nashville Banner*, April 17, 1902, p. 2.
5. "The Ramblers Are Coming," *Nashville American*, March 22, 1904, p. 2.
6. "T. Dwight Webb Slightly Hurt," *Nashville Banner*, June 4, 1907, p. 8.
7. *Ibid.*
8. *Ibid.*
9. "F. E. Shwab and T.D. Webb," *Nashville American*, June 4, 1907, p. 1.
10. "Treasurer Webb of Cumberland," *Chattanooga Daily Times*, June 4, 1907, p. 1.
11. *Ibid.*
12. "Felix Shwab Recently Shot Treasurer Webb," *Memphis Commercial Appeal*, June 18, 1907, p. 3.
13. "What about It," *Nashville American*, June 5, 1907, p. 4.
14. *Ibid.*
15. "Non-Enforcement of Law," *Nashville American*, June 7, 1907, p. 4.
16. "Card from Judge Baker," *Nashville American*, June 8, 1907, p. 7.
17. *Ibid.*
18. "V. E. Shwab," *Nashville Banner*, April 20, 1907, p. 23.

Chapter 19

1. Jim Hoobler, "Who Was Edward Carmack, and Why Is There a Statue of Him at the State Capitol?" https://tnmuseum.org/Stories/posts/who-was-edward-carmack.
2. *Ibid.*
3. William B. Eigelsbach and James S. Linder, "Drink, Death, and Politics: The Killing of Senator Edward W. Carmack," *Library Development Review* (1994–1995), p. 12.
4. Frank W. Lewis, "Political," *Nashville Tennessean*, December 8, 1909, p. 4.

Chapter 20

1. "Deputies Seize Cascade Plant," *Nashville American*, April 2, 1909, p. 1.
2. "Cascade Co. Makes Bond," *Nashville American*, April 4, 1909, p. 9.
3. "Cascade Co. Must Pay," *Vicksburg Herald*, August 11, 1909, p. 1.
4. "9,000 Barrels Liquor Seized,"

Chapter Notes

Memphis Commercial Appeal, April 2, 1909, p. 3.
 5. "Owners Now in Charge," *Nashville American*, April 6, 1909, p. 5.
 6. "Liquor Men Declare Sharp Plays Politics," *Chattanooga Daily Times*, April 4, 1909, p. 13.
 7. "On Thursday of Last Week," *Baptist and Reflector*, April 8, 1909, p. 1.
 8. "Compromise Likely in Cascade Case," *Nashville Banner*, July 12, 1909, p. 1.
 9. "Probably To-Day or To-morrow," *Nashville Banner*, July 14, 1909, p. 1.
 10. "To Investigate Charges," *Nashville American*, July 29, 1909, p. 9.
 11. "Cascade Case Compromised," *Clarksville Leaf Chronicle*, August 11, 1909, p. 1.
 12. "Schwab Must Pay Penalty," *Chattanooga Daily Times*, August 11, 1909, p. 8; "Cascade Co. Must Pay."
 13. "Frank P. Bond Reaches Home," *Nashville American*, August 14, 1909, p. 9.
 14. "Cascade Distillery Case," *Nashville American*, August 12, 1909, p. 4.
 15. "Uncle Sam Takes Cool Ten Thousand in Cascade Case," *Columbia Herald*, August 13, 1909, p. 1.
 16. "Cloud Appears on the Horizon," *Nashville Banner*, August 23, 1909, p. 10.
 17. "R.S. Sharp for Governor," *Nashville American*, August 22, 1909, p. 17.
 18. Frank Lewis, "Political," *Nashville Tennessean*, November 10, 1909, p. 4.
 19. "Property Is Rich in Iron," *Nashville Tennessean*, November 26, 1909, p. 9.
 20. *Ibid.*
 21. "Big Tract of Land in Hickman County Sold," *Nashville Tennessean*, September 29, 1910, p. 13.
 22. "The Marriage of Miss Augusta Shwab," *Nashville Tennessean*, December 17, 1909, p. 7.

Chapter 21

 1. "Cascade's Best Compliment," *Nashville American*, May 9, 1909, p. 7.

 2. "Where Liquor Men Will Go," *Nashville American*, May 9, 1909, p. 24.
 3. "Think It Is Temporary," *Nashville American*, December 24, 1909, p. 8.

Chapter 22

 1. "Reveals Plans of Liquor Men," *Nashville Tennessean*, December 31, 1910, p. 1.
 2. "Discussion of the Reif Letter," *Nashville Banner*, December 31, 1910, p. 1.
 3. *Ibid.*
 4. "High Handed Corruption," *Nashville Banner*, April 12, 1911, p. 1.
 5. "Allege Unfair Treatment," *Memphis Commercial Appeal*, April 14, 1911, p. 2.
 6. "Several Wholesale Liquor Dealers," *Nashville Banner*, April 15, 1911, p. 16.
 7. "Alleged Corruption of Members of Legislature," *Nashville Banner*, April 29, 1911, p. 1.
 8. "Tennessee Legislative Situation Approaches Revolutionary Stage," *Knoxville Sentinel*, April 28, 1911, p. 1.
 9. "Attempted Bribery Story Stirs the Capital," *Nashville Banner*, April 28, 1911, p. 1.
 10. "Sidelights from Jesse," *Nashville Tennessean*, May 1, 1911, p. 6.
 11. "That Reif Letter," *Journal and Tribune*, May 1, 1911, p. 4.
 12. "Denounces Story as Entirely a Fabrication," *Nashville Tennessean*, May 3, 1911, p. 9.
 13. "Who Favors the Election Bill?" *Nashville Tennessean*, May 4, 1911, p. 6.
 14. "Investigation of 'Slush Fund' Ordered," *Knoxville Sentinel*, June 26, 1911, p. 1.
 15. "Also Vetoes Resolution," *Chattanooga Times*, July 5, 1911, p. 1.
 16. "Officers of Golf and Country Club," *Nashville Banner*, December 5, 1912, p. 16.
 17. "Romantic Wedding Follows Elopement," *Journal and Tribune*, March 29, 1912, p. 5.
 18. "No Fatalities Among the Poor," *Nashville Banner*, January 10, 1912, p. 1.

Chapter Notes

19. "The State Press," *Nashville Banner*, July 8, 1913, p. 6.

Chapter 23

1. "Battle Royal Is Expected," *Journal and Tribune*, October 14, 1913, p. 5.
2. "The Nuisance Bill," *Nashville Banner*, October 13, 1913, p. 1.
3. "Battle Royal Is Expected," p. 5.
4. *Ibid.*
5. "The Tennessee Legislature," *Bristol Courier*, October 16, 1913, p. 4.
6. "Battle Royal Is Expected."
7. "John Barleycorn Knocked Out in Second Round," *Nashville Tennessean*, October 14, 1913, p. 1.
8. "Enjoin Alleged Liquor Dealers," *Nashville Tennessean*, June 13, 1914, p. 3.
9. *Ibid.*
10. "Federal Licenses to Sell Liquor," *Nashville Banner*, July 2, 1914, p. 14.
11. Notes from Evelyn Barton to Dick Wright. Ms. Barton was commissioned by Wright, of Stanley Industries, in 1959 to research the history of Cascade and GDC. The notes were provided to the author by Kay Baker Gaston.

Chapter 24

1. "Imposing Nashville Business House Is Sold," *Nashville Tennessean*, January 19, 1912, p. 1.
2. "Deed to Big Store Filed with Register," *Nashville Banner*, January 23, 1912, p. 9.
3. "New Structure Will Be Modern," *Nashville Tennessean*, April 26, 1914, p. 13.
4. "Announce Two New Buildings," *Nashville Banner*, April 25, 1914, p. 30.
5. "That Nashville Town Meeting," *Nashville Banner* (from *Memphis Commercial Appeal*), August 6, 1915, p. 6.
6. "Control of Carthage Bridge Changes Hands," *Nashville Banner*, January 17, 1916, p. 13.
7. "Elect Board of Directors," *Chattanooga Daily Times*, October 11, 1916, p. 10.
8. "N., C., & St. L. Elects Officers," *Memphis Commercial Appeal*, October 11, 1916, p. 4.
9. Elizabeth Ives, *The Belvedere Club: Shwab-Houston Memories* (Saginaw, MI: Self-published by the Belvedere Club, copyright 1969, Belvedere Club, Charlevois, Michigan), pp. 36–40.
10. *Ibid.*
11. *Ibid.*
12. "Death Comes to Mrs. Dickel," *Nashville Banner*, September 16, 1916, p. 18.

Chapter 25

1. Augusta Banzer Shwab will.
2. *Shwab v. Doyle*, Supreme Court of the United States, May 1, 1922.
3. *Shwab v. Doyle*, 269 F. 321, 1920, Circuit Court of Appeals, Sixth Circuit.
4. *Shwab v. Doyle*, Supreme Court.
5. "Shwab Resists Suit to Collect City Tax," *Nashville Banner*, December 7, 1917, p. 13.
6. "Wholesalers to Leave City," *Nashville Banner*, February 6, 1917, p. 1.
7. Harry Kroll, *Bluegrass, Belles, and Bourbon* (New York: A.S. Barnes, 1967), p. 208.
8. "Wholesalers to Leave City."
9. "Victor E. Shwab, Bank and Public Service Head, Dies," *Nashville Tennessean*, November 3, 1924, pp. 1, 8.
10. "V. E. Shwab Died Sunday," *Nashville Banner*, November 3, 1924, pp. 1, 7; "Victor E. Shwab."
11. "Cascade Distillery Burns as Owner Dies," *Chattanooga Daily Times*, November 6, 1924, p. 16.
12. "The Famous Cascade Distillery," *Berkshire Eagle* (Pittsfield, MA), November 7, 1924, p. 8.
13. "Tennesseans Pay Their Share to U.S.," *Knoxville Journal*, September 2, 1925, p. 20.

Epilogue

1. "Why the 1897 Bottled in Bond Act Still Matters to Whiskey Fans," *Tennessean*, September 18, 2022, p. 1d.
2. Author's interview with Nicole Austin, January 18, 2023.
3. *Ibid.*

4. "Nicole Austin of George Dickel," *Tennessean*, August 18, 2022, p. 5c.
5. Author's interview with Nicole Austin.

Appendix

1. "Harry C. Shwab," *Pittsburgh Daily Post*, March 17, 1887, p. 3.
2. "Harry Shwab," *Pittsburgh Daily Post*, June 16, 1895, p. 4.
3. "A Benefit to Popular Men," *Pittsburgh Daily Post*, April 5, 1896, p. 11.
4. "Testimonial Event," *Pittsburgh Press*, April 25, 1897, p. 4.
5. "Harry Shwab," *Pittsburgh Press*, September 12, 1897, p. 4.
6. "Harry Shwab Again in Charge," *Pittsburgh Daily Post*, July 30, 1898, p. 5; "Harry Shwab's Appointment," *Pittsburgh Press*, July 29, 1898, p. 8.
7. "Tried to Get in Theaters," *Pittsburgh Weekly Gazette*, May 31, 1902, p. 5.
8. Interview, *Philadelphia Inquirer*, January 1905, p. 30.
9. "Harry Shwab in Hospital," *Evening World*, April 14, 1906, p. 6.
10. "Goes Abroad for Gorilla," *Brooklyn Citizen*, July 1, 1906, p. 9.
11. "Friars' Festival," *New York Tribune*, May 10, 1908, p. 46.
12. "Friar's Club History," zippia.com/friars-club-careers-122923/history.
13. "Friar's Festival," p. 46.
14. "The Friars," John J. Gleason, *Theater Magazine* Volume 31. p. 478/9, 1920.
15. "Friar's Club History," zippia.com/friars-club-careers-122923/history.
16. "The 'forgotten' Trump roast: Relive his brutal 2004 thrashing at the New York Friars Club," Elahe Izadi, washingtonpost.com/news/arts-and-entertainment/wp/2017/04/29/the-forgotten-trump-roast-relive-his-brutal-2004-thrashing-at-the-new-york-friars-club/.
17. "There Was a Lively Tussle," *Pittsburgh Daily Post*, May 5, 1888, p. 9.
18. "Some Excited Supers," *Pittsburgh Daily Post*, March 13, 1895, p. 6.
19. "A Telegram Was Received," *Pittsburgh Press*, April 7, 1895, p. 12.
20. "Standing Head and Shoulders," *Pittsburgh Daily Post*, December 8, 1895, p. 9.
21. John Simkin, "The American Magazine," September 1997 (updated January 2020), https://spartacus-educational.com/USAamericanM.htm.
22. Maurice Brown Kirby, "The Siberian Wildman," *American Magazine* LXVI (May–October 1908), pp. 33–41.
23. Flora Shwab passport, United States Department of State, August 21, 1924.
24. U.S. Census Bureau, 1860 United States Federal Census.
25. "Resolutions," *American Israelite*, November 17, 1871, p. 10.
26. U.S. Census Bureau, 1880 United States Federal Census.
27. "The Death Call," *Pittsburgh Post-Gazette*, March 25, 1884, p. 4.
28. "Instruction in Music," *Nashville Tennessean*, September 7, 1889, p. 2.
29. "Music," *Boston Evening Transcript*, September 16, 1891, p. 7.
30. "Music," *Boston Evening Transcript*, October 5, 1897, p. 11.
31. For Louisville piano lessons, see "Musical," *Courier-Journal*, October 8, 1899, p. 5. Flora gave lessons in 1899 and also gave a number of recitals during this time. For Louisville recitals, see "Concerts for Young People," *Courier-Journal*, March 12, 1903, p. 2, and "Among Local Musicians," *Courier-Journal*, April 8, 1900, p. 14. For her enrollment at Columbia by 1903, see Flora Shwab's letter to Marian MacDowell, May 2, 1908, Box/Folder 49, Papers of Marian Nevins MacDowell, Edward and Marian MacDowell Collection, Special Collections, Music Division, Library of Congress, Washington, D.C. She states that she took MacDowell's classes at Columbia during his final year there, and left in February 1904, so she must have been there during 1903.
32. Flora Shwab to Marian MacDowell, undated, Box/Folder 49, Papers of Marian Nevins MacDowell, Edward and Marian MacDowell Collection, Special Collections, Music Division, Library of Congress, Washington, D.C.
33. "Music," *Boston Evening Transcript*, September 5, 1891, p. 13; "Music,"

Chapter Notes

Boston Evening Transcript, September 22, 1893, p. 9.

34. "Music," *Boston Evening Transcript*, September 24, 1897, p. 9.

35. "Music," *Boston Evening Transcript*, September 20, 1893, p. 9.

36. For evidence of active membership in the Louisville Musical Art Society, see "Musical Art Society's Plans," *Courier-Journal*, May 26, 1901, p. 16, and "In Society," *Courier-Journal*, June 2, 1901, p. 6. For charter membership, see Anna Hopper, "Keeping Alive the Spirit of Music in Louisville," *Courier-Journal*, April 20, 1913, p. 46, and "Music and the Drama," *Courier-Journal*, November 29, 1910, p. 4. For "Concerts for Young People," see note 9, as well as "Amusements," *Courier-Journal*, February 8, 1903, p. 20.

37. "Musical," *Courier-Journal*, October 8, 1899, p. 5.

38. "Miss Shwab's Recital To-night," *Courier-Journal*, April 10, 1900, p. 8.

39. "Old-Time Superstitions in Music," *Courier-Journal*, December 3, 1899, p. 15.

40. "Brief Points about People," *Courier-Journal*, June 20, 1902, p. 4.

41. "Points about People," *Courier-Journal*, October 25, 1903, p. 6.

42. "Musical Events in Louisville," *Courier-Journal*, November 27, 1910, p. 15; "Music and the Drama," *Courier-Journal*, November 29, 1910, p. 4.

43. "Music and the Drama."

44. "The Day's Concerts," *Boston Globe*, December 9, 1914, p. 12.

45. "Recital by Miss Shwab," *Boston Globe*, December 6, 1914, p. 36.

46. "Paragraph about Musical Matters Here and Elsewhere," *Boston Globe*, November 15, 1914, p. 59.

47. "In Louisville Society," *Courier-Journal*, March 9, 1924, p. 28; "Victor E. Shwab, Bank and Public Service Head, Dies," *Nashville Tennessean*, November 3, 1924, p. 8.

48. "In Louisville Society."

49. Flora Shwab to Marian MacDowell, undated, box/folder 49, Papers of Marian Nevins MacDowell, Edward and Marian MacDowell Collection, Special Collections, Music Division, Library of Congress, Washington, D.C.

50. For George's involvement, see the official report of Flora Shwab's death: "Report of the Death of an American Citizen," American Consular Services, United States Department of State, January 30, 1925.

Bibliography

Official Publications

Coffee County Deed Books 5–7.
County Court Minutes, February Term 1899. Coffee County, Tennessee.
Gaston, Kay Baker. "M. B. Sims and Wife to V.E. Shwab." Coffee County Deed Book, W, 14, March 1888, 267, p. 166.
Nashville City Directories, 1853–1854, 1859, 1860, 1866, 1903, 1905.
Shwab v. Doyle, 269 F. 321, 1920, Circuit Court of Appeals, Sixth Circuit.
Shwab v. Doyle, Supreme Court of the United States, May 1, 1922.
Tennessee Supreme Court finding, 1891.
U.S. Census Bureau, 1850, Louisville, Kentucky.
U.S. Census Bureau, 1860, United States Federal Census.
U.S. Census Bureau, 1870, Youngstown, Ohio.
U.S. Census Bureau, 1880, United States Federal Census.
U.S. 12th Census, Nashville, Tennessee, 1900.

Manuscripts and Records

Death certificate of Flora Shwab. January 26, 1925. Lausanne, Switzerland.
Early History of Temple Beth El, Knoxville, Tennessee. Temple Beth El internal history.
Fenn, Bert. "Ohio River Steamboats." Cincinnati Public Library Special Collections: "Cincinnati," 1987.
Flora Shwab passport, United States Department of State, August 21, 1924.
Flora Shwab to Marian MacDowell. Box/folder 49. Papers of Marian Nevins MacDowell, Edward and Marian MacDowell Collection. Special Collections, Music Division, Library of Congress, Washington, D.C.
Knox County Archives. East Tennessee Historical Society. April 24, 1860.
"Letter to the West Side Driving Club." Tennessee Archives.
Minutes of Davidson County Chancery Court. Book N, 38. 1864.
Minutes of Davidson County Circuit Court. December 23, 1886.
"Report of the Death of an American Citizen." American Consular Services, United States Department of State, January 30, 1925.
Testimony of detectives Charles Wood and Edmund Schlemann. City of Philadelphia Police records, September 29, 1859.
Testimony of officers H. B. Smith; Carloss; Tourolman. State of Tennessee Supreme Court, August 8, 1857.

Newspapers

American Israelite, "Louisville, Kentucky," July 18, 1901.
American Israelite, "Resolutions," November 17, 1871.
Baptist and Reflector, "On Thursday of Last Week," April 8, 1909.

Bibliography

Berkshire Eagle (Pittsfield, MA), "The Famous Cascade Distillery," November 7, 1924.
Boston Evening Transcript, "Music," September 5, 1891.
Boston Evening Transcript, "Music," September 16, 1891.
Boston Evening Transcript, "Music," September 20, 1893.
Boston Evening Transcript, "Music," September 22, 1893.
Boston Evening Transcript, "Music," September 24, 1897.
Boston Evening Transcript, "Music," October 5, 1897.
Boston Globe, "The Day's Concerts," December 9, 1914.
Boston Globe, "Paragraph about Musical Matters Here and Elsewhere," November 15, 1914.
Boston Globe, "Recital by Miss Shwab," December 6, 1914.
Bristol Courier, "The Tennessee Legislature," October 16, 1913.
Brooklyn Citizen, "Goes Abroad for Gorilla," July 1, 1906.
Brooklyn Daily Eagle, "There Is a Good Deal of Humor," August 13, 1899.
Brownlow, W.G. "Ramsey Drawn Out of Overton by a Soaped Pig." *Tri-Weekly Whig*, August 9, 1859.
Chattanooga Daily Times, "Bribery Investigation," February 17, 1901.
Chattanooga Daily Times, "Cascade Distillery Burns as Owner Dies," November 6, 1924.
Chattanooga Daily Times, "Elect Board of Directors," October 11, 1916.
Chattanooga Daily Times, "Schwab Must Pay Penalty," August 11, 1909.
Chattanooga News, "Tennessee Millionaires: How the Legislature Missed It by Failing to Get a Herald Report on Manny Shwab's Bank Account while in Session," May 1, 1901.
Chattanooga Press, "The Anti-Whiskey Element," January 16, 1903.
Chattanooga Times, "Also Vetoes Resolution," July 5, 1911.
Chattanooga Times, "Liquor Men Declare Sharp Plays Politics," April 4, 1909.
Chattanooga Times, "Sam Jones' Hot Shot," April 15, 1905.
Chattanooga Times, "Treasurer Webb of Cumberland," June 4, 1907.
Clarksville Leaf Chronicle, "Cascade Case Compromised," August 11, 1909.
Columbia Herald, "Uncle Sam Takes Cool Ten Thousand in Cascade Case," August 13, 1909.
Courier-Journal, "Among Local Musicians," April 8, 1900.
Courier-Journal, "Amusements," February 8, 1903.
Courier-Journal, "Brief Points about People," June 20, 1902.
Courier-Journal, "Concerts for Young People," March 12, 1903.
Courier-Journal, "In Louisville Society," March 9, 1924.
Courier-Journal, "In Society," June 2, 1901.
Courier-Journal, "Miss Shwab's Recital To-night," April 10, 1900.
Courier-Journal, "Musical," October 8, 1899.
Courier-Journal, "Musical Art Society's Plans," May 26, 1901.
Courier-Journal, "Musical Events in Louisville," November 27, 1910.
Courier-Journal, "Music and the Drama," November 29, 1910.
Courier-Journal, "Old-Time Superstitions in Music," December 3, 1899.
Courier-Journal, "Points about People," October 25, 1903.
Daily American, "Asylum of Nashville Commandery No. 1," June 13, 1894.
Daily American, "Capt. J. Hadley Clack, Chief of Police," May 14, 1893.
Daily American, "Cascade Distillery," March 3, 1891.
Daily American, "Circuit Court," March 7, 1890.
Daily American, "The Committee's Report," June 16, 1894.
Daily American, "A Confessed Murderer," August 3, 1891.
Daily American, "The Courts," October 13, 1886.
Daily American, "Died," August 4, 1891.
Daily American, "A Distressing Accident," August 29, 1885.
Daily American, "For Sale," November 18, 1886.

Bibliography

Daily American, "George A. Dickel & Co," May 18, 1881.
Daily American, "Growing Commerce," September 21, 1890.
Daily American, "Hooper Tragedy," June 28, 1877.
Daily American, "Limited Local Items," November 12, 1890.
Daily American, "Lost," May 22, 1885.
Daily American, "Personal," March 26, 1884.
Daily American, "Real Estate," January 12, 1887.
Daily American, "Real Estate Transfers," June 16, 1889.
Daily American, "The Sheriff Sued," January 30, 1892.
Daily American, "Wines and Liquors," August 11, 1889.
Daily American, "Yesterday's Fire," May 18, 1881.
Evening World, "Harry Shwab in Hospital," April 14, 1906.
Hopper, Anna. "Keeping Alive the Spirit of Music in Louisville." *Courier-Journal*, April 20, 1913.
Journal and Tribune, "Battle Royal Is Expected," October 14, 1913.
Journal and Tribune, "Clerk and Master Weaver," October 18, 1899.
Journal and Tribune, "Committee Which Investigates Charges," April 13, 1901.
Journal and Tribune, "Romantic Wedding Follows Elopement," March 29, 1912.
Journal and Tribune, "That Reif Letter," May 1, 1911.
Knoxville Daily Register, "Military Burial," March 12, 1862.
Knoxville Journal, "Dear Buck," January 18, 1892.
Knoxville Journal, "Tennesseans Pay Their Share to U.S.," September 2, 1925.
Knoxville News Sentinel, "Schwab Got It," February 23, 1901.
Knoxville Register, "State vs. A. Schwab," November 12, 1857.
Knoxville Sentinel, "Cpt. Shwab in Town," February 24, 1896.
Knoxville Sentinel, "Investigation of 'Slush Fund' Ordered," June 26, 1911.
Knoxville Sentinel, "Tennessee Legislative Situation Approaches Revolutionary Stage," April 28, 1911.
Lewis, Frank. "Political." *Nashville Tennessean*, November 10, 1909.
Lewis, Frank W. "Political." *Nashville Tennessean*, December 8, 1909.
Lucifer the Light-Bearer (Valley Falls, KS), "Our Press Censorship," September 1, 1893.
Memphis Commercial Appeal, "9,000 Barrels Liquor Seized," April 2, 1909.
Memphis Commercial Appeal, "Allege Unfair Treatment," April 14, 1911.
Memphis Commercial Appeal, "Felix Shwab Recently Shot Treasurer Webb," June 18, 1907.
Memphis Commercial Appeal, "N., C., & St. L. Elects Officers," October 11, 1916.
Memphis Commercial Appeal, "Value of a Title," May 1, 1890.
Minneapolis Times, "Fergus Falls Finally," June 23, 1895.
Nashville American, "After the Board," December 13, 1898.
Nashville American, "At the Press Banquet," February 28, 1901.
Nashville American, "Board of Directors Meet," March 5, 1898.
Nashville American, "Card from Judge Baker," June 8, 1907.
Nashville American, "Cascade Co. Makes Bond," April 4, 1909.
Nashville American, "Cascade Distillery Case," August 12, 1909.
Nashville American, "Cascade's Best Compliment," May 9, 1909.
Nashville American, "Cumberland's Head," March 1, 1905.
Nashville American, "Demurrers," January 25, 1898.
Nashville American, "Deputies Seize Cascade Plant," April 2, 1909.
Nashville American, "Emile Shwab," July 12, 1901.
Nashville American, "F. E. Shwab and T.D. Webb," June 4, 1907.
Nashville American, "Frank P. Bond Reaches Home," August 14, 1909.
Nashville American, "Largest Taxpayers," July 19, 1903.
Nashville American, "Last of Campaign ... Enthusiastic Meeting," May 17, 1905.
Nashville American, "Lily Whites Act," October 25, 1894.
Nashville American, "Non-Enforcement of Law," June 7, 1907.

Bibliography

Nashville American, "Owners Now in Charge," April 6, 1909.
Nashville American, "A Political Masquerade," October 26, 1894.
Nashville American, "R.S. Sharp for Governor," August 22, 1909.
Nashville American, "The Ramblers Are Coming," March 22, 1904.
Nashville American, "Selected a Ticket," October 24, 1894.
Nashville American, "Think It Is Temporary," December 24, 1909.
Nashville American, "To Investigate Charges," July 29, 1909.
Nashville American, "The Tribune," October 1, 1895.
Nashville American, "What about It," June 5, 1907.
Nashville American, "Where Liquor Men Will Go," May 9, 1909.
Nashville Banner (from *Memphis Commercial Appeal*), "That Nashville Town Meeting," August 6, 1915.
Nashville Banner, "Alleged Corruption of Members of Legislature," April 29, 1911.
Nashville Banner, "Announce Two New Buildings," April 25, 1914.
Nashville Banner, "Attempted Bribery Story Stirs the Capital," April 28, 1911.
Nashville Banner, "At the Tabernacle," November 3, 1894.
Nashville Banner, "Bought $40,000," April 28, 1892.
Nashville Banner, "Campaign in Full Blast," May 2, 1905.
Nashville Banner, "Capt. Clack to Dr. Kelley," June 24, 1893.
Nashville Banner, "Captain J. Hadley Clack," January 18, 1904.
Nashville Banner, "The Challenge Trophy Cup," June 25, 1895.
Nashville Banner, "Cloud Appears on the Horizon," August 23, 1909.
Nashville Banner, "Clubbed by Clack," September 27, 1893.
Nashville Banner, "Compromise Likely in Cascade Case," July 12, 1909.
Nashville Banner, "Control of Carthage Bridge Changes Hands," January 17, 1916.
Nashville Banner, "Damage Suits," September 23, 1886.
Nashville Banner, "Death Comes to Mrs. Dickel," September 16, 1916.
Nashville Banner, "Deed to Big Store Filed with Register," January 23, 1912.
Nashville Banner, "Democrats," April 15, 1895.
Nashville Banner, "Discussion of the Reif Letter," December 31, 1910.
Nashville Banner, "Dr. D.C. Kelley," July 1, 1893.
Nashville Banner, "Editorial," February 20, 1885.
Nashville Banner, "Federal Licenses to Sell Liquor," July 2, 1914.
Nashville Banner, "High Handed Corruption," April 12, 1911.
Nashville Banner, "The Investigation," June 5, 1894.
Nashville Banner, "Last Week's Outrage," April 11, 1895.
Nashville Banner, "Made Seven Arrests," June 11, 1894.
Nashville Banner, "Mr. G.A. Dickel Dead," June 11, 1894.
Nashville Banner, "Nashville's Big Fire," May 17, 1881.
Nashville Banner, "No Fatalities Among the Poor," January 10, 1912.
Nashville Banner, "The Nuisance Bill," October 13, 1913.
Nashville Banner, "Officers of Golf and Country Club," December 5, 1912.
Nashville Banner, "Political Matters," October 25, 1894.
Nashville Banner, "Postal Improvement," October 7, 1891.
Nashville Banner, "Probably To-Day or To-morrow," July 14, 1909.
Nashville Banner, "Reform," October 6, 1883.
Nashville Banner, "The Report," June 16, 1894.
Nashville Banner, "Several Wholesale Liquor Dealers," April 15, 1911.
Nashville Banner, "Shwab Resists Suit to Collect City Tax," December 7, 1917.
Nashville Banner, "The Situation Dry," January 16, 1892.
Nashville Banner, "Sold by Trimble & Co.," May 9, 1890.
Nashville Banner, "Southern Electrical Company Makes Sale," April 17, 1902.
Nashville Banner, "A Splendid Whist Victory," June 25, 1895.
Nashville Banner, "The State Press," July 8, 1913.

Bibliography

Nashville Banner, "Still at It," May 30, 1894.
Nashville Banner, "T. Dwight Webb Slightly Hurt," June 4, 1907.
Nashville Banner, "Tennessee Whiskies," December 14, 1889.
Nashville Banner, "The Ticket Named," October 18, 1894.
Nashville Banner, "The Ticket Named," October 24, 1894.
Nashville Banner, "V. E. Shwab," April 20, 1907.
Nashville Banner, "V. E. Shwab Died Sunday," November 3, 1924.
Nashville Banner, "V. E. Takes Shwab School Kids on Outing," ____.
Nashville Banner, "The Voice of the People," August 16, 1898.
Nashville Banner, "Wholesalers to Leave City," February 6, 1917.
Nashville Republican Banner, "Fire in Knoxville," April 7, 1860.
Nashville Tennessean, "Big Tract of Land in Hickman County Sold," September 29, 1910.
Nashville Tennessean, "The City," June 12, 1868.
Nashville Tennessean, "Denounces Story as Entirely a Fabrication," May 3, 1911.
Nashville Tennessean, "Destructive Fire," August 14, 1874.
Nashville Tennessean, "Died," October 5, 1872.
Nashville Tennessean, "Enjoin Alleged Liquor Dealers," June 13, 1914.
Nashville Tennessean, "Imposing Nashville Business House Is Sold," January 19, 1912.
Nashville Tennessean, "Instruction in Music," September 7, 1889.
Nashville Tennessean, "John Barleycorn Knocked Out in Second Round," October 14, 1913.
Nashville Tennessean, "The Marriage of Miss Augusta Shwab," December 17, 1909.
Nashville Tennessean, "Miss Shwab Entertains," December 12, 1901.
Nashville Tennessean, "Montgomery Bell," January 19, 1890.
Nashville Tennessean, "New Structure Will Be Modern," April 26, 1914.
Nashville Tennessean, "Property Is Rich in Iron," November 26, 1909.
Nashville Tennessean, "Reveals Plans of Liquor Men," December 31, 1910.
Nashville Tennessean, "Sidelights from Jesse," May 1, 1911.
Nashville Tennessean, "Society," August 16, 1890.
Nashville Tennessean, "Society," September 7, 1889.
Nashville Tennessean, "South Nashville Brewery," May 19, 1871.
Nashville Tennessean, "Victor E. Shwab, Bank and Public Service Head, Dies," November 3, 1924.
Nashville Tennessean, "Who Favors the Election Bill?" May 4, 1911.
Nashville Union and American, "Imported in Bond," November 8, 1872.
Nashville Union and American, "Mammoth Pears," August 25, 1871.
Nashville Union and American, "Off for Europe," May 22, 1870.
Nashville Union and American, "The Toll-Gate Tragedy," June 2, 1877.
Nashville Union and American, "Wholesale Liquor Trade," March 14, 1875.
Nashville Union and Dispatch, "Circuit Court of the United States," May 15, 1867.
New York Times, "Nashville, Tenn.," October 12, 1883.
New York Times, "The Occupation of Nashville," March 2, 1862.
New York Tribune, "The Organization Was Small in Numbers at First," May 10, 1908.
Philadelphia Inquirer, Interview, January 1905.
Pittsburgh Daily Post, "At the Theater," May 1888.
Pittsburgh Daily Post, "A Benefit to Popular Men," April 5, 1896.
Pittsburgh Daily Post, "Harry C. Shwab," March 17, 1887.
Pittsburgh Daily Post, "Harry Shwab," June 16, 1895.
Pittsburgh Daily Post, "Harry Shwab Again in Charge," July 30, 1898.
Pittsburgh Daily Post, "How Manager Shwab Is Getting Along with His Pup," February 11, 1888.
Pittsburgh Daily Post, "A Rousing Welcome Home," December 12, 1887.
Pittsburgh Daily Post, "A Sad-Eyed Man," March 24, 1888.
Pittsburgh Daily Post, "Some Excited Supers," March 13, 1895.

Bibliography

Pittsburgh Daily Post, "Standing Head and Shoulders," December 8, 1895.
Pittsburgh Daily Post, "Tales of the Stage," April 21, 1888.
Pittsburgh Daily Post, "There Was a Comic Scene," March 10, 1888.
Pittsburgh Daily Post, "There Was a Lively Tussle," May 5, 1888.
Pittsburgh Post-Gazette, "The Death Call," March 25, 1884.
Pittsburgh Press, "Christmas Is Over," December 27, 1895.
Pittsburgh Press, "Harry Shwab," September 12, 1897.
Pittsburgh Press, "Harry Shwab's Appointment," July 29, 1898.
Pittsburgh Press, "Playhouse Gossip," March 27, 1895.
Pittsburgh Press, "Shwab's Retirement from the Bijou Theater," May 5, 1888.
Pittsburgh Press, "A Telegram Was Received," April 7, 1895.
Pittsburgh Press, "Testimonial Event," April 25, 1897.
Pittsburgh Press, "Willa Cather," September 20, 1896.
Pittsburgh Weekly Gazette, "Tried to Get in Theaters," May 31, 1902.
Tennessean, "Nicole Austin of George Dickel," August 18, 2022.
Tennessean, "Statue a Reminder of Life Stories Left Untold," February 15, 2004.
Tennessean, "Why the 1897 Bottled in Bond Act Still Matters to Whiskey Fans," September 18, 2022.
Turney, Peter. "Liability of Abstract Companies for Defective Abstracts." *Daily American*, December 15, 1890.
Vicksburg Herald, "Cascade Co. Must Pay," August 11, 1909.

Articles and Periodicals

"Alton Military Prison Site." American Battlefield Trust. https://www.battlefields.org/visit/heritage-sites/alton-military-prison-site.
Blakemore, Erin. "During the Civil War, Gen. Ulysses Grant Began Expelling Southern Jews—Until Lincoln Stepped In." July 23, 2019. https://www.history.com/news/ulysses-grant-expulsion-jews-civil-war.
"The Champion Nashville Team." *Whist Journal* 5, no. 52 (September 1895).
Dickinson, W. Calvin. "Temperance." October 8, 2017. https://tennesseeencyclopedia.net/entries/temperance/.
Eigelsbach and Linder. "Drink, Death, and Politics: The Killing of Senator Edward W. Carmack." *Library Development Review* (1994–1995).
Fieth, Kenneth. "Samuel Jones." October 8, 2017. https://tennesseeencyclopedia.net/entries/samuel-jones/.
Gaston, Kay Baker. "George Dickel Tennessee Sour Mash Whiskey." *Tennessee Historical Quarterly* (Fall 1998).
Hoobler, Jim. "Who Was Edward Carmack, and Why Is There a Statue of Him at the State Capital?" https://tnmuseum.org/Stories/posts/who-was-edward-carmack.
Jones, James B., Jr. "Arthur St. Clair Colyar." October 8, 2017. https://tennesseeencyclopedia.net/entries/arthur-st-clair-colyar.
Jones, James Boyd. "A Tale of Two Cities Civil: The Hidden Battle Against Venereal Disease in Civil War Nashville and Memphis." *Civil War History* 31, no. 3 (1985).
Kirby, Maurice Brown. "The Siberian Wildman." *American Magazine* LXVI (May–October 1908).
Lewis, J. Eugene. "The Tennessee Gubernatorial Campaign and Election of 1894." *Tennessee Historical Quarterly* 13, issue 3 (September 1, 1954).
"Pittsburgh's First Indoor Ice Skating Rink." https://pittsburghhockey.net/arenas/schenley-park-casino.
Simkin, John. "The American Magazine." September 1997 (updated January 2020). https://spartacus-educational.com/USAamericanM.htm.
"The Slave Laws of Tennessee." Tennessee Genealogy Trails. http://genealogytrails.com/tenn/slavelaws.html.

Bibliography

"The Story of the Friars." October 25, 2008. Wayback Machine.
"Temperance Movement in Tennessee." Tennessee State Library and Archives. https://sharetngov.tnsosfiles.com/tsla/exhibits/prohibition/temperance.htm.
"Tennessee Centennial Exposition." Tennessee Virtual Archive (TeVA). https://teva.contentdm.oclc.org/customizations/global/pages/collections/centennial/centennial.html.
The Universal Jewish Encyclopedia. https://www.jewishencyclopedia.com.
Wheeler, W. Bruce. "Knoxville Archived, April 27, 2012, at the Wayback Machine Internet Archive." *Tennessee Encyclopedia of History and Culture*, 2002; retrieved February 28, 2008.
Witt, Wayne. "Climax Is Gone ... Memories Linger." *Tennessean Magazine*, July 8, 1973.

Books

Besmann, Wendy Lowe. *A Separate Circle: Jewish Life in Knoxville, Tennessee.* Knoxville: University of Tennessee Press, 2001.
Caron, Vicki. "Alsace." In *Antisemitism: A Historical Encyclopedia of Prejudice and Persecution*, Vol. 1, edited by Richard Levy. Santa Barbara, CA: ABC-CLIO, 2005.
———. *Between France and Germany: The Jews of Alsace-Lorraine, 1871–1918.* Stanford, CA: Stanford University Press, 1988.
Chamberlain, Chris. *Nashville Beer: A Heady History of Music City Brewing.* Charleston, SC: History Press, 2014.
Cook, Jerry Wayne. *Historic Normandy, Bedford County, Tennessee.* Normandy, TN: Cook, 1976.
Drake, Edwin. *The Annals of the Army of Tennessee.* Whitefish, MT: Kessinger Publishing, LLC, reprint 2007.
Fitch, John. *Annals of the Army of the Cumberland.* Philadelphia: J. Lippincott & Co., 1864.
Ives, Elizabeth. *The Belvedere Club: Shwab-Houston Memories.* Saginaw, MI: Self-published by the Belvedere Club, copyright 1969, Belvedere Club, Charlevois, Michigan.
Kroll, Harry. *Bluegrass, Belles, and Bourbon.* New York: A.S. Barnes, 1967.
Lowery, Thomas P. *The Story the Soldiers Wouldn't Tell: Sex in the Civil War.* Philadelphia: Stackpole Books, reprint 2012.
MacArthur, William. "Knoxville's History: An Interpretation." In *Knoxville: Crossroads of the New South*, edited by Lucile Deaderick. Knoxville: East Tennessee Historical Society, 1978.
Swift, Jonathan. *Thoughts on Various Subjects, Moral and Diverting.* 1706. Independently republished 2019.

Other

Augusta Banzer Shwab will.
Author interview with Kay Baker Gaston, May 13, 2022.
Author interview with Nicole Austin, January 18, 2023.
Author interview with Ridley Wills, December 9, 2022.
Gaston, Kay Baker. Letter from Parson Bremer, 1983.
Notes from Evelyn Barton to Dick Wright.
Stock certificate: Cumberland Telephone and Telegraph Company (Became Bell South) Henderson, Kentucky, 1884. https://scripophily.net/cumberland-telephone-and-telegraph-company-became-bell-south-henderson-kentucky-1884/.

Index

Numbers in **_bold italics_** indicate pages with illustrations

A. Schwab & Co. 16, 47, 119; ads in *Knoxville Register* 27, **_27_**; Brownlow vs. 25–28; as a clothing company 40; selling liquor to slaves 18–20; smuggling (court records and testimonies) 31–35; as wholesale liquor dealers 17, 21, 27; *see also* George A. Dickel & Co. (GDC); Salzkotter, Meier; Schwab, Abraham
Adams Bill 134
Ake, Joseph 71
Alsace 16, **_16_**
American Israelite 136
American Protective Association (APA) 104, 106–109
American Whist League (AWL) 113–115; *see also* Shwab, J. Emile
animals, cruelty to 130–131; *see also* Humane Society
Annals of the Army of the Cumberland (Fitch) 31
anti-abortion laws 173
Anti-Saloon League 132, 176, 178
anti–Semitism 15–16, 20, 89
anti-slavery sentiment 18
Apollinaris 54, **_54_**–**_55_**
Austin, Nicole 78, 195–196

backset (liquid from a previous sour mash distillation) 78
Baker, Judge 143, 145–146
Baker, Lieutenant 94–95, 99
Banzer, Emma *see* Shwab, Emma Banzer
Baptist and Reflector 153
Barthell, Ed 138
Barton, E.M. 123
Baskette, Gid 86
Battle, Fannie 172

Beesley, Jesse C. 170
Belle Meade Country Club 171
The Belvedere Club (Ives) 184
bicycle 87–88
Biddle Cup 113
Bluegrass, Belles, and Bourbon (Kroll) 188
Boalen, Thomas C. 101
Board of Public Works, Nashville 60, 90, 94, 100, 130–131, 137, 138, 141
Bond, Frank 152–155, 182
bone-dry bill 188
Boston Conservatory of Music 86, 112
Bradford, J.C. 102
Bragg, Braxton 72
Bremer, Parson 36
Brooklyn Daily Eagle 115
Brown, John 72
Brownlow, W.G. "Parson" 25–26, 28, 48
Buell, Don Carlos 30
Buist, John 29
Bumpous, T.J. 138
Burkholz, John 63
Burns, Robert 175
Byrum, Mose C. 90–91

Caldwell, James E. 82, 123, 138, 140–141, 152, 171, 192
Campbell, M.R. 178
Cardoni, Flavius 46
Carmack, Edward Ward 36, 147–149
Carroll, W.S. "Bill" 150, 152–153
Carroway, P.M. 87
Carter, John 126
Cascade Creek 71
Cascade Falls 72, **_73_**
Cascade Hollow Distillery (Cascade Whisky) 71–78, 127–130, 178; advertisement 159–161, **_160_**; background

233

Index

71–72; bottles, jug, and pint bar glass *129*; cleanest white hominy 76; competition 75; forest fires destroying *193*, 194; Manny obtaining full ownership 130; reputation 74–75; seizure 9, 150–158; sour mash process 76–77; tax burden 9, 153; violation of internal revenue acts 151–153; *see also* George A. Dickel & Co. (GDC)
Castner-Knott Building 179–183
Castner-Knott Dry Goods Company 179
Cate (Memphis sheriff) 174
Centennial Exposition Company 122–123
Chambers, William 68
Chattanooga & St. Louis Railway 183
Chattanooga Brewing Company 166
Chattanooga Daily Times 143, *163*
Chattanooga News 133–134
Chattanooga Press 137
Chattanooga Times *108*, 109, 143, 153, 154, 170, *193*
Chicago Sunday Sun 90–91
Citizens' Reform Ticket 56–57
Clack, J. Hadley 89–101, 124, 126; attributes 90–91; Byrum's case 90–91; investigated and arraigned 91–92; Kelly and 92–94; obituary 90; Waller's investigation 95–99
Clarksville Leaf Chronicle 154
Climax Saloon 62–65, 66, 71, 161, 179; customers 64; interior 65, *65*; profitability 64
Coca-Cola 9, 159
Columbia Herald 155–156
Columbia University 87
Colyar, A.S. 105–108, 124–126
convict release system 107
Coochee Coochee Dance 126
Cook, Jerry 71
Cooper, Duncan 147, 148
Cooper, J.S. 171
Cooper, Robin 147–149
cruelty to animals 130–131; *see also* Humane Society
Crump, E.H. "Boss" 173–175
Cumberland Telephone and Telegraph 123, 137, 138–139, 140–141
Cunningham, F.E. 72

Daily American 39, *54*, *55*, *58*, *60*, *69*, 84, *90*
D'Arcy 9, 159, *162–164*, 165

Davidson County Chancery Court 123, 187
Davidson County Grand Jury 168
Davis, McLin "Kie" 72, 74, 127, 128, 196
Davis, Norman 128, 130
Davis, Paul McLin 130, 158, 192
Davis, Thurman 127, 128
Democrats/Democratic Party 153, 156, 167, 169, 175, 193; election of 1894 102–108; Legislative Convention 102; merchants 56; municipal elections 138, 139; primary for governor 147; Prohibition and 149, 168; saloon advocates 149
Detroit Trust Company 186
Diageo 10, 110
Dickel, Augusta Banzer 45, 50, 110, 187; death 184, 185, 186; injunctions issued to 176; obituary 184; will 185
Dickel, George 50; arrest 40, *41*; barley award 38; birth 36; community affairs 51, 52–53; death 110; faith in future of GDC 110; generosity 39; as German immigrant 189; gold-headed cane 39, *39*; horse-riding accident 110; as a liquor wholesaler 38; obituary 38, 110, *111*; as a shoe- and bootmaker 38, 40; will 110
Dickerson Pike property 82–84
Dryfous, Henry 17, 24, 32

East, E.H. 123
Edison, Thomas 126
Eighteenth Amendment 178, 189
election bill 168–171
elections of 1894 102–109
electric streetcar 82, *83*
equalization of wantage 152
Essenger, Rachel 45
Estate Tax Act 186–187
evangelical ire 109; *see also* Jones, Sam
Evans, Henry Clay 107

federal seizure *see* seizure of Cascade Hollow
First National Bank 85, 171, 190
First Savings Bank & Trust 171
Fitch, John 31
Fitzgerald & Co. 27
Fletcher, R. 68
Forrest, Nathan Bedford 92
four-mile law 131, 133, 134, 173
Friedenberg, Isaac 34
Friedenberg, Mike 34

234

Index

Gage, John 71
Gage Creek 71
Gaston, Kay Baker 3–4, 36, 74, 127
General Electric 141
General Order No. 11 *34*, 35
General Order No. 146 72
George A. Dickel & Co. (GDC) 9, 10–11, 14, 41, 47, 49, 178; advertisements and notices 84–85, *86*, 159–165, *160*, *162–164*; Apollinaris and 54, *54–55*; beer 49; expansion 48–49; fire of 1881 and 54, 56; headquarters 56, *57*; lawsuit against Jack Daniel 60, *60*, *61–62*; local politics and 56; owners 50; partners and their roles 60, 62; production moved to Louisville 165; specialties 49; vision 54; wholesale distributorship 49
George Dickel Bottled in Bond (Tennessee whisky) 195
German immigrant population 39, 40
Gerst, William 49, 176
Gerst Brewing Company 39
Globe 120
Goodpasture, E.C. 169–170
Gordan, J.B. 102
Grant, Ulysses S.: General Order No. 11 *34*, 35
Gray, Gilda 64
Gray, J.J. 157
Great Southern Telephone & Telegraph Company 123

Hard Rock Café 80; *see also* Silver Dollar Saloon
Hauck Brewing Company 133
Hayes, James 133
Highland Company 178
Hill, A.S. 51
Hill, W.T. 100–101
Historic Normandy (Cook) 71
Hooper, Ben 171, 173
Hooper, Leonard K. 51, 52, 53
Hospital Number Fifteen *see* Soldiers Syphilitic Hospital
Hoss, Dr. 132
Howse (Senator) 138, 139
Huckleberry, Pink 90
Humane Society 130–131

injunction bills 176
Internal Revenue Service (IRS) 72, 74, 75, 110, 188
international revenue tax 156

Jack Daniel's 9, 10, 50, 60, 161, 188
Jews: in France 15–16; General Order No. 11 *34*, 35; moratorium on debts owed to 15–16
"John Barleycorn" *174*, 175, *177*
Johnson, D.M. 132
Jones, Sam *108*, 109
Jourlman, R.D. 24
jug bills 175

Keith, S.J. 123
Kelley, D.C. 92–94
Kennedy, J.L. 95–97, 124, 125–126
Kentucky Chew method 78
Knoxville News Sentinel 133
Knoxville Register 19
Knoxville Sentinel 112, 169
Kroll, Harry 188

Lackey, William 27, 28
Lampblack Republicans 104, 105
Landis, A.L. 90
Landrith, Ira 132
law enforcement 89–101; *see also* Clack, J. Hadley
Lea, Luke 182–183
Lester, Frank 152
Levy, Solomon 30
Lewis, Frank W. 149, 156–157
license(s) 176–177; an act of 1832 and 18; for clubs and fraternal orders 177; for medicinal purposes 176, 188; for operating saloons 48; prostitution 67; rectifying liquor without 40, *41*; tippling without 168
Lilywhite Republicans 104–105
Lincoln, Abraham: General Order No. 11 35
"Liquor Men Declare Sharp Plays Politics" 153
London, Jack 175

MacDowell, Edward 87, 119, 120
MacDowell, Marian 119, 120
Magen David Society 17, 58
USS *Maine* 127
Maney, George 38
Marshall, Mit 126
Marshall, W.R. 178
mash processes 78
Maxwell House Hotel 55, 64
May, Philip *55*
Maynard, Horace 25
McCarthy, Spot 65

235

Index

McDonald, J.Q. 169–170
McKenna, Joseph 187
McKinley, William 121, *122*
McQuiddy, David 74
"Mellow as Moonlight" 74
Memphis Commercial Appeal 82–83, 143–144, 168, 181–183
Memphis Tennessee Brewing Company 166
Men's Quarter 63, 68, 78
minyans 17, 58
Morris, T.O. 139
Motlow, Lem 176, 188
Mt. Olivet plot 110, 120, 193
Muller, William 32
municipal elections 137–139
Murphy, Francis 117

[n-word] election bill 149
Nance, A.C. 51–52, 53
Nance, Bell 51–53
Nashville Abstract Company 83–84
Nashville American see *Nashville Union and American (U&A)*
Nashville & Decatur Railway Company 183
Nashville Banner 55–56, 58, 74, 85, *86*, *87*, 153–154
Nashville, Chattanooga & St. Louis Railway 157
Nashville fire 54–56
Nashville Golf and Country Club 171
Nashville Power Company 11
Nashville Railway & Light Company 171
Nashville Republican Banner 27–28, 55, 56, 58, 74, 82, 84, 85–86, *86–87*, 90, 91, 92, 94, 99, 102, 103, 104, 105, 106, 107–108, 110–111, *111*, 112, 113, *115*, 124, 125, 138, 143, 144, 153–154, 167–169, 172, 176, 181, 182, 184, 188
Nashville Tennessean 13, *14*, *44*, 46, 49, 86, 102, 107, 115, 135, 149, 156, 157–158, *162*, 166, 170, 175, 176, *177*, 179–180, *180*, 181–182, *191*, 192, 195, 196
Nashville Union and American (U&A) 9, *39*, *41*, *46*, *47*, 51–53, 54, 55–56, 59, 99, 102–105, 106, 108–109, 113, 131, 132, 136, 139, 140, 141, *142*, 143, 144–145, 147, *151*, 153, 154–156, 159, *160*, 161, *162*, *163*
Nashville Whist Club 112, 114, *114*
Neil, A.B. 175
Nelson, Charles 85

Nelson's Green Brier Distillery 85, 188–189
nepotism 45–46
Nestor, Michael 95, 96, 99
New York Friars Club 116
New York Herald 133, 134
North Cherry Street 84
Nuisance Bill and Act 173, *174*, 175, 176

open-air debates 137–138

Pacific States Telegraph Company 141
Palmer, Walter 192
Patterson, Malcolm 147, 148, 149, 150
Peabody Teacher's College 179
Peeler Bill 131–132
Penrose, Ida 22, *23*
Pinewood Ore Company 158
Pittsburgh Daily Post 117
Pittsburgh Post-Gazette 58
Pittsburgh Press 118
Prohibition/Prohibition laws 10, 15, 48, 64, 131–134, 189, 192, 195; bone-dry bill 188; cities in states unaffected by 161; election bill and 168–171; election of 1894 and 102–109; GDC and D'Arcy advertising 159, *163–164*; Kentucky and 178; law enforcement and 89–101; seizure of Cascade distillery 150–158; Shwabs' efforts to repeal 166–172; whiskey for medicinal purposes during 188
Prohibitionists 147–149, 168, 170, 172
prostitution 15; legalized and regulated 66–68

Quart Law 48

Ramblers 141, *142*
real estate properties: Manny 82–84, 123, 178, 179–183, 185, 193; Meier 69
"Reform: A Strong Pull and a Long Pull All Along the Line" 56
Reform Party 60
Reif, Charles 166
Removal Act 175
Republicans/Republican Party 35, 102, 104, 107, 149, 155, 156, 166, 168, 169; Lampblack 104, 105; Lilywhite 104–105
Roosevelt, Theodore 159
Ross, Jim 70
Runnells, John 192
Rust, William 98–99

236

Index

Rye, Thomas C. 188
Ryman, Thomas G. 103, 104, 107–108, 109

saloon(s) 11; advocates 149; Climax Saloon 13, *36*, 62–65, 66, 71, 78, 99, 161, 179; converted to soft-drink stands 176; licenses for 48; Silver Dollar Saloon 13, *36*, 78–81, 137, 179; Sunday tippling laws 110–111; three "jug bills" 175; *see also* Anti-Saloon League; Nuisance Bill and Act
Salzkotter, Felix 41; death 46; obituary *44*; statue *44*, *45*, 46–47
Salzkotter, Meier 17, 21, 28, 31, 49, 50, 63, 150; apprehension and testimony 32–34; burial 69–70; as a capitalist 69; death 69, 70; Felix (son) *see* Salzkotter, Felix; marriage and divorce with Cecelia 17, 22–24, 40–41, *42*, 47; marriage with Essenger 45; obituary 69, *69*; overseas explorations for best products 54; passport 41, *43*; retirement 68–69; role at GDC 47, 60, 62
Schenley Industries 189, 195
Schlemin, Edward 22
Schorr, J.W. 166
Schwab, Abraham 11, 40, 41, 42, 71, 119, 150, 192–193; as an Alsatian Jew 15, *16*, 57–58; arrest 19; Brownlow and 25–28; census of 1850 and 17; citizenship declaration *16*, 28; contacts in France 27; death 57, 58, *58*; faith-based associations 17, 58; family 16, 17; French wines and liquors 16, 27; lawsuit against city of Nashville 187–188; minyans 17, 58; in Nashville city directory of 1853–1854 17; obituary 58, *59*; political allegiances 28; selling liquor to slaves (court records and testimonies) 18–20; wine and liquor businesses 16, 58
Schwab, Annie 21, 42, 119, 136
Schwab, Cecelia 16, 17, 21, 28, 119; Bilger and 22–23; marriage, infidelity, and divorce 17, 22–24, 40–41, *42*, 47
Schwab, Joseph 16, 17, 21, 28; burial 29–30; death 29; gravestone 30, *30*; Rock City Guards and 29
Seay, William P. 22
seizure of Cascade Hollow 9, 150–158
Sharp, R.S. 150, 153–156
Shwab, Augusta 158
Shwab, Bertha Wehle 136
Shwab, Bessie 135, 183, 171

Shwab, Emma Banzer 38, 45, 50, 87, 135, 184, 189, 193; accident, news coverage, and lawsuit against city 58–60, *60*
Shwab, Felix Emile 36, 47, 50, 135, 140, 141–145, 184
Shwab, Flora 42, 58, 82, 86–87, 112, 193; as a concert pianist 119–120; death by committing suicide 120; early life 119; MacDowell and 87, 119, 120; mental health struggles 120
Shwab, Gene Mason "Gunga" 78
Shwab, George, IV 119
Shwab, George Augustus 50, 87–88, 133, 150, 166–167, 178; criminal indictments against 168
Shwab, Harry Clay 116–119, 193; date of birth 119; death certificate 118–119
Shwab, Hugh 135, 158, 165, 178, 188
Shwab, J. Emile 21, 22, 42, 50, *81*, 82, 87, 136; in city directories 112; death 136; funeral 136; obituary 115–116, 136; whist and 112–115
Shwab, John Buist 29, 50, 135, 136, 137, 140, 188, 189
Shwab, Louis Banzer 50
Shwab, Louise 135, 183, 184
Shwab, Louise Prichitt 68, 136, 189
Shwab, Paul Eldridge 190
Shwab, Victor Emmanuel "Manny" 9, 10–11; architectural aesthetics 179; burial 193, 194; as a capitalist 13; character and familial devotion 50; city directories and 50; Clack and 89–101, 124, 126; Climax Saloon and 62–65, 66, 71, 161, 179; criminal indictments against 168; death 11, 13, 190; as a debaucherer 181–182; Dickerson Pike property 82–84; family 50, 135–137, 183, 184; father's death announcement 58, *58*; financial, social, and charitable circles 171–172; fishing incident 146; Humane Society 130–131; income tax 1924 194; injunctions issued 176; Jewish heritage 43; lawsuit against city of Nashville 187–188; lawsuit against federal government 186–187; marriage 45; municipal elections and 137–139; obituaries 11, 13, *14*, 190–193, *191*; as a "one-man Tammany Hall" 11, 13; pneumonia 190; profile photograph *190*; Prohibitionists vilifying 172; prominence and reputation 58; real estate portfolio 82–84, 123, 178, 179–183, 185, 193; Silver Dollar Saloon

237

Index

78–81, 137, 179; wife of *see* Shwab, Emma Banzer; World War I and 189; *see also* Cascade Hollow Distillery (Cascade Whisky); George A. Dickel & Co. (GDC)
Shwab School 84, *85*
Shwab v. Doyle, Collector of Internal Revenue 186–187
Sidebottom (chief of police) 124, 125, 126
Silver Dollar Saloon 78–81, 137, 179
Sims, Matthew 72, 74
Sixth Circuit Court of Appeals 187
Slapp, Thomas 150
slave: sales 18, *18*; selling liquor to 18–20
slush fund 167, 169, 170
smallpox outbreak 34
Smith, H.B. 18–19
smuggling 31–35
soft drink dealers 176
Soldiers Syphilitic Hospital 68
Southern Bell Telephone and Telegraph Company 123, 138–139
Southern Electric Company (SEC) 141–142, *142*
Spaulding, George 67
sporting houses 63; *see also* saloon(s)
Stainback, George 95, 96, 99
State Association of Whist Clubs 112
statue of Felix Salzkotter *44*, *45*, 46–47
steel bridge 183
Stifel and Pfeiffer brewery 38–39, 49
Stitzel Distillery 165, 178, 188
Stokes, Walter 183
Sunday tippling laws 94, 110–111
Swift, Jonathan 104
Sykes (councilman) 100
syphilitic paresis 118

Taft, William 156
Tanguay, Eva 64
Tate, Benjamin E. 171
tax evasion 151–152, 156
Tennessean see *Nashville Tennessean*
Tennessee Centennial and International Exposition 121–123

Tennessee Historical Quarterly 74
Thomas, Major 121
Thompson, Frank 176
Tri-Weekly Whig 25–26, *26*, 28
Turney, Peter 107
Turolman, R.D. 19

United Electric Railway Company (UER) 82
U.S. Supreme Court 185; *Shwab v. Doyle, Collector of Internal Revenue* 186–187

Van Tien, J.W. 142–143
Van Winkle, Pappy 9, 165, 188, 196
V.E. Shwab Building *see* Silver Dollar Saloon
venereal disease 67–68, *69*
Vertrees, John 152–153, 186
Vicksburg Herald 154
Vine Street Christian Church 193
Vining, Thomas 97–98

Waddell (representative) 108
Walker, John 150
Waller, Claude 95–99
Warner Iron Company 157
Watkins, R.H. 159
Watts, F.O. 152, 183
Webb, T. Dwight 141–144, 145
Wells, Ida B. 147
West Side Club House 121–122, *122*
Western Electric Company 123
Whiskey Advocate 195
whist (bridge whist) 112–115
Whist Journal 113–114
Williams, A.E. 139
Williams, Charlie 99
Williams, John 99
Wilson, Ephraim 67
Wilson, Woodrow 130, 178
women: legalized prostitution 66–68
Wood, Charles W. 22–23, *23*
World War I 10, 178, 189

Zwicker, Julius G. 79–80

www.ingramcontent.com/pod-product-compliance
Lightning Source LLC
Chambersburg PA
CBHW032037300426
44117CB00009B/1098